Julian Hawthorne

Saxon Studies

Julian Hawthorne

Saxon Studies

ISBN/EAN: 9783337075606

Printed in Europe, USA, Canada, Australia, Japan

Cover: Foto ©Paul-Georg Meister /pixelio.de

More available books at **www.hansebooks.com**

The "Dresdener Nachrichten" on "Saxon Studies."

(Translation.)

As if to mark his exultation at the injuries of all kinds which the inhabitants of Dresden have sustained at the hands of the monster Thomas, another American, Julian Hawthorne, of Boston, has perpetrated an outrageous libel on Dresden. It is entitled "Saxon Studies," and is full of every kind of falsehood and insult, ostensibly calumniating Dresden, Leipzig, and Saxony only; but in reality conveying aspersions against the whole of Germany. Fortunately, this opinion of the work is that held in America itself, as appears by the *New Yorker Staats Zeitung* of the 12th January, which has been forwarded to us. We extract from this honoured newspaper the following vigorous defence of Germany:—"It is well known that the Saxons are esteemed the best-mannered, most affable people in Germany. They are renowned for their politeness; their style of living is in many respects more refined than is the case in the north and south of Germany; and if, therefore, the bulk of the Saxon population is described as stupid and coarse, rude and dirty—if, during a three years' residence in Germany, the author failed to meet with a single pretty face among all the Saxon ladies, who, on the contrary, impressed him only by their ugliness, silliness, hypocrisy, great fondness for beer, and unappeasable appetite for dancing—if all Saxons without exception, so often as they came in contact with this author, exercised a most disagreeable influence on his sense of smell—if the residences of even the highest classes are far inferior in their lack of comfort, their bareness and formality, their want of all those

refinements demanded by æsthetic taste, to the most moderate requirements of respectable housekeeping—if all this, **we say, is the** case in **Dresden** and Leipzig, it would really **be hard** to name any **spot in** Germany which would not appear to this bumptious American [*anspruchsvollen Amerikaner*] in **a** much more perverse light. According to Hawthorne's view, the Saxon mind—that is, **the** German mind in general—certainly possesses a great aptitude for the acquisition of knowledge, but this knowledge is not digested, is not assimilated into flesh and blood, and does not make the Germans a wise people. And therefore Goethe, Schiller, Heine, and the other great thinkers of Germany are either not Germans, or they are **the** only true Germans ever born. Immediately after this assertion the author goes on to say that Dresden barmaids have composed very pretty poetry in his presence, that they understand playing on the piano, and that he was fairly amazed by the many-sidedness of their accomplishments, and the skill with which **they** expressed themselves. But alas! the unfortunate **Saxon** women are forced to work like slaves. They **must** attend to the housekeeping and earn the means of livelihood at **the same** time; nay, he has met women in his walks who were harnessed along with a dog to a waggon, while the husband sat smoking like a sultan within. The misuse of dogs, who are employed, contrary to the intention of nature, as draft-animals, **is** certainly not uncommon in Dresden; and if, occasionally, a woman helps a dog in his labour, she does it out of a humane feeling for the animal, and a desire to lighten his toil: and it is rank absurdity to paint such a picture as the above of a service of friendship like this.—Even in the judgment of an American newspaper printed in the English language, the whole book is nothing but a caricature; and what more lenient judgment is possible when, for example, we read that the author has nowhere heard worse music than in Saxony—where music is interpreted in the most impassioned manner, and whose musical institute is renowned for its excellence throughout all Europe? The author affirms **that true**

music cannot be appreciated by Saxon ears, because it were else incomprehensible that people at a garden-concert, while a **symphony** of Beethoven was being given, quaffed from time to time a mouthful of beer, or munched the sausage which lay on the plate before them, and immediately afterwards intimated their approval of the majestic harmonies by clapping their hands, nodding their heads, and rolling their eyes. But space fails us to expose all the nonsense which, under the pretentious title of 'Studies,' this book contains: but we have already said enough to show that the author is a snobbish blockhead, who cannot enough wonder that all Saxons do not live in the same style as wealthy people on Fifth Avenue in New York. Because he was unable to gain admittance to the respectable society of Dresden and Leipzig, and found himself confined to association with the masses, he revenged himself by describing the habits and customs of the lowest orders as if they were those of the whole people: as when, for example, he asserts that the only way the dance-loving Saxons dance is for the man to grasp the woman round the waist with both hands. Were a European traveller to take a fancy to make studies of society in New York after such a fashion as this, what a distorted picture of American life might he paint: and yet he would not find it necessary to sin half as much against truth as the author of this book has done, in order to produce no less repulsive an effect. Without doubt there may be many imperfections in German social life; but the extenuation of circumstances must be allowed for; and in order to form a fair opinion, the observer should not fail to compare the social results in Germany with those in other countries." To these admirable remarks we will append the observation that we are far from classing the numerous Americans living in Saxony in the same category with their self-conceited fellow-countryman. They are our beloved and honoured guests, and clearly demonstrate by the fact of their presence among us, their disagreement with the views of this clownish upstart [*Gleichheits-Flegel*].

New York Times, Jan. 9th.

"We get, instead of criticism and glorification [of German literature and people], of which the world nowadays has enough and too much, a series of very interesting and often very amusing sketches of real life. . . . The actual dulness of his subject does not repress the vivacity of a thoughtful and skilful writer, as Mr. Hawthorne amply shows. . . . 'Saxon Studies' take place in the class of literature to which Emerson's 'English Traits' belongs. It is of lighter calibre than that sententious study of our English cousins, but it may therefore be more generally attractive. Not that it is lacking in thoughtfulness, far from it; but that it is easy and unconscious in its manner of thought and very pleasing in its style."

Appleton's Journal, Jan. 8th.

"No amount of quotation could do justice to a work whose most impressive effect lies in the cumulative character of its contents. . . . His contempt becomes a genuine literary inspiration. . . . He subjects [the Saxons] to an analysis so incisive, so ingenious, so searching, and so pitiless, that the reader feels at times as if he were himself upon the rack. . . Among noted examples of satire and invective, 'Saxon Studies' is wholly unique. Junius's scorn was confined to persons and a party; the humour of Swift carries a genial element into his most ferocious satire; but if ever the literature of hate comes to be classified, 'Saxon Studies' will easily take the first place among its classics. It alone suffices to counterbalance, from a literary point of view, all the adulation that Germany's success has extorted from the world."

New York Evening Post, Dec. 27th.

"The good points of 'Saxon Studies' are readableness, vivacity, and pictorial power."

SAXON STUDIES

SAXON STUDIES

By JULIAN HAWTHORNE.

STRAHAN & CO., PUBLISHERS
34 PATERNOSTER ROW, LONDON
1876

PRINTED BY
M'CORQUODALE AND CO., "THE ARMOURY,"
SOUTHWARK.

TO

EDWARD D. HOSMER, ESQ.,

OF CHICAGO,

A SOUVENIR OF ONE OR TWO WELL-REMEMBERED YEARS.

FROM HIS FRIEND

THE AUTHOR.

PREFACE.

When the ostensible subject of a book is one with which everybody believes himself familiar, the legendary gentle reader becomes rarer than ever. The author of the present compilation, however, has not consciously written anything calculated practically to avail the least instructed visitor to Saxony. Under cover of discussing certain aspects of Dresden life, he has stolen entrance to a far wider field of observation and remark—so wide, that though the whole world of analysers and moralists crowded into it, there would be space and to spare for each hobby to curvet its fill. He is free to admit that his interest in Saxony and the Saxons is of the most moderate kind,—certainly not enough to provoke a treatise on them. They are as dull and featureless a race as exists in this century, and the less one has to do with them the better. But, the plan of his work requiring some concrete nucleus round which to group such thoughts and fancies as he wished to ventilate, and the Saxon capital happening to have been his residence of late years, he has used it, rather than any other place, to serve his turn in this respect. So far, therefore, from being abashed at any critic's discovering nothing essentially Saxon in "Saxon Studies," he would insist upon thinking such a verdict complimentary.

On the other hand, the author by no means desires to evade the responsibility of whatever opinions, on matters of Saxon life and character, the ensuing pages chance to contain. He has perhaps been led to speak home truths more often than he would otherwise have done, by reason of the mawkish tendency, very observable of late, to make Germans, of all people in the world, and Saxons with them, the object of sentimental hero-worship. But nothing that he has advanced in this direction errs not on the side of mildness rather than of severity; and no deliberate assertion as to matter of fact that he has made, is controvertible upon any grounds whatever.

Probably none would more readily admit this than the better class of Saxons themselves. It is true that these chapters, while appearing serially, were bitterly denounced in some of the Dresden journals, as well as elsewhere. But the author has before him, as he writes, the programme of a "Native and Foreign Mutual Interest Protection Company," dated at Dresden, June, 1875, and signed by Baron von Stockhausen as president. This company aims to remedy some of those very abuses, for mentioning which the "Studies" have been assailed. The reform is a necessary, if not a particularly hopeful one; but in any event, the present writer is very far from claiming either credit for the enterprise or interest in its success: and would be hugely diverted to find himself masquerading in a character so alien to his ambition and capacity as that of a patcher-up of dilapidated manners and morals.

"Saxon Studies" own no such exalted pretensions. That they may be an amusement and relaxation to the reader, as they have been to the writer, is the best the latter cares to wish for them. Providence would never have been at the pains to create man the only laughing animal, had it not first made him the most laughable of all.

TWICKENHAM,
    Dec., 1875.

CONTENTS

		PAGE
I.—DRESDEN ENVIRONS	...	1
II.—OF GAMBRINUS	...	52
III.—SIDEWALKS AND ROADWAYS	...	95
IV.—STONE AND PLASTER	...	153
V.—DRESDEN DIVERSIONS	...	203
VI.—TYPES CIVIL AND UNCIVIL	...	258
VII.—MOUNTAINEERING IN MINIATURE	...	321

I.

DRESDEN ENVIRONS.

I.

THE capital of Saxony, although not devoid of some pleasant interior features, improves, like the Past, as we walk away from it; until, seen from a certain distance, it acquires a smack of Florence. But cross this line in either direction, and the charm begins to wane. Here erects itself a moral barrier, which the temperate traveller should not transgress. A like mystic circle of greatest enjoyment surrounds all delights; though, unfortunately, we are aware of it only after it has been overpassed. The right perception of mutual distances is a Philosopher's Stone, for which the wise, from Solomon down, have been experimenting.

The true end of travel is, to reconcile us to our homes. We study foreign countries and customs, not for their intrinsic sake, but in order to compare them disadvantageously with our own: and thus the mere cosmopolitan misses more than he gains. But man's eyesight sharpens as his intellect expands; and he begins to hold aloof from his surroundings. The tendency is not an unhealthy one, and, had Paradise never been lost, we should scarce have heard so much about its attractions. Lovers, it is true, appear to prefer contact to vision; but hearts—sweet-hearts at all events—see with some faculty transcending ordinary eyesight, and unattainable by common-place travellers. Nevertheless, we shall do wisely, on starting out into the world, not quite to disencumber ourselves of our affectional luggage. It restrains too extended wanderings, and tempers glances else too keen for perfect truth.

As for Dresden, I think its main charm lurks in the towers of its churches and palaces. They elevate the city's outline and make it seductive; albeit thereby somewhat falsifying its true character. Dresden is less romantic than the promise of its spires: for that matter, it is doubtful whether any city could maintain the standard of a cluster of minarets. Surely, the veriest atheist—if there stir within him any vestige of what less rational beings call a soul—must bless Eternal Nothingness that superstition still puts steeples on her churches. Religion may be folly, but all creeds admit the beauty of a dome. It gives unlimited enjoyment, and covers a **multitude of** sins. What **is** there, **in** this upward-tapering, slender-pointing, worse than practically useless structure, that so ensnares the **fancy?** Certainly, a spire is an outrage to logic and to common sense. Yet the practice of building them has outlived many a seeming-wiser custom, and will, I trust, be one of the latest-cured follies of mankind. The idea **was** first, perhaps, suggested by an aspiring lamp-flame; and **it** may continue in vogue so long as fire—and that finer fire we call soul—tends heavenward.

At all events, had I a grudge against Dresden, with power **to** back it, I would overthrow her towers. Had they never been erected, the city would to-day have been unknown. The traveller, downward-gazing from yonder long-backed hill, and beholding a flattened swarm of mean-featured houses spreading dingily on both sides of a muddy river, would have hastened on, to carry fame and fortune elsewhere. Not here had the Sistine Madonna chosen her abode.

But, **as** it is, these dusky minarets are **loadstones** whose **attraction** it is not easy to resist. In absence, they rise in memory **and woo us** back. Nevertheless, if we have once escaped, we shall do wisely to revisit them no **more.** The tall pinnacles lose nothing in the light of **recollection**; rather, a second look would find them less **refined** and lofty than at first. Beautiful were they as we gazed upon them; but perfect, only when we have turned away.

II.

From the summit of this grassy upland we may see the city lie below us in the broad and shallow valley through which the Elbe prolongs a lazy S. Under the influence of the early sunbeams, a thin brown mist rises above the red-tiled roofs, and is trailed away by the indolent breeze. This valley is a notable wind-conductor, and many an epidemic has been put to flight by the sturdy northern gales—fortunate medicine for a most constipated system of drainage.

We turn our backs on the city, and ramble country-wards for to-day. We may walk as leisurely as we like, pausing whenever the humour takes us. For my own part, I refuse at the outset to be hurried, or to stick to the main road when the bye-path looks more inviting. The day is before us: and it is better to acquire something of country lore before attempting the city.

As the sun of planets, so is Dresden centre of a spattering of villages. It is observable, that, although the central body is greatly larger, and presumably older than its satellites, yet the latter are more antique in aspect and conservative in character. Like the smallest babies, they have the oldest faces, and are furthest behind the age. Their limited constitutions do not easily assimilate new food: the short-paced intelligence of the offspring fails to keep pace with the parent's far-striding civilization. Dresden is, at present, not very far behind the age in some respects: it knows something about velocipedes, tramways, and expensive living. But the villages are still early in their eighteenth century. The ignorance of the average Saxon peasant is petrifying—all the more in view of the fact that, of late years, he has begun to learn reading and writing. Such acquirements appear to be a poor gauge of intelligence. Of the march of events—the news of the day—of all such knowledges as the American infant sucks in with the milk from his feeding-bottle—your Saxon peasant has no inkling. Often, he cannot tell you the name of the king beneath whose palace walls he lives. A tradition is current that the last king but one (who was safely buried about thirty years ago) still survives in a neighbouring castle, a captive to the ambition of his relatives.

In short, like better men than they, when truth is not readily to be had, they swallow lies with at least equal relish. The Saxon mind is capacious of an indefinite amount of information; but its digestion is out of proportion weak. There is not power to work up the meal of knowledge into the flesh and blood of wisdom. I have observed in the faces of the learned an expression of mental dyspepsia,—bulbous foreheads and dull pale eyes. As for Schiller, Goethe, Heine, and the rest of that giant conclave, they are either not German, or else they are the only true Germans ever born. Immense, truly, seems to be their popularity among their later countrymen: but is the sympathy so officiously asserted, genuine stuff? It sometimes puts me in mind of the reflection of sublimity in mud puddles.

There is, or used to be, a symmetricalness and consistency about these peasants, unattainable by the more enlightened. They lived near the earth, like plantains; but their humbleness was compensated by some wholesome qualities. It is uncomfortable to reflect that cultivation will vitiate them—has already begun to do so. Such manure as they are treated to will cause them either to grow rank and monstrous, or to rot away. Broad-based scepticism is sometimes maintained to be better than deep-rooted prejudice; but it does not seem to withstand storms so well.

If progress must progress with these people, why not a little modify the method? The heart of the peasant is, perhaps, as valid as other men's: but his brain is perniciously weak. Yet reformers address themselves solely to the latter, and force it to an empty activity. The cone is thus inverted, and the learned peasant topples over. In the best of men, the brain, however large, has always been outweighed by the heart. Were education filtered into the peasant through the latter channel, it could never hurt him. It might work in more slowly, but would always remain pure and sweet, and never overfill the vessel.

III.

Barriers against civilisation are rather physical than moral,—a matter of good or bad roads. We need not consult books for the history of past times; all ages since the Deluge live to-day, if the traveller direct his steps aright. How old is the world? Shall we measure its antiquity by Babylon or Boston? Time sleeps beneath immemorial ruins at one spot, while he mounts the telegraph pole at another.

The Nineteenth Century, accordingly, while it ambles easily down the current of the Elbe, and along the high-roads and railways, seldom exerts itself to climb a hill or wind its way into a sequestered valley. There are retreats but a few miles from Dresden, where still lingers the light of centuries sunk beneath the general horizon. The "Guttentag" affords a ready test of the matter: the distribution of this flower of courtesy marks the boundaries of progress.

Try yonder peasant, for instance, as he passes us on the road.—Did he stare at us stolidly? or go by, awkwardly unconscious, with averted gaze?—We are at an easy distance from Dresden, and the roads are good. But, did he touch his cap, meet our glance with humble frankness, and speak the "Good-day" with a pleasant gruffness of cordiality?—Alas, poor fellow! he lives in a savage gorge, accessible only by an uneasy footpath. Though he appear scarce thirty, he was born at least one hundred and fifty years ago. He knows nothing about the Neue-Continental-Pferd-Eisenbahn-Actien-Gesellschaft lately started in Dresden. May we not almost say, seeing that he has never breathed our Nineteenth Century air, that he has no real existence at all?

This same flower of courtesy depends for its growth not solely on the locality, however, but somewhat also on the individual. In one and the same household we may meet with it under all conditions of luxuriance or starvation. As a rule, it flourishes best with the very old and with the very young—those who have either lived too long to be affected by modern gospels, or have not yet grown tall enough to reach up to them. It is in the hands of the well-grown youth that the flower is most apt to droop, or wither quite away: they it is who dream most of emigrating to America, and who meantime practise some American virtues in their native cottages. Much unhappiness is no doubt in store for them: but posterity may glorify their stripes with stars.

Their newly gained culture has not yet sunk so deeply into these peasants, however, as to be incapable of occasional disconcertment. If we first salute them, they will almost invariably return our greeting: or the magnet of an overbearing or calmly superior glance will often draw the words from our man, or startle them out of him. For no Saxon, of whatever degree, understands the maintenance of self-respect in the presence of what he fancies a superior power.

In treating of Saxon manners, it might be supposed that the illustrations should be drawn elsewhere than from the peasantry. But I find among them the original forms of many social peculiarities, which, on higher planes, are almost unnoticeable by reason of their conventional dress: conventionalism being the true cloak of invisibility. Superficially, a best-society drawing-room in Germany and in England appear much alike; but go to the corresponding villages, and we see plainly points of difference, which exist no less—although outwardly imperceptible—higher up. The thin, satiny skin of the polished man-of-the-world is a better veil of his soul, than is the canvas-like hide of the coarse-grained labourer.

But, indeed, all Saxons know how to be polite, and

often seem to take pleasure in elaborate exhibitions of civility. Few things do they enjoy more than to take off their hats, smile, nod, and exclaim "Ja! Ja! Ja!" It is curious and strange to watch the antics of a group of acquaintances who have by chance encountered one another at a street corner. After a brief but highly animated conversation, they proceed to make their adieux. It is on his powers in this respect that the Saxon chiefly prides himself. Behold, therefore, our friends who stand waving their hats, smiling, nodding, gesticulating, peppering one another with broadsides of Ja's. They become every moment more and more wound-up. Their excitement permeates every part of their bodies, and approaches ecstacy. It resembles the frenzy of Dancing Dervishes, or the more familiar madness of our own Shakers. This is the Saxon's mystic religious dance. To this height of fervour rises the warm-heartedness for which he is noted. Politeness is common in Saxony—provided only that it cost no more than in the proverb.

IV.

American Emerson says, "I have thought a sufficient measure of civilisation is the influence of good women." He is said to be the most popular foreign essayist in Germany; and it is certain that these people are most fond of such literature as is furthest beyond their comprehension. Nevertheless, no true Saxon would subscribe to that particular dogma. For, yonder market-waggon, high-piled with country-produce, and drawn by a woman and a dog tugging on either side the shaft, while the husband driver walks unencumbered alongside,—is so far from being a singular spectacle that, after now some six years daily familiarity with it, I confess to a difficulty in quite sympathising with the indignation of a new-comer. But, indeed, this is nothing : only, at nightfall, we shall meet the same waggon homeward-drawn by the same team : and lo ! seated upon the empty hampers, smokes serene the man and master of all. Let us be rational : why walk home when our woman and dog are at hand to carry us ?

Why do not the woman-emancipationists come to Saxony, and see with their own eyes what the capacities of the sex actually are? Here women show more strength and endurance than many of their husbands and brothers do. They carry on their broad backs, for miles, heavier weights than I should care to lend my shoulders to. Massive are their legs as the banyan-root; their hips are as the bows of a three-decker. Backs have they like derricks; rough hands like pile-drivers. They wear knee-short skirts, sleeves at elbows, head-kerchiefs. As a rule, they possess animal good nature and vacant amiability.

But at twenty or twenty-five they are already growing old.

Growing old, with them, is a painful process, not a graceful one. The reserves of vitality are dry, and the woman's face becomes furrowed, even as the fields she cultivates. Her eyes fade into stolidity and unintelligence. Her mouth seldom smiles. Thirty finds her hollow-cheeked, withered, bony. At fifty—should she live so long—she is in extreme old age. Meanwhile she has been bearing children as plentifully as though that were her sole employment. But such labours secure her scarce a temporary immunity from other toil. I have seen her straining up a long hill, weighted with more burdens than one.

Pleasanter is it to consider her in the hayfield, before youth has dried up in her. Her plain costume follows her figure closely enough to show to the best advantage its heavy but not unhandsome contours. Seen from a distance, her motions and postures have often an admirable grace. Her limbs observe harmonious lines. In raking, stooping, tossing hay, her action is supple and easy. As she labours in the sun, she keeps up a continuous good-humoured chatter with her companions. Her bare arms and legs are bronzed by summer exposure to heat—and dirt; and her visage is of a colour almost Ethiopian. But an American Southerner might see in her more than the dark complexion, to put him in mind of former days and institutions.

The Greeks had slaves who took the edge off the work, but were not intended to bear Grecian children. Saxon slaves are not let off so easily. A nation, whose women keep their houses, saw their wood, cultivate their crops and carry them to market on their backs, and bear children in season and out of season, may indeed go to war with full ranks, for a time. But what use to conquer the world, if our sons and daughters are to grow up cripples and idiots? For, does that pregnant woman whom we saw straining uphill with her heavy basket injure only herself?

I have already remarked that the ground-plan of high society may best be studied in the nearest village; and so the best way to become acquainted with a Saxon lady is to observe her peasant-sister who sweats and tugs in fields and on country roads. The spirit of chivalry never throve among these people, high or low; what is more serious (and, perhaps, too much so for context so light-toned as this), the bulwarks of female chastity, where they exist, are rather mechanical than moral. In Saxony, therefore, suspicion justly has the weight of conviction. The best result of this system is an insecure and exaggerated innocence—the rest needs not further to be enlarged upon.

Women are what men make them; and thus we come back to our Emersonian text. The nation that degrades its women, cuts off the wings and darkens the light which should lift and guide it to an enduring standpoint. I cannot but feel a misgiving about these German triumphs in field and cabinet, when I see men helping themselves before women at table—and elsewhere.

How many of us have dreamt romantically about the ideal German peasant-girl? She appeared to us pretty to the edge of beauty—perhaps a step beyond. She was blue-eyed, and flaxen braids fell over shapely shoulders. Her gown was charmingly caught up at one side; she was often seen with a distaff, and was apt to break out in sunny smiles or pathetic little songs. Goethe and Kaulbach have much to answer for! And yet, among many imperfect Gretchens, I have sometimes fancied that I caught a glimpse of the real, traditional heroine.

Handsome and pretty women are certainly no rarity in Saxony, although few of them can lay claim to an unadulterated Saxon pedigree. We see lovely Austrians, and fascinating Poles and Russians, who delicately smoke cigars in the concert-gardens. But it is hard for the peasant type to rise higher than comeliness; and it is distressingly apt to be coarse of feature as well as of hand, clumsy of ancle, and more or less wedded to grease and dirt. Good blood shows in the profile; and these young girls, whose full faces are often pleasant and even attractive, have seldom an eloquent contour of nose and mouth. There is sometimes great softness and sweetness of eye; a clear complexion; a pretty roundness of chin and throat. Indeed, I have found scattered through half-a-dozen different villages all the features of the true Gretchen; and once, in an obscure hamlet, whose name I have forgotten, I came unexpectedly upon what seemed a near approach to the mythic being. She was at work on the village pump-handle, and her management of it was full of grace and vigour. She bade me good-morning in a round, melodious voice, and looked healthy, fresh, bright, and almost clean. I gave but one glance, and then a subtle inward monition impelled me to hurry away. For, although a second look might have recognized her as the long-sought one, yet it might have brought disappointment, and, therefore, was too much to risk. Meanwhile, so much was gained—I cannot say that I have failed to find her.

But this is sentimental nonsense. English, French, Italians, Spaniards, Russians—each and all surpass their German sister in some particular of beauty; and the American, of course, in all combined. Gretchen will always have unlovely hands and shapeless feet; her flaxen braids will be dull and lustreless, and her head will be planed off behind on a line with her ears. This is no anti-climax: for most of the qualities which make a human being humanly interesting, are dependent upon a goodly development of the cerebellum.

V.

We sallied forth this morning in quest of a representative Saxon village; but, save as regards situation, one is as representative as another. The same people inhabit all, and follow the same customs, submit to the same inconveniences, partake of the same ignorance, and are wedded to the same prejudices and superstitions. Moreover, the names of fifteen out of twenty of these villages end in the same three mystic letters— "itz." What "itz" signifies, I know not; but I should fancy that whoever lives in a community whose name terminates otherwise would feel like a kind of outlaw or alien. Loschwitz, Blasewitz, Pillnitz, Pulsnitz, Sedlitz, Gorbitz,—all are members of one family, and look, speak, and think in the family way. It is admirable the care they take to post up their names on a signboard at each entrance of the village, doubtless a safeguard against the serious danger of forgetting their own first syllables. Were some mischievous person, while the honest villagers slept, to interchange all their signboards, there would be no hope of their ever identifying themselves again. Perhaps, indeed, they would fail to perceive the alteration. Pillnitz or Pulsnitz—what odds? It can matter little to a pebble what position on the beach it occupies; and I dare say the members of various families might be substituted one for another, and nothing be noticed much out of the way on either side.

Many of these little flocks of houses have settled down from their flight in realm of thought along the banks of a stream which trickles through a narrow gorge, between low hills. The brook is an important element in the village economy, fulfilling the rather discordant offices of public drain, swill-pail, and wash-tub; and moreover serving as a perennial plaything for quantities of white-headed children and geese. It is walled in with stone; narrow flights of steps lead down at intervals to the water's edge, and here and there miniature bridges span the flood. The water babbles over a pebbly bottom, varied with bits of broken pottery and cast-away odds-and-ends of the household; once in a while the stream gathers up its strength to turn a saw-mill, and anon spreads out to form a shallow basin. Stiff-necked, plaster-faced, the cottages stand in lines on either bank, winking lazily at one another with their old glass eyes, across the narrow intervening space. Above their red-tiled roofs rise the steep hill-ridges, built up in irregular terraces, overgrown with vines or fruit-trees. Nobody seems to stay at home except the geese and the babies.

Such little settlements hide in country depths, whither only grassy lanes and footpaths find their way. Others there are, mere episodes of the high road, dusty, bare, and exposed, with flat views over surrounding plains; with a naked inn—" Gasthaus "—in their midst, where thirsty teamsters halt for beer, and to stare with slow-moving eyes at the pigmy common with its muddy goose-pond, and to pump up unintelligible gutterals at one another. Others, again, are ranged abreast beneath the bluffs on the river bank; a straggling footpath dodges crookedly through them, scrambling here over a front doorstep, there crossing a backyard. Women, bare of foot and head, peer curiously forth from low doorways and cramped windows; soiled children stare, a-suck at muddy fingers; there are glimpses of internal economies, rustic meals, withered grandparents who seldom get further than the doorstep; visions of infants nursed and spanked. A strip of grass intervenes between the houses and the Elbe river; through trees we see the down-slipping current, bearing with it interminable rafts and ponderous canal boats, and sometimes a puffing steamer, with noisy paddle wheels. At times we skirt long stretches of blind walls, from the chinks of which sprout grass and flowers; and which convey to us an obscure impression of there being grape-vines on the other side of them.

Or, once more, and not least picturesquely, our village alights on a low hill-top, where trees and houses crowd one another in agreeable contention. The main approach winds snake-like upwards from the grass and brush of the valley, but on reaching the summit splits into hydra heads, each one of which pokes itself into somebody's barnyard or garden, leaving a stranger in some embarrassment as to how to get through the town without unauthorized intrusion on its inhabitants. Besides the main approach, there are clever short-cuts down steep places, sometimes forming into a rude flight of stone steps, anon taking a sudden leap down a high terrace, and finally creeping out through a hole in the hedge, at the bottom. The houses look pretty from below; but after climbing the hill their best charm vanishes, like that of clouds seen at too close quarters. In Saxony, as well as elsewhere, there is a penalty for opening Pandora's box.

VI.

As for the cottages themselves, they are for the most part two-storied boxes, smeared with stucco and gabled with red tiles: thatch being as rare here as it is common in England. In fact, these dwellings are not real cottages, but only small inconvenient houses.

They are never allied to their natural surroundings—never look as though they had grown leisurely up from some seed planted æons ago. They never permit us to mistake them for an immemorial tree-stump or mossy rock, which rustic men have hollowed out, and improved into a home. The oldest of them have a temporary, artificial look, conveying the idea that they have been made somewhere else, and set down in their present situation quite by accident, to be tried in a new place to-morrow. A Saxon never sees the spot he builds in, but only the thing he builds. German toy-villages, which charmed our childhood, are more accurate copies of the reality than our years of discretion would have supposed. Magnify the toy, or view the reality from a distance, and the two are one and the same.

This unstable impression results from the fact that Saxon souls have no home-instinct. The peasant thinks of his house as a place to sleep in—and to eat in before and after sleep. He knows no hearth, around which he and his family may sit and chat; instead, there stands a tall glazed earthenware stove, which suggests the idea rather of a refrigerator than of a fire, until we burn our fingers on it; a hypocritical, repellant thing, which would sooner burst than look comfortable. And how can a man converse rationally or affectionately over-night, with the woman whom he means to harness to his cart in the morning? His only resource is to go to the inn, and drink flatulent beer in company with a knot of smoky beings like himself. He seldom gets drunk; indeed, I doubt whether the "Einfaches" beer which he affects is capable of producing anything worse than stolid torpidity—which is perhaps not a wholly undesirable condition for a homeless man to be in. On gala-days he drinks and eats more than usual, and sometimes puts on a suit of remarkable black broadcloth—with the comfortless grandeur thereto appertaining. He plods on foot to the next village, and sits in the "Restauration," or bowls in the alley, or talks crops and prices with his peers. Be that how it may, the gala ends, for him, so soon as he turns his face homewards.

Partly answerable for this barrenness of soul is, no doubt, the form of government, which pokes its clammy, rigid finger into each man's private concern, till he loses all spirit to be interested in them himself. But yet more, must it be said, is it traceable to that cold, profound selfishness which forms the foundation and framework of the national and individual character, in every walk of life: the wretched chill of which must ultimately annul the warmth of the most fervent German eulogist, provided he be bold enough to bring his theoretical enthusiasm to the decisive test of a few years' personal intercourse and conversation with the people.

At this early hour of the day, however, our peasant is off to his work, and we may examine his abode without calling into question the qualities of the owner. It is by no means devoid of ornamentation, both natural and artificial: which, if in harmony with the temporary character of the house itself, is, not the less, often tasteful and pretty. Whenever possible, the house is made the nucleus of a bunch of flowers and verdure. Brightly coloured blossoms crowd the narrow windows, winter and summer; and the greater number of the cottages have attached to them tiny gardens—some hardly bigger than large flower-pots—where grow pansies, pinks, marigolds, and roses, in gaudy profusion. Flower cultivation is a national trait; and I have seen very unæsthetic-looking people plucking wild-flowers in the fields. Wild-flowers are easily obtainable, it is true, but the spirit that uses them is less common. Here seems to be a contradiction, and a pleasant one, in the Saxon peasant's character. We look in vain from his house-windows to those of his face; there are no traces of flowers there; albeit plenty of soil in which to plant them. Nevertheless, were there not germs of grace and beauty somewhere hidden in him, such blossoms would scarcely adorn his outward life.

For my part, I like to believe that the women thus make amends to themselves, a little, for the moral sterility of their earthly existence. The flowers that we see in their windows may bloom there to a better purpose than elsewhere. Perhaps, too, they may be prophetic as well as emblematic of good.

Besides his flowers, the peasant often drapes the front of his house with a thick green apron of woodbine or grape. The latter is never out of place: but woodbine impresses me as being insincere and artifical —the antipodes of the strong and faithful ivy. It does not cling to its support of itself, but must be fastened up; and a mischievous wind-gust may snatch it from its moorings. It grows rapidly; but its tendrils do not twine round the heart; nor does it endure long enough for the eye to become lovingly familiar with its twists of stem and massings of foliage. Compared with ivy, it is meretricious; flourishes with superficial luxuriance, but has no real pith; makes a gaudy show in autumn; but in winter its splendours fall away, and leave a straggling nakedness. It does not uphold, but is upheld, and must fall when the support is withdrawn. It endures but a few years at best, and dies unlamented, for another may readily be had to fill its place. It has no modesty; but obtrudes itself officiously, flaunting its glossy, fragile leaves with an unbecoming freedom. It lacks the tender traditions which ivy owns. Seen from a distance, an incautious eye might mistake the one for the other; but when I find my ivy turn out woodbine, I feel the same kind of disappointment which follows upon addressing, to a stranger, the sentimental remark intended for a friend.

The grape is, on the whole, perhaps the most suitable vine for cottage purposes, because it has to do with the life of the present; whereas the ivy more resembles a pall than a wedding garment, and is chiefly associated with ruins and crumbling traditions. The grapevine hangs its shaggy green beard from eaves and window-sills; and when the fruit is ripe, the cottage seems the realization of an Arcadian dream of luxury. Howbeit, if we attempt still further to realize our dream by putting forth our hand to pluck and eat,— the awakening comes; for every cluster has a market as well as æsthetic value. It is well to be pastoral and romantic, but I must first pay so many groschen for the grapes. Thus is sentiment made ridiculous now-a-days; all the fine pictures have a reverse side, whereon is daubed a grinning caricature, named Common Sense, or Practical Experience. Some clever person is almost always at hand to spring this reverse upon us; but not the less, in solitude, or in rare companionship, we will sometimes forget the parody in musing on the poem.

VII.

As at present used in reference to the works of man, picturesque is rather a vague term. If it may not be directly defined as ignorance, it is at least opposed to what is understood as classic beauty. A picturesque house or street is one which, though meant for use, is practically inconvenient to the verge of uselessness. From this point of view, it will be doing no violence to polite usage to describe these Saxon villages as eminently picturesque. The dwellings are seldom so comfortable as a right economy of materials would have allowed; they huddle together irregularly, drawing in their toes, as it were, and ducking their heads between their shoulders. Some few are built of hewn logs, the second storey projecting like a ponderous eyebrow; and these have I know not what quaint charm, which distinguishes them from others in the memory. They are more primitive. It is the yoking of poverty with some so-called modern improvements that makes real, unlovable ugliness. Justly to harmonize itself, poverty should wear a garment of antiquity, proportioned to its degree.

The front door is not always the mouth through which proceeds the true utterance of the house; in many it is uniformly closed, and wears an aspect of wooden formality. We behold, on jambs and lintel, an uncouth display of architectural ornamentation; and here are inscribed the date of erection, the name or initials of the founder, and some baldly pious motto—a scriptural proverb, or other scrap of religious truism. "Im Gottes Segen ist Alles gelegen," "Wer Gott vertraut hat wohl gebaut," and so on indefinitely. These may be, and I suppose they generally are, taken as evidences of a childlike simplicity and faith. But I would rather they had been written on the inner side of the lintel. The introduction of God's name to every base occasion is a trait of this people, and crops out in their daily conversation to a degree quite astonishing. It is not a sincere or wholesome practice, rather a kind of religious snobbishness.

Although the front door has not always this pharisaical character, but is sometimes made genial by an ample porch and worn steps and balusters—yet as a general thing the back-door manifests more vitality and frankness. It opens on an unevenly paved court: above, the tiled roof stoops affectionately; here sits the old man with his porcelain pipe, and watches the old woman peeling potatoes; while the baby at their feet is happy with the potato-skins. Here we see the earthen pots and copper-kettles of Dutch painters; here detect makeshifts and undress rehearsals. Here is a fine irregularity of light and shade; and, in the heat of summer, a grateful gloom and dampness. That man must be puritanically upright and above-board who never cherished a secret partiality for back-doors. There are easy back-door ways of doing and saying things, such as can never make their appearance on the front doorstep.

The curiosity which may have prompted me to peep into a Saxon farm-yard was never justified by what I saw there. Two sides of the enclosure are bounded by a high blind wall rough with dirty plaster; the other two, by barns and outhouses. There is always a melancholy excess of space: objects which should be grouped together, languish apart. Here is a pump; in that corner huddles a cart; yonder is a heap of straw. Lonely hens straggle here and there, presided over by a preoccupied cock, who seldom crows. An ill-humoured dog barks at me from a distant kennel, and rattles his rusty chain. It is vain to look for the warmly-hospitable atmosphere, for the bustle, the sound, the busy repose that should belong to farmyards. The ground is roughly paved with cobble stones; infrequent men and women shuffle, woodenshod, across and along, but I see no one who looks a farmer. The Saxons do not appreciate the earth; they sow without affection, and reap without thankfulness. Their selfish stolidity cannot sympathize with warm-hearted, generous, slow, majestic nature; they grudge the labour of co-operating with her, and would rather steal the milk from her breast, than claim it by the sacred right of children. But though they be sulky, nature never is; she yields nourishment to them as to others; and there is gracious humour in the smile wherewith she hears them grumble at the pain of suckling her.

Hard by the farm-yard are the hillocks and headstones of the village cemetery. Were there any warmth in the dead, they lie close enough here to create a very genial temperature. The monumental devices stand shoulder to shoulder, each striving to outdo its neighbour, either in stylishness or in extravagance of eulogistic inscription. There can be no safer gauge of culture in a people than the aspect of their graves. They bury their bodies out of sight; but their superstition, their vanity, their truth or falsehood —these nowhere declare themselves so undisguisedly as on the tombstone. We must read the carven inscription, like some kinds of secret writing, between the lines; and how different is the hidden from the ostensible meaning! What traits of character and condition are pourtrayed in the design, ornament, and material of this last milestone of earthly life! In what a solemn light it stands; and with what eyes must the soul regard it, which looks from beyond the grave! Pitifully awry must the least pretentious appear, from that standpoint; but what of these gilt, gingerbread affairs, with their records of titles and virtues? Green grass is the tombstone which best bears all tests. It tells only of the life which springs from decay.

From of old, humourists have made capital of the follies of headstones; but there is something ghastly in the smile which such jests create. I prefer to let the poor, fantastic records remain in peace, to crumble or endure, as sun and rain may choose. Most of these Saxon memorials are made of wood, garnished with more or less of symbolic atrocity. The graveyard, as a whole, wears an aspect of grisly gaiety, impressing the beholder as a subtle stroke of malignant satire. In the silent sunshine of a summer day, or beneath the yet more voiceless moonlight, the strained discord of the spectacle is protest sufficient against itself.

VIII.

I have already made passing mention of the geese; but they are entitled to more than a brief notice. They constitute a goodly proportion of the village population, and they are invariably at home. When not paddling and gobbling in their mud-puddle, they dawdle in lines along the streets, or anent the back-yards, where may perchance be found some kind of food dear to the goosey heart. There is admirable unanimity in a flock of geese, as though each were magnetically conscious of all his companions' sentiments and emotions. All wish to do the same thing at the same time; and fortunately the conditions of their life permit the indulgence of this desire. Yet is each goose a kingdom to himself; pride waddles in his gait, and unbounded self-complacency wallows with him in the dirt. You may easily put him to flight; but out of countenance—never! So soon as his pursuer's back is turned, the fugitive hisses as briskly as though he had been heroic from the beginning.

There is something very human in their hiss, and in their expression in giving vent to it. I have never heard precisely such a sound from a human being, or seen a human neck stretched in just such a way. But I fancy that many souls, were they visible, would appear not otherwise than as hissing geese; and that the spirit of their speech is a similar sibilation.

Though intolerant of strangers, geese fraternize with their fellow villagers, albeit never on terms of such familiar confidence as hens maintain. The character of the goose, with its fine distinctions from those of other domestic fowls, has never been sufficiently set forth. The goose should not be made typical of stupidity, save as it may be the essence of stupidity to see all things through the medium of one's self. He is the symbol of the lowest form of egotism: barring that, he is as astute as any animal of his order. I am always surprised to hear of a pet goose: there seems to be no way of caressing him, except to feed him; for though egotists are not as a rule averse to being made much of—as witness cats—yet the goose is too full of himself to care for endearments. Furthermore, his self-conceit is not of a wholesome external character, like that of the turkey or peacock: it subsists little on the consciousness of outward attractions, but seems to build upon a suppositious mental or moral worth,— with an assurance, ludicrous, yet too human to be agreeable. What causes the goose to bend his head in passing beneath the farm-yard gate, except the persuasion that his towering spirit overtops the world? Unlike that of the eagle, however, the goose's self-esteem has nothing lofty or noble in it: it is the conceit of vulgarity—pride inverted, because based on petty self.

It is agreeable to harmony to observe how constantly the goose affects muddy water. They are the pigs of the bird race. They prefer muddy water, and glory in it. If muddy water be not a good emblem of spiritual uncleanness and perverted truth, I know not where to find a better. The proud severity of swans leads them to pure lakes and streams, and the naïve innocence of the duck attaches him to ponds whose faults are mitigated to duckweed and minnows. But nothing suits the goose so well as a barren mud-puddle. The sleekness of his coat presents a sinister contrast to the undisguised grossness of his interior. He is an epitome of certain human vices; and even when prepared for the table, a slice too much of him fills the soul with heavy disgust.

I once met with a quaint theory, according to which the dumb companions of man were held to be the reflection of his own ruling thoughts and affections. Thus the character of the savage is revealed in the wild beasts he hunts; that of pastoral nations, in their peaceful flocks; of the chivalrous and warlike races, in their thorough-bred and fiery steeds. As the man's nature changes, so do the animals around him die out or multiply. For every wild beast that becomes extinct, there expires some fierce passion of a human soul. For every dove that coos on the roof, there dwells in some heart a thought of innocence and gentleness:—a pretty fancy, arbitrary at first sight, perhaps, but to a deeper consideration revealing glimpses of a profound inward significance.

How happens it, now, that there should be so many geese in Saxon villages? Geese will grow as readily in one place as another; yet here are twice as many geese, in proportion to the human population, as elsewhere. I fear there must be an occult vein of sympathy between them and their owners, reaching deeper than the flavour of roast goose, or money value, can explain:—some mutual consciousness of similar dispositions. Geese, I say, are symbolic of self-seeking, self-glorifying, short-sighted human vanity; and where geese abound, such vices are rife. If this be not the solution of the mystery, the sole alternative lies in the fact that, at Strasbourg, they make pate-de-fois-gras. In justice to the theory, I must admit that there are at least half as many pigeons as geese in Saxony. These I take pleasure in construing as representative of the love of mothers for their babies, and the innocent thoughts of the babies themselves. If we must have pies, let us fatten pigeons rather than geese.

IX.

A noticeable quietness pervades these villages; as though they had dropt asleep ages ago, not to awaken in this century at any rate. The houses stand voiceless, like empty shells, and the narrow road wanders lonely between them. The inhabitants are abroad—in Dresden, in the fields, wherever their work may have taken them. Within the village limits remain only those who are either too old or too young to be away: these, with the proprietor of the Gasthaus, and a shopkeeper or two, are all.

But even were every one at home, we should never see anything resembling the omnipresent activity of a New England or Western village. They are born quiet, these people: a Saxon baby has but little cry in him, and no persistent noisiness. In infancy he is stiffened out in swaddling-clothes, and lives between two feather pillows, like an oyster in his shell: moving only his pale blueish eyes and pasty little fingers. A greasy nursing-bottle is poking itself into his mouth all day long. He has a great, hairless, swelled head, like an inflated bladder. His first appearance out doors is made in a basket-waggon, planted neck deep amidst his pillows; the hood of the waggon being up and closely blue-curtained. Sometimes he rides double, his brother's or sister's head emerging at the opposite end of the little vehicle. They seldom die under this treatment: indeed even a soul would find difficulty in escaping from those feather pillows, and through the crevices of those close drawn blue curtains. When they have colic (but they seldom muster energy sufficient), they uplift a meagre cry, as though aware that something of the sort would be expected of them. But it often happens, as I am credibly informed, that they must be dashed with cold water in order to bring their lungs into action. A dash of cold water would be apt to produce a spasm in a Saxon of whatever age.

Thus early begins the subjection to law and custom. When the child gets to be thirty inches high, or thereabouts, it is sent to school; whither it paces temperately, with little noise; racing, horse-laughing and all disorder are tacitly discouraged. The little girls link arms and gossip as they go; while the boys march soldier-like with their small knapsacks, precocious in discipline and conservatism. When the play-hour comes, they engage in a mutually suspicious manner, as though self-conscious of hypocrisy and make-believe.

By and by some of them grow up,—more of them than would be supposed. But the habit of following authority and precedent in all concerns of life grows with them. They will never feel quite safe about blowing their noses, until they have seen the written law concerning that ceremony, signed and sealed by the king, and countersigned by Prince Bismarck. They swim everywhere in the cork-jacket of Law; and, should it fail them, flounder and sink: or even lose their heads and are betrayed into some folly which helps them to the bottom.

It is that early experience of swaddling and feather-pillowing, I suppose, which implants in all Saxons their sleepless dread of a draught. I fancy their very coffins must be made more air-tight than other people's, and the sod must be pressed down more closely over their graves. Summer or winter, nothing will hire a Saxon to sit beneath an open window, to stay in the same room with an open window, or to sleep with an open window in the house. Why windows in Saxony were made to open, is a mystery. The Saxon turns up his coat-collar and glares intolerant at the mere rattling of a window sash. He will risk a broken head in the cause of bad air. The atmosphere of the lecture-rooms in schools and universities, lies thick and foul as stagnant water. Those rooms are atmospheric sewers, with no outlet. If you become giddy and nauseated with the breathing-material, you must seek relief out of doors: no fresh air may trespass on the hallowed impurity of the interior.

As might be imagined, such lung-food as this gets the native complexion into no enviable state: in fact, until I had examined for myself the mixture of paste and blotches which here passes for faces, I had not conceived what were the capacities for evil of the human skin. I have heard it said—inconsiderately—that the best side of a Saxon was his outside: that the more deeply one penetrated into him, the more offensive he became. But I think the worst damnation that the owner of one of these complexions could be afflicted with, would be the correspondence of his interior with his exterior man.

The Saxon can no more be influenced to moderation in this matter, than the wind can be persuaded not to blow. His argument declares that a cold is more to be dreaded than poison, and influenza than a two-edged sword. Whereas, at worst, an influenza can but kill; but foul air means diseased life. It is surely better to die in the freedom of the mountains, than to exist in however luxurious a polluted room. Nevertheless, the Saxon does not merely endure pollution,—he likes it—and it likes him.

It is an ill-built, ill-favoured race, and of an unhealthy constitution. As for the soldiers, they are in all respects a forced product; compelled to exertion and hardship so long as their term of service lasts, they make up for it by dying early. They are machines, working marvellously while the driver's hand is over them; then coming to a rusty standstill for ever.

Despite their closeness within doors, in summer the Saxons much affect the open air. They will sit all day beneath the beer-garden trees. Yet do they return, without sigh or shudder, to their atmospheric sties at night. And they seem to carry their atmosphere about with them. Meeting a party of them on the breeziest summit of the Saxon Switzerland, anon we have a subtile reminiscence of stale tobacco and beer. Is there nothing in the souls of this people congenial to the fair and pure influences of nature? They admire—who more vociferously?—a fine view or picturesque vista. Howbeit, the very fact of their being able glibly to utter profundities, casts a sinister suspicion upon the genuineness of their title-deeds thereto. What true lover of nature, should she in a fortunate hour reveal her beauty to him, would not blush and stammer in the attempt to compliment her to her face? She abashes his praise to silence. That eloquent stanza which, as he sat at home, seemed to him the full utterance of the best his eyes could discover, shrinks now from his lips, and shows pale and vulgar. He must turn his back upon living nature, and forget the better part of her, before he can remember her eulogies aright.

Not so the Saxon, who not only delights to wear his heart upon her sleeve, but is himself the daw that pecks at it. He loudly approves that which transcends approval. The pure and chaste loveliness of nature, which should be viewed only reverently and in silence, he levels with the allurements of a harlot, which every charlatan may canvass with praise or blame. And, such is the bad power of this low spirit, the true lover's reverence is disturbed, and he is vexed with a miserable suspicion of that sanctity which he had fancied secure from all base approach. But in truth it is no mysticism to say that the essential Nature is in each man's soul; it is the soul, and the soul's mood, which quickens and colours her; and, womanlike, she changes with our change.

The Saxon's sentimentalism is vitiated by his

moral and physical ill-health. He is continually doing things false in harmony, and incomprehensible, as all discord is. Who but he can sit through a symphony of Beethoven's, applauding its majestic movements with the hand which has just carried to his lips a mug of beer, and anon returns thither with a slice of sausage? It seems as if no length of practice could marry this gross, everlasting feeding to any profound appreciation of music. He frowns down the laughter of a child, the whispering of a pair of lovers, as disturbing the performance: but the clatter of knife and fork, the champing of jaws, offend him not. He seems to recognize the noble beauty of the theme; he nods and rolls his eyes at the sublimer strains. Does he comprehend them? He reminds me of the Jews, who, indeed, possess the Bible; written moreover, in their native Hebrew; who peruse it daily, and can repeat much of it by heart; and who yet have never read so much as a single line of the word of God.

X.

We have wandered through the village, its extreme outpost is behind us, and we tread once more upon the smooth white highway. The road is lined on both sides by interminable rows of trees, defining its course when itself is out of sight. There are cherry, apple, and, less often, poplar trees. On the whole, the effect is tiresome. I do not like to see my path marked out before me. Moreover, I am kept perpetually in mind of the nearness of mankind. Each tree was planted by a man; and, if it happen to be a fruit tree, men must often visit it. The road itself, to be sure, is also man's handiwork. But it does not obtrude itself; at most it is but the amplification of a natural pathway, and so falls quietly in with the order of nature—provided only it be not too immitigably straight.

It is a noticeable trait of this country—the impossibility of getting beyond every-day limits. There is no seclusion, whereof we may feign ourselves the first invaders, and, as such, secure from pursuit or encounter. There is no profound wildness, even where the surroundings seem least tame. The woods are supervised by foresters, in green uniforms and glazed caps, who take care that the trees shall be planted in straight lines, and affix its label to every tenth trunk. Who but a hypocrite would pretend to lose himself in a forest, all whose trees were numbered? Nay, in some places (the royal park for instance) are certain respectable-looking old vegetables, which no one would suspect of such enormity, which are provided with names and titles into the bargain. We may find them set forth in the Forester's book thus: "No. 27. Oak. Heinrich the Stout." "No. 28. Elm. Karl the

Long-legged." What is to happen to a people who can do such things as this?

We cannot fly beyond the possibility of a Saxon, so long as we remain in Saxony. No matter where we are, he has been there just before us; and hark! his step approaches from behind. Yonder thickly-wooded dell seems the abode of nymphs and hamadryads, unprofaned as yet by any human presence: let us plunge into it, and woo its sweetly shy inhabitants. Virgin moss yields beneath our feet, we hear Arcadian twitterings of birds. The bare exterior world is shut out and forgotten. We listen for the light step of the wild nymph amidst the bushes, and scan closely the rough bark which seems ready to start asunder at the magic pressure of the hamadryad's finger. We strike a path leading to the nymph's grot—'tis a smartly painted beer-cabin, with square, yellow wooden chairs and tables. The nymph and the hamadryad, in soiled petticoats and rolled-up sleeves, are scrubbing the floor and window; while Pan stands yonder in a swallow-tailed coat, with a napkin under his arm, and answers to the title of Kellner. Bring your best beer, waiter, and draw it cool. We need refreshment!

I know few spots more beautifully unkempt than is a certain rocky pass in the Saxon Switzerland. The steep sides are rank with mossy verdure—cool and moist with trickling springs. Tender ferns bend greenly athwart dark backgrounds of stony clefts. Beside the rugged pathway bubbles over rocks the glancing soul of a cold brook. High up, the slope whispers with thick-growing pines, mingled with trees of less austere foliage. Highest of all, grey crags crowd abrupt and angular against the sky, and cast jagged shadows on the opposite steep. Listening closely, we hear only the brook, and the pines, and a dapper bird or two, and a torrid hum of invisible insects. Here, surely, is the unprofaned retreat so long desired in vain.

But, looking again at that immemorial battlement which the siege of centuries has so grandly scarred, we see painted, just at its base, a spruce white square, on which is recorded in accurately formed letters and numerals, white and red, the position of this point relatively to the Government Survey Base Line, and its elevation in metres above the mean level of the North Sea. Immediately the secluded pass seems peopled with the shapes of Saxon engineers, uniformed and equipped. Those pines were set out, at so much per dozen, by the king's landscape gardeners, who, likewise, grouped the rocks by aid of a steam derrick. The brook was a happy after-thought; but owing to the scarcity of water, it runs only during the season. There is a model in plaster of our entire surroundings in the Engineer's Bureau, with a pin sticking in the very spot where we now stand. I repeat there is no escape. The presence of man journeys with us like the horizon, go we never so fast or far.

Indeed, there are the stone-breakers, who take up their abode along our whole line of march. They are a class by themselves; I cannot imagine their following any other profession. They are mostly time-gnawed old fellows, whose bones seem to have been cracked long ago by their own hammers. They wear great goggles of wire-gauze, which give them an impressive air of gloomy cadaverousness. A huge wooden-soled shoe protects their foot from stray knocks. On frequented roads a canvas screen is set up, to protect the passer by from flying stone-sparks. We hear the dull intermittent beat and crack, but see only the head of the hammer as it rises occasionally above the screen for a harder stroke.

The men seem to take an interest even in such work as this. An extra hard bit of stone arouses their combative instinct; and they have a sensation of pleasure when a fragment divides into pieces of the proper size and shape; while, if it weakly crumble, they damn it with contempt. Thus with their hammers do they sound the whole gamut of the emotions. Occasionally they pause from labour, straighten their stiff old backs, and glance at the sun, to see how far he is from dinner time. Before falling to work again, they look critically at their next neighbour's stone pile, and exchange a grunt or two with him. Like other world toilers, they sometimes think themselves hardly used—the sport of fortune—and grumble that they would have done better as watchmakers, or painters on porcelain. In point of fact, however, stone-breaking is all they care about on earth, and, were they compelled to forego it, they would break their old hearts in default. Even and regular stand their stone-heaps, end to end, and each is provided with its number, painted on a larger piece of flat rock. Labelling and classification is carried thus far, in Saxony; and I cannot kick a pebble from my path without more or less disorganizing the schemes of the Government at Berlin.

XI.

I am continually oppressed with the idea that immeasurable possibilities for fine scenery are wasted in Saxony. The Saxon Switzerland is, to be sure, as picturesque as could be desired. But it is an abrupt topographical anomaly, uprearing itself in a reactionary manner out of a tedious extent of plain. From a great distance we see the vast square-built rocks lifting their shoulders a thousand or twelve hundred feet skyward; they seem to own no relationship to the silly fields that smile at their feet—no sympathy either of form or substance. I find a shrewd correspondence between this typographical anomaly, and that mental one which uplifts, above the low level of ordinary German intelligence, the enduring group of cloud-capped giants which has given the land its reputation.

Why so flat and tedious, O Saxony! as though some enormous incubus had for ages been rolling its heavy length across your unfortunate face, till your every feature was obliterated? Is there any remedy? I see none, short of a general eruption, whereby the whole surface might be broken up in volcanoes, and become a Switzerland indeed. And may the physical upheaval be prophetic of a moral one; for it is of significance that mountainous tracts are ever inclined to freedom.

However, the country is not flat in the prairie fashion. It appears so only as the eye sweeps it from a distance. But, traversing the seeming plain, we find it everywhere seamed by narrow gullies, in which the villages lie; so that it were better described as an agglomeration of low table-lands. Beautifully verdant they are in spring and in summer, and pleasingly variegated with squares of many-tinted grain and produce. Moreover, there is an extraordinary abundance of wild flowers—rather an abundance than a variety. I have seen tracts of seven acres actually carpeted with pansies, whose myriad little faces show at a distance like a purple haze. Amidst the green young wheat grow deep azure corn-flowers and scarlet poppies: an armful might be gathered in a few minutes. The banks of country lanes are often blue with harebells; and anon we pass great clover-meadows, humming with bees. This commonness of beauty perhaps mars that finer enjoyment which needs rarity as the finishing flavour. Nevertheless, it affords a broad triumphant satisfaction.

A more concrete taste may be gratified by the cherries—a staple produce of Dresden neighbourhoods. In spring, so thick are the blossoms, the trees resemble white branching coral; but the perfume is faint, as is likewise the flavour of the fruit itself. Flavour or not, they are agreeable eating in warm weather, and cheap enough to tempt to imprudence. We may sit on the bench beside the cherry-booth, and see our plateful gathered from the tree over our heads: or, for a consideration, mount the tree ourselves, and work our will upon it. The cherries are of all kinds and colours, from black to white, and are recommended by the vendor as good for the blood. We devour them, therefore, with the self-complacency of a health-seeker added to the palatal enjoyment; and were it not that they are dismally apt to be wormy, our pleasure would be without alloy.

Agreeably suggestive are the booths themselves— little board huts, planted in the green midst of the cherry country. The season lasts from the end of June on into August—the mellowest slice of the year;

and if enjoyment of nature be ever unconsciously possible, the cherry-people must be happy. Material cares have they none, for their business can lose them nothing, and is apt to pay them well. Each merchant hires a number of trees for the season, paying a percentage—not on what they bear, but on what he sells. The only danger for him is a total failure of the cherry yield, in which case he would be liable for ground-rent; but this occurs only thrice a life-time.

The booth contains a single room, in which sleep the merchant and his family, like caterpillars in a web. The cooking-stove is wisely put outside on the grass, and the interior thus kept free from smoke and heat. The wife sits in the doorway nursing the baby, while the other children, who are incredibly dirty, but all the happier therefor, play together in a desultory way, or tease a cross-grained cur, who is always an outspoken foe of intending customers. At noon, when the baby goes to sleep, mamma gets dinner: the family gather together: in the afternoon the man smokes his pipe: and so the day passes on.

Delightful—all this: the leisure; the trees, beneath whose shade we sit, all the time working for us and supporting us; the amusement of watching our guests —their various fashions of eating, their remarks and questions, their discontent or satisfaction, their manner of payment and of departure. With what independence would we prepare our noonday meal, and how appetising a fragrance would go up from our fried trout and our bacon and greens. Then light we the after-dinner pipe, whose blue smoke ascends skywards through the green leaves of the tree beneath which we recline. At night, how comfortable to lie on our matting, amidst the country hush, hearing the summer winds come soft-footed up the valley and pause at our window; occasional cherries dropping, over-ripe, with a gentle pat on the roof above; half-conscious, during the night, of the whispering passage of a shower; to fall asleep, secure in the watchfulness of the dog on the threshold; to dream of Arcadian shepherdesses; to awake, fresh, in the early morning, gather betimes our basket of fruit, and sit down to await our first customer. But I suppose the real life, especially when there are babies, does not run on quite so unexceptionably. A prolonged rain, or a wind perverse enough to blow the smoke in at the hut door, would impair our ideal humour.

XII.

We must turn our steps homeward: at yonder crossing is a guide-post, which should tell us our way, and the distance. Small risk of getting lost in Saxony, if guide-posts can prevent it: though their usefulness is sometimes impaired by the illegibility of the names inscribed upon them: the "nach" is the only part of the direction which is always distinct. Nor are the estimates of distances often of much service, especially when couched in terms of "Stunde." Theoretically, two Stunde go to a German mile; but, in practice, they vary as the length of various men's legs. What is an hour's walk for one, another may accomplish in half the time; and a dim recognition of some such fact has led the people to qualify their Stunde by an array of adjectives, which complicate if they do not relieve the difficulty. The government milestones, however, are distinct from the guide-posts—are a newer institution, and as rigidly accurate as their elder brethren are lax. Solid and orderly are they, arched over the top, and consecrated with the government monogram. They look like gravestones, beneath which we may fancy the particular mile recorded on them to be interred. German miles are so long, that we never get on such familiar terms with these milestones as we do with English ones; and the decimal fractions are a sore trial of friendly forbearance.

As we descend the slope towards Dresden, the long panorama is rich with peaceful beauty. There rise the spires and domes, mellowed by the western sun; the white-gleaming river; the further shore dotted with white villas; the pine-shaded horizon; and, wide and high above all, the grand phantasmagory of cloudland.

It is in this point of cloud-scenery that Dresden surpasses all places I have seen. The time will some day come, after we have learnt to travel by telegraph, and have become familiar to satiety with terrestrial beauty, that there will be pilgrimages, not to the Alps and to Niagara, but to the land of superbest clouds. Clouds never can become hackneyed, for their forms and tints are infinite, and no Murray or Baedekker can lay down rules and usages about the seeing them. In any true sense of the word, they are indescribable—save by lady-novelists, new to their profession, whose ideas are apt to be cloudy. In every way they are the most elevating part of nature—entrapping our eyes at the horizon, and leading them zenith-ward. Without clouds, the bare, blue, unchanging sky would become intolerable. Man cannot bear unmitigated heaven, any more than he can do without clothes. Clouds are the garments of the sky, and each new costume seems fittest of all. Throughout the world it is the garment that is beautiful. Trees have their leaves, rocks their moss, soil its grass, the earth its blue atmosphere, the atmosphere its clouds.

These vapoury mountains quite outdo their solider rivals; but inspire the imagination with promise of celestial prototypes yet fairer than they. With their unlimited range of form and shade, they may arouse all sentiments from grotesque to sublime; and they prepare the untravelled mind for all the best that earth can show. No alps, no castles by the sea, no palaces in Spain, can surprise him who from his own house door has seen the sun set. And not the traveller only, but the wit, the humorist, the student of character, may find stimulus for thought and food for reflection in the clouds—find his noblest fancies outdone, his completest theories proved inadequate. But how is this? Yonder celestial cloud-pinnacle, up whose steep acclivity our high-flown thought was clambering, has subtly sculptured from its facile substance a set of demoniac features, which twist themselves into a sardonic grimace of mockery at our enthusiasm. Our parting digression has carried us too far: we must get back once more to the sober highway. But we return, also, to the opinion which has accompanied us throughout our day's ramble—that the solidest attractions of Dresden and its suburbs are the impalpablest ones, and the least describable. If so it be, the Saxons need not repine. Only the baser part of things is communicable, and doubtless the pleasanter features of the Garden of Eden are those whereof no tradition has come down to us.

II.

OF GAMBRINUS.

I.

LIFE is a tissue of mysteries. One is, that if the feelings be touched the palate never complains. An egg, hard-boiled over the fire of the affections, outdoes an omelette by Savarin. A half-pint of schnapps, poured into an earthern mug by the hand of the affections, has a finer aroma than old wine in crystal goblets, less finely presented. Or what rude bench, cushioned by the emotions, is not softer than satin and eider-down? The spiritual not only commands the sensual—it may be said to create it. The banquets of the gods are divine only in so far as they harmonize the two. This is the whole secret of nectar and ambrosia.

The theme so expands beneath the pen, that we were best bring it to a head at once. Suffice it introduces us to the modest establishment of Frau Schmidt, just beyond the outer droschky limits: a favourite resort of mine, though better beer, easier chairs, and more accessible sites be discoverable elsewhere. I cannot baffle the reader's insight—the outweighing attraction is Frau Schmidt herself. Yet she is not a widow—nay, she is fonder of her husband than is the case with most Saxon women; and he is really quite a fine fellow. Moreover, her personal charms are not bewildering. She appears before us a grey-clad little woman, with plain, pleasant, patient visage, and low, respectful voice: she puts down our schoppen of beer on our accustomed table near the window, smiles a neutral-tinted little smile of welcome; and we pass the compliments of the day. Twice or thrice during our stay she returns to chat with us; and her big, grave, reticent husband stands beside her, and puts in a rumbling word or two. Anon they are off to serve their other customers—mostly common workmen out of the street, thirsty, rough fellows, with marvellous garments and manners. Evidently, the spell that draws us hither is one which works beneath the surface. Well, we are not going to draw aside the veil just yet. Let us first discuss our meditative beer: in the dregs of the last glass, perhaps, we shall find the secret revealed.

From our window is a view of the river and the town. A tree rustles in the little front yard: beyond curves a dusty stretch of road. It is about four in the afternoon, and we have the room almost to ourselves. Till sunset we will sip, and muse, and moralize, and hold converse with the spirit of the great Gambrinus. Mighty, indeed, is he! Kings and emperors may talk, but to Gambrinus belongs the true fealty of Germans. We have only eulogy for him—his is a spell to disarm ill-nature's self. He is author of the most genial liquor in the world; his wholesome soul bubbles in every foaming glass of it. We could have forgiven Esau, had he yielded his birthright for a glass of German beer; nor would himself have regretted the exchange. The national song of Germany, which now pretends to be chiefly concerned about some sentimental "Wacht am Rhein" or other, were much better altered as follows :—

> "Lieber Land! Kannst ruhig sein;
> Fest steht und treu"—das Bier-Verein!

Try we a mouthful or two; how fresh, how wholesomely bitter—the texture how fine and frothy : mark the delicate film it leaves upon the glass. Lighter than English ale, of a less pronounced but more lastingly agreeable flavour: we tire of it no more than of bread. We may drink it by the gallon; and yet a little will go a long way. It seems not a foreign substance, but makes itself immediately at home. In colour it ranges from brightest amber to deepest Vandyke brown, and in strength from potent Nuremberg to airy

Bohemian. It is both food and drink to many a poor devil, whose stomach it can flatter into hypothecating a meal. To be sure, an unwelcome flabbiness and flatulence will, in the long run, reveal the deception. Rightly used, however, it makes thirst a luxury.

This liquor can be neither brewed nor exported beyond the fatherland; nay, a journey of but a few miles from its birthplace impairs its integrity. Why, is a romantic and poetical enigma. In America the brewing is more elaborate and careful, but the result is nervous and heady. The broad Gambrinian smile becomes a wiry grin, or even a sour dyspeptic grimace. If exported, no matter with what care of cork and tinfoil, ere it can reach its destination some subtle magic has conjured away the better part of it. *Et calum et animam mutat.* Gambrinus has laid a charm upon it: it is the life-blood of the country, and shall not flow or rise in alien veins.

A profound political truth is symbolized here, if we would but see it; it elucidates the subject of emigration and the effect of locality on temperament. The varieties of German beer are innumerable; each tastes best on the spot where it was brewed; and each has its supporters as against all others. Now, the Berlin Government seems desirous of proving (what we Americans have already proved to the world's satisfaction, if not to our own), that people living, no matter how far apart and under what different circumstances, may be united in mind, sentiment, and disposition as one man. To this end, what method more effective than to ordain a universal beer, and forbid the brewing or drinking of any other? Condense into one the many inconsiderable principalities of Gambrinus. True, though men can apparently be induced by the proper arguments to accommodate themselves to whatever political or moral exigencies, beer is of a more intractable temper, and persists in being different in different places. But surely Prince Bismarck, who can do so much, will not be beaten by a beverage: the difficulty will be ultimately overcome, if military discipline and legislation be worth anything. Two alternatives suggest themselves at once. The first, to create a uniform climate, soil, and water throughout the Fatherland—not an impossibility to German science, I should suppose;—the second, to brew the beer nowhere save in Berlin, to be drunk on the premises. Berlin would thus be secure of becoming the centre of attraction of the empire; and if, as is believed, Germans are Germans by virtue of the beer they drink, if all drank the same beer, of course they all would become the same Germans.

Moreover, if this may be done with the nation, why not apply the principle to the individual? A nation is but a larger, completer man; and if a nation may be concentrated at a single point, as Berlin, why not concentrate the persons composing it into a single individual, as Bismarck? Having swallowed his countrymen, the Prince could thereafter legislate to please himself; and might ultimately proceed to swallow himself into a universal atom.

Pending these improvements, we are consoled with the reflection that there are advantages connected with the undigested form impressed upon men and states by their original creator; for example, there is much entertainment in the discussions between various beer-cliques as to the merit of their respective beverages. Saxons, like other people, most enjoy disputes the least important and adjustable. A perverse instinct, no doubt, but universal, is that of asserting the worth of our opinion and individuality against all comers. It remains to hope, that Saxony, and Germany with her—leading the world in other departments of civilization—may, before long, resolve themselves into a homogeneous mass—according to modern lights, the only true form of union.

II.

Another pull at our schoppen: we must avoid overheating ourselves with transcendental controversy. The genius of beer is peaceful; and there is a mild unobtrusive efficacy about it which is a marvel in its way. The flavour, although highly agreeable, does not take the palate captive, but introduces itself like a friend of old-standing; the liquor glides softly through the portals of the gullet, and grows ever more good-humoured on the way down. We swallow a mouthful or two, and then put down the glass to pause and meditate. The effect upon thoughts is peculiar and grateful. It gently anoints them, so that they move more noiselessly and sleekly, getting over much ground with little jar. It draws a transparent screen between us and our mental processes—as a window shuts out the noise of the street without obstructing our view of what is going on there. Upon this screen are projected luxurious fancies—coming and going we know not whence or whither—and we become lost in following them. Slight matters acquire large interest; with what profound speculation do we mark the course of yonder leaf earthwards floating from its twig, over-weighted by the consideration we have bestowed on it. The striking of a church clock, a mile away, echoes through vast halls of arched phantasy. The babble of those good people at a neighbouring table foregoes distinctive utterance, and is resolved into a dreamy refrain. Our own voices seem to come from far away; our prosaic thoughts take on the hues of poetry and romance. We seem to chant rather than speak our sentences, and perceive a subtle melody in them. We feel comfortable, peaceful, yet heroic and strong; surely there is somewhat superb and grand about us, which, till now, has been but half appreciated. We sit full-orbed and complete, and regard our fellow-men with the sweet-tempered contempt of superiority.

That peculiar kind of friendliness and sociability which distinguishes Saxons would soon languish if deprived of its inspiring beer. As sun to earth, is their beer to them—the source of their vitality. Colourless and bloodless enough were they without it. If Gambrinus may not be said (such an assertion would indeed be treasonable) to be Germany's immediate sovereign, he at least renders her worth being sovereign over. It is well to make slaves and puppets of men, but he also deserves credit who gives the puppet a soul to be enslaved with.

Happy Saxons! have they themselves an adequate conception of the part beer plays in their economy—of the degree to which their ideas and acts are steeped in it? Only Germans can properly be said to possess a national drink; beer takes with them the place of all other beverages; an American bar, with its myriad eye-openers and stone-walls, would be absurdly out of place here. The Saxon's palate is not tickled with variety; one thing suffices him, which he loves as he loves himself—because it has become a part of him. It fascinates him, not as aught new and strange, which might be potent for a time, but eventually palls. But it is dear to him as are the ruddy drops which visit his sad heart—a steady, perennial, exclusive affection, constant as his very selfishness. Who calls the Saxon cold?—is there any devotion, he asks, warmer than mine to me?

I like to hear him call for his beer—as though he had been wrongfully separated from it, and claimed it as his Saxon birthright. There is a certain half-concealed complacency in his tone, too; arising partly from pleasureable anticipation, partly from patriotic pride that there is so good a thing to call for. Having got it, he never shows to such advantage as with it in his hand —never so like an apple of gold in a picture of silver. It seems a pity, then, that he should ever strive to be aught sublimer than a beer-drinker. For nothing else is he so fit; nothing else, perhaps, renders him so genial and happy; and surely there are many things which do him more harm. Gambrinus, the mightiest of Germans, not only did nothing else—he owes his greatness to that fact. Methinks there is a deep significance in the story how, when Satan called to claim his bargain, the German Bacchus trusted to no other weapon than this single beer-drinking faculty of his, and therewith got the better of his enemy. He played a manly part: a smaller man would have fallen to evasion, forsaking his true stronghold for another with which he was unacquainted. Gambrinus succeeded, as do all men who know their power and rely upon it. Doubtless, he might have wasted his time in making himself a fair philosopher, politician, soldier, or what not; but all would not have saved him from the devil. Saxons, here is food for reflection.

I am bound to admit, however, that this luxury, like all others, may be indulged in to imprudent lengths, and thereby lead to consequences anything but peaceful or meditative. A legend is current of a certain evil demon, Katzenjammer by name, who is as hateful as Gambrinus is genial; and it is whispered that between the two there is a mysterious and awful connection. When the jovial monarch's symposium is at its maddest height, when the guests are merriest and the liquor most delicious—then it is that this hideous presence lurks most nigh. The lights may blaze upon the festive board; but out of the shadow below, and in gloomy alcoves here and there, the boon companions shudder at the glimpse of his ghastly features. Those who have met him face to face (and such men live) describe him as sallow, cadaverous, blear-eyed, and unwholesome: his countenance overspread with a gray despair, as of a creature born from joy to misery, and retaining, in his wretchedness, the memory of all that makes life sweet, and the yearning for it. Moreover— and this is perhaps the grisliest feature of the legend— he is said to bear a villanous and most unaccountable resemblance to Gambrinus himself; insomuch that, when encountered the morning after a carousal, the beholder can scarce free himself from the delusion that it is Gambrinus's self he sees—fearfully changed, indeed, yet essentially the same. I fear there is some disagreeable secret at the bottom of all this, and that poor old Gambrinus did not quite escape the devil's claws, after all. However, if we can be resolute not to commit ourselves too far with the god, we may be tolerably secured against falling into the clutches of the hobgoblin. Meanwhile, excellent **Frau Schmidt**, another pint of beer!

III.

What may be the subtle principle according to which liquors depend for their flavour upon the form and fashion of the vessel from which they are quaffed, I know not; but certainly German beer should be drunk only from the schoppen. For a long time I put my faith in an Oxford mug of pewter with a plate-glass bottom; but, in the end, I reverted to the national tankard, with its massive base, its scolloped glass sides, and its lid enamelled with pictures and mottoes. The rest of the world might produce port glasses, hock glasses, sherry glasses, absinthe glasses; it was reserved for Germany to evolve the schoppen. Whether Gambrinus was the first to invent it, I am not precisely informed, but am inclined to consider it a supreme product of modern civilization.

I once visited the Antiken Sammlung in the Museum of the Zwinger; and judging by the wild experiments in the way of drinking-vessels on exhibition there, I should have thought the ancients must half the time have been in doubt what they were swallowing. There were elephants, fishes, Chinese pagodas, legless human figures which, unlike their living prototypes, would never stand upright even when they were empty; huge silver-mounted horns; ingenious arrangements to rap the drinker's pate if he spared to drink all at a draught, or to prick his tongue if he drank not fast enough. Some goblets there were of the capacity of seven quarts—so the guide assured me; and he added, in a quiet tone, that the mighty ones of yore thought nothing of emptying these without drawing breath. He was a tall, thin, courteous, amenable fellow, that guide —yellow-eyed, curly-bearded, with hands gloveless, unclean, and very cold. Near at hand stood a marble bust of Washington, placid, respectable, and rather dirty. How often had he heard that lie reiterated, without once being able to knit his marble brow at the liar, or wink a pupil-less eye at the visitor, not to be taken in. But I doubt not that the fact of the bust's being there deepened the guide's crime.

Of a less barbarous age are the ivory tankards,

elaborately carved, to be found in the windows of curiosity shops throughout Dresden. There, moreover, stand tall green glasses of Bohemian manufacture, jewelled and painted with arabesques and figures. But all are but approximations to the excellence of the clear glass schoppen of to-day, which, though it holds but a pint, may be replenished a hundred times a day, and is vastly more manageable than the seven-quart affair. They are usually some seven or eight inches high, and twice as much in girth—just the proportion of a respectable toper; but this model is varied within certain limits: and some of gothic design, with peaked lids, are as beautiful as heart could wish; and a pewter mannikin an inch and a half high, staggering under the weight of a barrel of liquor, is perched above the handle. The lids are a distinguishing feature, necessary to retard the too rapid evaporation of the foam. They must be kept down, like those of a maiden's eyes; should we neglect this precaution, not only is our beer liable to stale, but any impertinent fellow sitting near may, by beer-law, snatch a draught of it without saying, By your leave!

We may, of course, hurl the mug at him; there are few better missiles than a good schoppen, and every Saxon knows how to use it in this way also. The schoppen-throwing spirit is latent in the most seeming-inoffensive of the race, and will crop out on occasion.

We do not know our friend until we have seen him at such a moment. He has no tendency to individual action; he loves a majority, though not ignorant of how to turn the contrary position into a virtue. With a crowd to back him, he will sling his mug at anybody; and it is instructive to observe, when once his victory is secure, how voluble, excited, and indignant he becomes—how implacable and overbearing towards his foe; the same Saxon in his beer-saloon as at Sedan!

In reflecting upon the amount of beer consumed by the average Saxon during the day, I am inclined to believe with Rabelais that drinking preceded thirst in the order of creation, since the want postulates the habit: and that he drinks, not because his throat is parched, but in order that it may not be. It is no paradox that the thirstiest men are the smallest drinkers: therefore Saxons can never be thirsty, but drink either out of mere bravado, or else from a belief that to drink steadily the first half of their lives, will secure them from thirst during the second. If this creed be not a popular fallacy, it is a most important truth. Nevertheless, it would perhaps be safer to continue the remedy throughout the decline of existence, and so float comfortably into the other life.

IV.

From our present point of view, Dresden might be described as a beer-lake, of which the breweries are the head-waters. The liquid, however, is divided up into reservoirs of all sizes, from thousand-gallon tuns to pint bottles. The fishes are the Dresdeners themselves, who, instead of swimming in the lake, allow it to swim in them—a more pleasant and economic arrangement. This lake resembles the ocean in having hours of flood and ebb; but the tide never runs out so far as to leave the fishes high and dry. The periods of high beer, or full fishes, are, roughly speaking, from twelve to two at noon and from six to ten in the evening.

It is really not easy to exaggerate the importance of beer-saloons to the city economy. Beer, like other valuable things, has a tendency to lodge humbly: is fond of antique, not to say plebeian, surroundings; and is so thorough a demagogue that it not only flatters the multitude, but harbours in their midst! Now, so uninviting are some Dresden neighbourhoods, we must believe that, except for the beer-saloons in them, they would speedily be left without inhabitants. Thus beer equalizes the distribution of population. What is of more moment, it provides employment either directly or indirectly for a vast proportion of the people. Not to speak of the architects, coopers, glass-workers, and numberless others to whose support it largely contributes, it actually creates the landlords, waiters, and waitresses. We may go further, and point out that it is the vital principle, if not the cause, of the popular concerts, as well as of summer excursions into rural suburbs, whose healthful beauties would else remain unexplored. The student "Kneipen" owe what life they have more to their beer than to either their traditions or the Schläger. In short, society, among the mass of the people, is clustered round the beer-glass; and the liquor of Gambrinus is not more the national beverage than it is the builder-up of the nation.

The beer-saloon is the Saxon's club, parlour, and drawing-room, and is free alike to rich and poor, noble, and simple. The family-man as well as the bachelor, the old with the young man, is regular and uniform in his attendance, for Saxons have no homes, nor the refinement which leads most creatures, human or other, to reserve for themselves a retreat apart from the world's common path and gaze. It must not be inferred that the husband objects to taking his wife and children along with him: the broad Saxon tolerance never dreams of ostracising woman from the scene of her lord's conviviality. Though seldom present in large numbers, there is generally a sprinkling of them in every roomful of drinkers. I have not observed that they exercise any restraint upon the tone of conversation: considering the light in which woman is regarded, it is not to be expected that they should; and as for children, they are not regarded at all. The wives watch the conversation of their masters much as a dog might do, seldom thinking of contributing to it; or if they do, it is not in womanly fashion, but so far as possible in imitation of the men's manner. They drink their fair share of beer, often from the men's glass; but I cannot say that the geniality thus induced improves them. Until pretty far up in the social scale, there is little essential difference between the lower orders of women and those above them especially after Gambrinus has laid his wand upon them. In the German language there are no equivalents for the best sense of our Lady and Gentleman; and perhaps the reason is not entirely a linguistic one.

Female Saxony is very industrious; carries its sewing or embroidery about with it everywhere, and knits to admiration. When in its own company, it chatters like magpies, and we watch it with an appropriately amused interest. But our interest is of another sort when, as sometimes happens, a man enters with his newly-married wife, or sweetheart. The untutored stranger observes with curiosity the indifference of the couple to the public eye. Towards the close of the second glass, her head droops upon his shoulder, their hands and eyes meet, they murmur in each other's ear, and fatuously smile. It is nothing to them that the table and the room are crowded with strange faces. The untutored stranger, if he imagine these persons to be other than of perfect social respectability, commits a profound mistake. They are Saxons of the better class, and are utterly unconscious of anything coarse or ungainly in thus giving publicity to their mutual endearments. The untutored stranger had perhaps believed that publicity of love, to be sublime, must be manifested under very exceptional circumstances. He had read with pleasure how the beautiful woman threw herself upon her lover's bosom, so to intercept the fatal bullet; or his heart had throbbed at the last passionate embrace of wife and husband on the scaffold steps. But he is extravagant and prejudiced : not instant death, but a quart or so of beer, is pretext all-sufficient. Nay, may it not be that our Saxon sweethearts would find death put their affection out of joint, and therefore do wisely to be satisfied with the easy godfathership of Gambrinus? At all events, our criticisms are as gratuitous as untutored. The mixed assembly in which the exhibition takes place considers it so little extraordinary, as scarcely to be at the trouble of looking at it or away from it. Nevertheless there seems to be a spiritual nudity about it, which, if not divine, indicates a phase of civilization elsewhere unknown.

I have introduced this scene because it typifies a universal trait. Saxons cannot be happy except in public and under one another's noses. The edge of pain is dulled for them if only they may undergo their torture in the market place; and no piece of good luck is worth having which has not been dragged through the common gutter. Each man's family is too small for him—he must take his neighbour's likewise into his bosom. Is this the result of a lofty spirit of human brotherhood? or is it a diseased vanity, which finds its only comfort in stripping the wretched fig-leaves alike from its virtue and its vice? Nevertheless, most Saxons, if charged to their faces with being the first of nations, admit the impeachment; which proves how little true greatness has in common with the minor proprieties.

It would be pleasant to study this trait in its effect upon gossip and scandal. If a man denudes himself in presence of my crony and me, does he not deprive our epigrams of their sting, and make our inuendoes ridiculous? Backbiters, thus rudely treated, must miss that delicate flavour which renders a dish of French scandal the delight of the world. But the guild dies hard, and even in the face of a persecution which should go the length not only of confessing discredit-abilities, but of taking a pride in them, will still find some husks to fatten upon.

V.

It is high time for us to make some pleasant acquaintances; and if we will let our imagination wander citywards, I know a spot where we may meet some. Turning aside from the venerable Schloss Strasse, we traverse a narrower side thoroughfare, and soon arrive at a low and dark-mouthed archway. We vanish beneath it, and, feeling our way along the wall, come presently to a door which, opening almost of itself, admits us into an apartment remarkable alike for its smokiness, its narrowness, and its length. The opposite wall seems to press against us, and we instinctively adopt a sideways motion in walking down the room. Full five out of the seven or eight feet of narrowness are taken up with the square brown chairs and tables, of which there must be enough in Saxony to cover a third of the country's area. The walls are panelled breast high; the ends of the room are indistinct in the smoky haze. All the world is sitting down except ourselves and buxom Ida, who comes tripping along behind us, with both her plump hands full of beer. Let us hasten to be seated.

The Saxon habit of sitting down to everything is, by the way, one which Americans would do well to imitate, especially when they eat or drink. Man is the only animal that can sit squarely down upon a chair—it is as much his prerogative as laughing or cooking. The moral effect of sitting down is to induce deliberation, and we Republicans should have too much self-respect as well as prudence to stand up to a luncheon or liquor-bar like so many sparrows: while our Saxon brother finds his knees giving way at no more than the sight of a toothpick. That foolish relic of barbarism, the practice of rising to toasts, does, it is true, obtain in Saxony no less than elsewhere; but internal evidence justifies the prediction that Saxons will lead the world in refining it away.

Having thus got comfortably seated, buxom little Ida caresses the back of our chair, while she lends her ear and ear-ring to our order. Ida is always on the best of terms with her company, while maintaining a feminine ascendancy over them. She responds cordially if we summon her by name, but is deaf to the unceremonious rattling of the schoppen-lid, which is the usual way of calling for attendance. She sustains the many personal compliments wherewith she is plied with a rare complacent equanimity, repaying them with a softened cadence of tone and an approving smile. She has her favourites of course, but so manages matters as not to obtrude the fact unpleasantly upon the less fortunate. When, at parting, we take occasion to slip into her palm an eleemosynary coin, she allows her short fingers to close for a moment over ours in mute friendly acknowledgment. She is a brisk, round, smooth little body, with no feature or expression worth mentioning, and a figure consisting mainly of rounded protuberances. She knows her duties well, and deftly remembers the idiosyncrasies of her guest, after the first few visits have made him familiar. I have never seen in her face any record or passage of thought: she even adds up her accounts without thinking, and this is possibly one reason why so many small perquisites make their way to her plump pockets. When she finds herself at leisure—usually for an hour or so during the morning and afternoon—she has a well-conditioned little nap in a corner, never bothering her small brain-pan with life-problems past or to come. It is a mystery how a body and soul, combined in such very unequal proportions, should produce so pleasant and cheerful an effect. Is Ida ever naughty? I should as soon think of applying moral standards to a jelly-fish as to her; meanwhile, the worst wickedness I have detected in her is a funny fat slyness in that matter of perquisites. Her conscience —which probably is less fat and more gristle than any other part of her body—is, I am sure, untroubled.

Ida can scarcely be taken as a representative of her class—a fact which is probably less to their credit than to hers. German beer-girls are harder worked than English bar-maids—since in addition to late hours, they are obliged to walk from ten to fifteen miles a day, carrying to and fro heavy loads of beer-glasses. Though they may equal their English sisters in education, they are far behind them in intelligence and the appearance of refinement. They are often pretty, however, and, withal, healthy and substantial-looking: and I dare say their labours, arduous as they appear, are luxury compared to those of the peasantry, from which class most of them spring. More deleterious than the physical work is doubtless the moral wear and tear consequent upon receiving day by day the jokes, caresses, compliments, or insults of a rabble of men of all ranks and tempers. They generally acquit themselves with some tact and more good humour; and they are subjected to a freedom of speech and behaviour from the sterner sex which, in any other country, would be met by a thoroughly deserved box on the ear. It appears to be understood that the right of embracing the beer-girl is included in the price of the beer. In one respect, these young women compare pleasantly with the men-waiters: that whereas we may bind the latter body and soul to our service by a judicious administration of fees, in the minds of the former we can at best only create a conflict between their interests and their affections. We may fee a Kellnerin to the limit of her desires; yet, if that be our best charm, all will not prevent her enjoying her whisper in the corner with her poor soldier, who never gave her anything more valuable than a kiss, while our beer-glass stands empty. This is more agreeable than anything in the male character. Women were never so necessary to the world's welfare as now, if only they will be women. Let them steep their brains in their hearts, or else dispense with the former altogether. What becomes of these waitresses later in life, I know not. Let us hope they are happy with their soldiers.

The little clique which makes Ida's beer-saloon its nightly resort is of a character complementary to Ida's own. They are elderly men, and represent the most thoughtful and enlightened class in Dresden. They are patriots of '48, who, having been banished by their government, owe their recall to the progress of those opinions for which they suffered exile. Most of them are now members of the Council, and amuse themselves by occasionally voting against an increase of the king's income. They are among the few Saxons whose patriotism does not consist in being selfish, conceited, and intolerant of criticism. They desire, not to defend their country for what she is, but to help her to what she might be: if they do not sympathize with their unenlightened countrymen, they would like to render them worthy of sympathy. In the face of so stiff a job, I cannot but admire their uniformly jovial and well-conditioned aspect. There is nothing of the melancholy, wild-eyed, long-haired, collarless enthusiast about them. Probably they have the wisdom to use those qualities in their opponents which can be made to serve their own ends, and thus have become prosperous.

We may hold agreeable converse with these men, for their draught of the outer world has permanently improved their mental digestions, and allows us to talk discursively without fear of giving offence. When the beer has loosened in them the reins of those faculties which their experience has developed, they become very good company. Yet, when all has been said, there remains a secret sense of dissatisfaction. We have coincided upon many points, but on what one have we melted together? The objection may seem fantastic, but it is true and of significance. Many a hard head and intractable judgment do we meet, who yet in the dispute lets fall a word or tone which makes the eyes fill—we know not why—revealing a deeper agreement between us than any of opinions. We fight such men more lovingly than we ally ourselves with others, whose creeds, perhaps, fit ours like the lines of a dissecting map.

VI.

Besides the politicians, there is a sprinkling of the learned class, who are often shabbier in external aspect than men of far less consideration. In addition to their undeniable beer-drinking powers, they have quaffed deep of the Pierian spring, and are no less interesting than the books which they compile. There is a little human glow in them, however, and their erudite talk reminds of conversations printed on a page: it lacks the unexpectedness and piquancy of original or spontaneous thought. They are wood of a straight, close grain—displaying none of the knots and eccentric veins which make a polished surface attractive: nor do they possess the rich, pervading colour which might compensate for plainness of structure. Their faculties are useful to the world in the same way that printing-types are—they may be arranged to form valuable combinations, but are not therefore intrinsically captivating—have none of that fascination which attaches to a black-letter MS. Geniuses not only never repeat themselves, but never use the same material twice. Each fresh work is done in a new way, with new tools; and retains an unhackneyed aroma, be it ever so irregular or imperfect.

But the talents of the Saxon sages are limited in number and overworked; and the very fact of their limitation and want of idiosyncrasy seems to be the cause of their application to all sorts and amounts of labour. But a man who can get anything out of himself, all on the same rule and scale, should perhaps be especially careful to confine himself to only one thing. Original men change colour, tone, and key with every new idea; and as no idea can ever be twice the same, so is their manner of entertaining it never twice identical. Otherwise they are machines; and I think the Saxon sages often have a tendency to be mechanical.

Nevertheless, there are some originals among them. One gentleman I remember, who was by profession a lawyer, but had dabbled in literature, was the author of some poetry, I believe, and ranked himself among the Klopstocks and Heines. He had fine features, and a high, bald forehead, which he seemed always trying to heighten by passing his hand up it, and tossing back the thin locks of grey hair which hung down to his shoulders. He was dressed with small care, and less cleanliness; his shirt, in particular, was enough to make the heart ache. Reverses, perhaps, or disappointed ambition, had enrolled this personage among the sworn disciples of Gambrinus, and it was his daily custom to pledge that monarch so deeply that by evening his heart was full and ready to overflow on small encouragement. One night he entered late, and proceeded, without warning, to be ardently enamoured

of an unobtrusive young man who happened to be of
our party, and whom he had never seen before. "Sir,
you are dear to me! I love you, sir! my heart is
yours!" In proof of his regard, he presently began to
declaim a great deal of poetry; and never have I
heard those pieces more finely and eloquently interpreted. The scene, perhaps, took its rise in the
whim of a half-tipsy brain, but, as the actor wrought
upon himself, it assumed a hue of grotesque pathos.
The man became stirred to his depths; now tears
ran down his cheeks; now his eyes flashed, and
he manned himself heroically; and now again he
paused to empty his beer-glass and sign to Ida for
more. But the liquor he drank, instead of disguising
him, dissolved the mask of his inner nature. Heaven
knows what confused memories of joy and grief were
at work within him; but it was evident that, through
the miserable absurdity of circumstance, he gave us
distorted glimpses of what had been best and highest
in his character—that he was laying bare to us the
deepest heart he had. And it is on this account—
not for purposes of ridicule—that I have brought
forward the episode. His sincerity no one could have
doubted, least of all himself: yet it revealed nothing
genuine; the man's very soul was artificial, and in
the heat of his self-abandonment, he could not be
natural. His sentiment and passion could only have

moved unconscious hypocrites like himself. He had been very eminent in his profession, and all he did was marked by exceptional talent: he must once have been an exceeding handsome man; and, above all, he was a thorough German, in accord with the genius of his countrymen. But for those who are not Germans, the heart is the gunpowder whose explosion gives the bullet of thought its effect, and they cannot be pierced with the subtlest intellectual missile which lacks this projecting power.

After Ida's, my favourite resort was a mediæval-looking apartment in the Neustadt, near the head of the venerable, historic bridge which connects the main thoroughfares of the old and new towns. Werthmann, the proprietor, is a man of taste and feeling, and has adorned his saloon with intent to realize, so far as he may, the ideal of a Gambrinian temple. We enter a square room of a moderate size, wainscoted to a height of five feet from the floor with dark carved wood. Above the wainscot the wall is divided lengthwise into two compartments, the upper one exhibiting designs of highly-coloured groups of figures in fourteenth-century costumes, relieved against a dark-blue background; while the other is devoted to scraps of convivial poetry, appropriate to the paintings, and executed in the black-letter character; which poetry, if not always unexceptionable, either from a moral or poetical point of view, matches well enough the tone of the surroundings. Over the doorway is inscribed the legend " Kommt Herein, Hier ist gut sein!" which is certainly an improvement upon some of those religious perpetrations which I have noticed further back. In other places we spell out such agreeable truism as " Gerste mit Hopfen giebe gute Tropfen;" and here, again, is Doctor Martin Luther's famous couplet. The windows are sunk nearly three feet into the walls, with black oak sills and panels, and command a view of the ugly old market-place, with its rough cobble pavement and its tanned market women, presided over by the ungainly equestrian statue of Augustus the Strong, his gilding sadly tarnished by the weather. There is an inner room, much in the fashion of the first, save that the background of the frescoes is golden instead of blue ; and still beyond is the billiard-room, whence issues a buzz of voices and click of balls. At certain hours of the day Werthmann comes in—a portly, imposing, but thoroughly amiable figure, bowing with serious courtesy to each of his assembled guests. This done, he seats himself at a table with his favourite gossips and a glass of his particular beer. Among the frescoes on the walls there is more than one portrait figure of Herr Werthmann in the character of Gambrinus himself—and he supports the *rôle* well. But he is not for show only. One morning I caught him on a chair, amidst half-a-dozen workmen, clad in an enormous pinafore, and bespattered with the whitewash which he was vigorously applying to the ceiling. He is a good type of Saxon landlords, who, as a rule, are among the pleasantest and most conversable men in town. Much of the success of their business depends on their genialty, and practice makes it their second nature.

The attendants here are both male and female, though the former perhaps predominate, in their regulation black swallow-tails. I have often noticed a singular effect which uniforms have upon the analysis of character; it is nearly impossible to form an unbiassed judgment of a man whose coat and hat mark his profession. Inevitably we regard him, not as a simple human being, but through the coloured medium of his official insignia. Thus, if the Kellners wore ordinary clothes, it would be much easier to pronounce upon their peculiarities of disposition and behaviour. As it is, their sable dress-coats—which seem to have been born with them and to have grown like their skins—their staccato manner, their fallacious briskness, their elaborate way of not accomplishing anything, and their fundamental rascality, appear to be the chief impressions of them left upon my mind. They do not contrast well with the English waiters; there is seldom any approach to neatness in their condition, and they never attain the cultured, high-bred repose which we see on the other side of the Channel. In their swindling operations they manifest neither art nor delicacy; moral suasion is unknown to them, nor do they ever attempt to undermine us on the side of abstract justice and respectability. They simply and brutally retain the change, and meet any remonstrance on our part, first with denial, secondly with abuse, and finally with an appeal to the police.

Some few of these men have grown old in the service, but the majority are between eighteen and thirty. Often they are the sons of hotel-keepers, serving an apprenticeship at their trade. Their wages are very moderate, but I fancy few of them retire from the profession without having accumulated a tolerable fortune. Unless treated with a politic mixture of sternness and liberality, they are apt to be either brusque or preoccupied, if not altogether oblivious. Possibly their darker traits may be the effect of continually wearing black tailed-coats, and when they put them off, they may also lay aside their tendency to theft and falsehood. But my researches have not gone so deep as to warrant me in more than offering the suggestion.

VII.

In summer, however, we have no business to sit between four walls; Dresden is full of beer-gardens, where, if the beer is sometimes inferior, its flavour is compensated by the soft pure air and the music. Our difficulty will be, not to find a pleasant spot, but to fix upon the pleasantest. Sauntering beneath a mile-long avenue of chestnut-trees, we might climb to the Waldschloesschen Brewery, resting on the hillside like a great yellow giant, whose hundred eyes look out over a lovely picture of curving river and hazy-towered town. Here, sitting on the broad stone terrace, beneath trees so dense of foliage that rain cannot penetrate them, we are on a level with the tops of trees below, which have the appearance of a green bank suspended in mid-air. Far off on the river the white steamboats crawl and palpitate, and the huge canal-boats spread their brown wings to help along as best they may their unwieldy bulk. Here, too, the beer is of the best, and we may drink it to the tune of Mozart and Strauss.

Somewhat similar are the attractions of the Bruelsche Terrasse, which is also more accessible and more exclusive. It is fine in the evening, when it sparkles thick with coloured lamps and throbs with music; and the river, above whose brink it stands, is a black, mysterious abyss, revealed only by the reflected lights which wander here and there across its surface, or range themselves along the length of the distant bridge, and cast long wheeling shadows of unseen people passing to and fro across it. But even here we find imperfections; the beer glasses are scandalously small, and the waiters, who wear not only dress-coats but silver buttons, are more rapacious and remorseless than harpies.

After all, however, the best place is the Grosser Wirthschaft, in the Royal Park. There we are in the midst of a small forest; but a vista, opening through the trees and broadening over a wide green meadow, yields us a glimpse, at a mile's distance, of a grey dome and two or three tapering spires. The square open court, some sixty yards in width and closely planted with trees and street-lamps, is partly closed in on two sides by low buildings; the orchestra occupies a third, while on the fourth stands sentinel a gigantic tree. During the pauses of the music, a few steps will bring us to sweet secluded walks, where we might almost forget that such things as houses and Saxons existed in the world. During the heat of the season concerts are given here at five in the morning, and are attended by crowds of tradespeople, who thus secure their half-holiday before the day has fairly begun. If we can manage to get up early enough to go to one, the effect of the spectacle upon the imagination is very peculiar. Reason tells us that it is long before breakfast time; but the broad sunshine, the crowd of people drinking their beer, the music and the wide-awakeness of everything, proclaim four o'clock in the afternoon. The fact that the sun is in the wrong quarter of the heavens only increases our bewilderment, and we are almost persuaded either that the whole scene is a wonderful mirage, or that we are phantoms, accidentally strayed into the material world.

Surely, only hypercriticism could find anything to complain of in all this. We do not, I suppose, expect Saxon beer-gardens to be like the land of the lotus-eaters, where dreamy souls recline on flowery couches, and know not whether the music in their enchanted ears comes from without or within. Moreover, cane-bottomed chairs are in many ways better than flowery couches, and to sit at a table with three or four other people, even if we do not happen to know them, is preferable to having no table at all. Lovers of music should not object to receiving in exchange for five groschen, a piece of paper with the musical programme on one side, and a bill of fare on the other; nor should they allow themselves to be disturbed by the continual repassing, during the performance, of unsympathetic waiters, who never allow a beer-glass to become empty through any lack of solicitation on their part to have it refilled. If the ground beneath our feet is reddish-brown gravel instead of turf, it is all the safer for delicate constitutions; and if trees, tables, and lamp-posts are rigidly aligned, it is all the better for order and convenience. As for the music, it surely could not be finer; and the fact that every individual of the orchestra may be seen sawing or puffing himself red in the face over his horn or violin, ought only to make the pleasure more real and tangible.

Who can deny all this? Nevertheless, all the world knows that to possess good things is only to foster the notion that they might be improved. Any strictures against Saxon beer-gardens would certainly apply with equal force anywhere else, and perhaps it is chiefly because they are good enough to suggest dreams of something better, that such dreams venture to assert themselves. Were I inclined to pick flaws, the first would be that the gardens disappoint from being half gardens and half something with which the spirit of gardens is quite irreconcilable. Music, whispering leaves, summer skies—what combination could be more charming? but if we descend—as we must—beneath the leaves, the disenchantment is all the harsher. Nature is put in a strait-jacket, her tresses are shorn, and she is preposterously decked out with artificial ornament. These gardens are aptly symbolised by the Sirens, who made fascinating music and had lovely hair, and who, seen from a proper distance, seemed all delightful. But they turned out to be less attractive below. Thus, if we walk in the secluded paths near the Grosser

Wirthschaft, catching snatches of the melody, and glimpses of the gay crowd shadowed by the cool foliage, the effect is captivating; but the stern utilitarian features which a nearer view discovers, are the Siren's claws.

But my quarrel strikes a deeper root than this, and will not, I fear, gain much sympathy. I question whether music can be heard as well in company as in solitude, save when the company is in very exceptional accord. Certainly, any strange or unwelcome presence jars like a false note continually repeated. Lovers, I should imagine, might listen to sweet music with a multiplied pleasure and appreciation: or a great assembly, ablaze with some all-inspiring sentiment, doubtless take additional fire from the sound of an appropriate strain. But to lavish the mighty symphonies of great musicians upon an ill-assorted crowd, brought together, ticketed and arranged of malice aforethought, is to pawn pearls at less than their value: isolation—harmonious seclusion—are the only terms upon which a perception of subtle musical jewels can be obtained, and even these are often insufficient.

The Bible tells us that Divine Presence can be better invoked by two or three than by one; but music, like nature, not being an infinite divinity, seldom reveals her more exquisite charms save to the solitary worshipper. Human beings are terribly potent things: we admire the shrewd scent of wild animals, but what is it compared with the keenness of man's spiritual scent for his fellow?

Furthermore, musicians, unlike little boys, should be heard but not seen. Perhaps a beautiful singer may be an exception, because, in her, facial expression may aid the interpretation and give it richer colouring; and possibly the cultured grace of a master-violinist may impart form and vividness to his rendering. But the grace and beauty, not to be offensive, must, at least, equal that of the theme. A visible orchestra is like a dissected Venus: to lay bare the springs and methods of the sweet mystery of harmonious life, is to sin alike against art and nature.

VIII.

I should not have been tempted to go so far, had it not been my purpose to go one step further, and announce the remarkable discovery that the Saxons have a less correct ear for music than any people with which I am acquainted. I am sure they think quite differently, and no doubt, after the first surprise is over, they will be grateful for having had their error pointed out. Undeniably, the greatest musical composers have been of German blood: just as in ancient times, by a sort of revenge of nature, giants and pigmies were made to live together. Moreover, there is nowhere more good music than in Saxony: nor anywhere better soldiers: the reason being, not that Saxons have any especial aptitude for war or music, but that they are exhaustively and indefatigably trained. Bismarck and Wagner are at the bottom of it.

The average Saxon orchestra learns its music by rote, and its perception of harmony is not intuitive but mechanical. They regard a false note as a mistake—never as a sin; and it is only rigid drilling which enables them to do so much as that. Listen to a party of young students singing together, as is the custom of young students all over the world: they sing loudly and in perfect good faith, conscious that they are Saxons, and therefore fancying that they are infallible. But there will be more discords to a stave, than an equal number of young men of any other country could produce. There may be something pathetic about this, but there is certainly much that is disagreeable. Again, the audiences of the garden concerts are affected by tunes and slight airs, and are invariably enthusiastic in their applause of a solo, however imperfectly rendered; because, having actually beheld a man stand up before them and produce, with more or less physical exertion, a variety of musical sounds, they are convinced that they have heard what is, or ought to be, music. But they pass by the great, sublime compositions with significant silence. Now, animals are moved by tunes, and parrots and magpies can be taught to whistle them. When the tunes are what is called national—enhanced, that is, by some glorious or inspiring tradition, the consideration of whatever musical worth they may have is as nothing: such tunes influence mobs, and Saxon mobs no less than others. A tune is to music what an automaton, with its little round of recurring movements, is to a living man with his infinite variety of manifestation, which yet observes a distinctive form and purpose.

Music in Saxony, like the army, is a forced product, having no root in the nature of the people, and destined to wither away when the artificial inspiration is removed. There is surely something sacred about music: those who are born to it will seek it out through all obstacles; but to obtrude it upon persons who have no vital understanding of it, is to do injury both to the music and to them. The commonest of concerts in Saxony, and elsewhere in Germany, is everywhere admired: they are too common, perhaps, and may be lowered by low appreciation. Nothing beautiful can be driven into a man from without: the only result will be to disfigure him and desecrate the thing of beauty.—But we are getting heated again. Another glass of beer?—No, we must bid Gambrinus farewell, for it is late. We have found more than we bargained for in our schoppen.

IX.

Good little Frau Schmidt comes up, with her pleasant but not quite cheerful smile, to see us to the door, and bid us not forget to return. We had made a little mystery about her, at the beginning of our session, with the understanding that it should be cleared up before we went away. The mystery does not amount to much, after all, but its elucidation may serve also to explain why Frau Schmidt is more of a favourite of ours than any Saxon woman we have known.

The fact is (for we have not skill further to prolong the suspense, even were there any longer reason for doing so) Frau Schimdt is an Englishwoman, born, she tells us, within hearing of Bow bells. She met in London the big, silent Saxon, with the fine massive head and serious bearing, who was destined to win her love and marry her. He, perhaps, was at that time a political refugee. Certainly he was more a man than the average: there was a force and largeness in him rare among Saxons; and individual excellence is an uncomfortable possession in a land governed as is this.

But when a good many years had passed, and an altered administration could pardon Herr Schmidt's political virtues, the memory of his birthplace continually haunted him: his health began to fail, and he fancied that only a breath of his native air could restore him. His wife doubtless shrank at first from the thought of leaving England, and settling among strange faces and barbarous tongues, in an unknown land. Yet her heart would not let her hold him back, and without her he could not go. They came, therefore, and Herr Schmidt, having purchased a small beer-saloon on the banks of the river he had known in boyhood, looked forward to health and quiet happiness.

But all was somehow not right—not as he had expected. Was Dresden changed, or had his memory played him false? There stood Dresden, with her domes and steeples; there flowed the well-known Elbe beneath the old historic bridge. Around him were Saxon tongues and faces; yet the city, the people of his remembrance were not there. Perchance, save in memory, they had never been at all. Ah, Herr Schmidt, in leaving England, I fear you were not wise. Had you remained, two good countries would have been yours: England, good enough in all conscience for those who have never known a better,— and the Saxony of your remembrance, without doubt superior to England, to Saxony itself, or to any other place whatever. But you were not wise, Herr Schmidt, and therefore both countries are lost to you.

And how of Frau Schmidt, the little grey-clad Englishwoman? She loves her Saxon husband, and would rather be with him than anywhere; yet, perhaps, amidst her many cares and few amusements, she finds now and then a moment wherein to be decently wretched. When, on my first chance visit to her little saloon, I happened to let fall an English word, I shall not soon forget with what a thirsty eagerness she caught up the old familiar tongue; with what an almost tremulous pleasure she stood and talked— talked for the mere pleasure of once more talking English; delighting in it as a child does over a long-lost toy; yet saddened by that very delight, because it made her recognize how rare the luxury was and must ever be. Well, she does her best to be a good wife, to make her guests welcome, and worthily to serve King Gambrinus, hoping secretly that in time he will reward her from his treasury, and enable her at least to die in England. That time will never come, patient little Frau Schmidt; but meanwhile may evil befall me if ever I neglect to send you that occasional English newspaper for which you once with hesitating earnestness besought me.

III.

SIDEWALKS AND ROADWAYS.

I.

PEOPLE live surrounded with themselves, and in their own atmosphere, and feel at ease in proportion as what is without is attuned to what is within. The religious devotee still gravitates towards his pew, the student towards his library, the drunkard towards his gin-shop. We never feel sure of a man until we have met him at his own fire-side, clad in his dressing-gown and slippers. If we happen to have made acquaintance beforehand with the dressing-gown and fireside, we shall already have gone far towards getting the measure of their proprietor. With this background to relieve the figure, a brief examination will reveal to us more than protracted study without it. But were it possible wholly to isolate a man from all surroundings, he would appear—if he appeared at all— an incomprehensible monstrosity.

As with the individual, so with the community. If

we wish to picture a people to alien minds, we shall do wisely to eschew direct description and analysis, and rather seek to indicate our subject by analogies from its encompassment; by suggestion, and subtle inference. Otherwise, our rendering is apt to appear crude and lifeless; for many delicate but important shades of character, too evanescent to be caught from the living man, are indelibly and permanently impressed upon the four walls between which his life is passed.

Men are a kind of hieroglyphic writing hard to decipher; but they translate themselves into their houses, and we may read them there at our leisure, without danger of being influenced by the sphere of human personality to falsify the conclusions of our cool and sober judgment. A man may, by virtue of his personal magnetism, juggle me into the belief that his black is white; but a glance at his designs in brick and mortar, at his pictures and paper-hangings, will go far to set me right again. As Emerson would put it, his expenditure is him; and he must be a shrewd man indeed who can falsify his expenditure.

Now, all communities, from families to nations, have each their distinctive flavour, insomuch that a Bostonian, or a Cockney, can be identified almost as readily as if he were coloured blue or green. In logical correspondence with this truth is the fact that the material London or Boston from which they come has recognizable peculiarities, distinguishing it from all other cities; the streets and houses are so built and laid out that they occupy a separate and particular place in the memory. To the vulgar mind the word city conveys the idea of streets and houses, and nothing more; or at best (if they have read Blackstone), of a town which has or had something to do with a bishop. Strictly speaking, however, these walls and pavements are but the incarnation of the true city, which primarily inheres in the brains and wills of the citizens. Their expenditure being them, and the city being unquestionably their expenditure, it follows that the city, as a whole, is an exposition of the modes of thought and temper of its inhabitants. Whatever discrepancies exist are due solely to the limitations of man's control over matter. Swedenborg, a profounder and broader seer than either Emerson or Blackstone, touches the core of the question when he says that cities represent doctrines.

Flesh and blood being thus related to stone and mortar, the delineator of the latter must become to some extent the portrayer of the former—a circumstance in no small degree to his advantage. For, let him describe what he will—a paving-stone or a doorknob, a window-blind or a church-steeple—he can always rebut the charge of triviality by admonishing the critic of a hidden symbolism contained in the passage, the vital significance of which only ignorance or levity could overlook. And if, in the course of his narrative, he happen on some bit of personal gossip, some human characteristic, humorous or pathetic, let him admit it without fear of inconsistency: it is but a more direct and undisguised method of painting a Dutch interior, or of giving relief and solidity to his sketch of yonder picturesque old castle-turret. Such a person is as infallible as the Pope; but, unlike the Pope, his infallibility is a comfort to him, and productive of both profit and amusement.

In these days of the ballot, and of universal suffrage, some enthusiastic elector may object, that the true representatives of a people's doctrines are, not the cities they live in, but the gentlemen they return to Congress or to Parliament; and that, consequently, a detailed analysis of these gentlemen's character and personal appearance will serve all the purposes of a moral and material estimate of the towns which they represent. Fifth Avenue—or Mayfair, as the case might be—would be discoverable in the representative's high arched nose; Wall Street, or Lombard Street, in the calculating glance of his sharp eyes; Five Points, or Seven Dials, in the ungainly shape of his mouth and feet. His intellectual and affectional nature would be a compendium of his electors', no less than his political opinions and prejudices. And the biography of the man would be a symbolic history of the city.

The suggestion is a valuable one, but action upon it would at present be premature. Every man is a microcosm, but some advance must be made in uniformity of condition and opinion, and in consistency of belief, before it would be possible for him, humanly speaking, to become a micropolis. His incongruities would kill him, in real life; even the creations of modern fiction could scarcely fulfil the exigencies of the position. Moreover, granting our micropolis, there is still a heavy deficiency to be made up in our capacities for analyzing him. Though our insight may be keen enough to distinguish the business quarters of his town from the aristocratic or plebeian ones, as portrayed in his features; yet, when we descended to the minutiæ upon which the general effect in so great measure depends, we should be apt to find ourselves at fault. Where, for instance, should we find recorded the order of architecture of the city hall? or how determine whether the streets were stone-paved or macadamised? But science, and the enlightenment of the masses, can work miracles; and far be it from us to question its ultimate mastery of trifles such as these. Meanwhile, however, we are fain to continue our lucubrations under the first-mentioned system.

II.

It would be of convenience to me could I declare at the outset what the distinctive characteristics of Dresden streets and houses are: whether the streets were all narrow, dark, and devious; or broad, straight, and open: whether the houses were invariably gabled, quaint, and crooked; or erect, fair-proportioned, and spacious: whether the city were one of magnificent distances, or contracted within the limits of a bow-shot. Unfortunately any such definite generalities are out of place in speaking of Dresden. Its only distinctive characteristics, so far as my observation goes, are its ubiquitous evil odour and its omnipresent dirty plaster. For the rest, what it asserts in one quarter it contradicts in another, and hardly allows us finally to make up our mind to either condemnation or approval.

There is one thoroughfare which, under five different names, traverses the city from north to south, as a diameter its circle. This fickleness in the matter of names becomes less surprising when we consider that the street has been several centuries growing, and that its course takes it through nearly every phase of life which the city affords, excepting only the lowest. Traversing its two or three miles of length from end to end, we shall make as thorough an acquaintance with the genius of Dresden streets as it suits our purposes to do. If once or twice we make a short incursion to the right or left, it will only be for the end of recreation.

It begins—locally if not chronologically speaking—in the Neustadt, on the northern bank of the Elbe, being known there as the Haupt Strasse. Considered in itself, this Haupt Strasse is the finest street in Dresden. It is sixty yards or more in width, and nearly a mile long; down its centre runs a broad walk bordered with trees; on either side is a carriage-way and sidewalks. But the street dwarfs the houses, which are here quite low and mean, and shops into the bargain. Shops and, still more, shop-signs, however intrinsically attractive and brilliant, are not consonant with architectural dignity; and these Saxon shop-signs, with their impossible names and grotesque announcements, would turn a street of Parthenons to ridicule. The Haupt Strasse merges at either extremity into an open place or square, that towards the north-west presided over by the new Albert-Theater, while the south-western one is forced to be content with that foolish old Augustus, surnamed the Strong —bare-headed, bare-armed, bare-legged, and astride of an incredible steed which squats on its hinds legs, and paws the air with its fore-feet like a gigantic kangaroo. Standing in the shadow of this worthy, we see the street pass on over the ancient bridge to the

Altstadt; on our left, across the market-place, is the hospitable door of our old friend Werthmann's beer-saloon, while nearly in front of us lies the black guard-house, like a sullen mastiff, whose glittering teeth are the stacked arms before the entrance, while his eyes are the sentry pacing to and fro, on the look-out for officers and royal carriages.

If the street dwarfs its houses, it pushes its sidewalks out of sight. Dresden is sometimes said to bear a distant resemblance to Florence; and, hearing this, the Dresdeners perhaps thought it incumbent upon them to dispense with all invidious distinctions between road and footway. But they proceeded upon a mistaken principle in so doing; for whereas in Florence the streets are all sidewalk, in Dresden the sidewalks are all street, or nearly so. The houses edge forward their broad stone toes towards the curb, and often quite overstep it; or, if otherwise, the path is mounded up to such a ticklish height, that walking upon it becomes precarious. In some districts, the matter is compromised by putting the sidewalk in the centre of the street, where it ekes out a slender existence, forming, on rainy days, the bed of an unsavoury little torrent which bears away in its current such domestic superfluities as the adjoining houses find it inconvenient to retain.

This, however, more accurately describes the condition of things ten years ago. An improvement-spasm has seized Dresden of late, and sidewalks have begun to broaden here and there, and laws have been made as to the conditions under which they are to be used, which are rigidly enforced by the police. It is observable, nevertheless, that although sidewalks are coming into existence, the Dresdeners either do not know how to use them, or do not much care to do so; they prefer the pavement. They stray on to the sidewalk in an incidental sort of way, but do not find themselves at home there, and soon return to the gutter. To a foreign mind a sidewalk is desirable not so much on account of its utility as because it assists, like a decent hat and coat, in the preservation of a certain self-respect and dignity. As men, we wish to separate ourselves as far as we may from the chaos of the roadway, where we are on no better a footing than the dogs, horses, peasant-women, and other draught animals. Sidewalks are, in our view, the etiquette—the courtesy of streets; as significant there as tasteful upholstery in a drawing-room. The Saxon, however, either has a soul above such considerations, or, shall we say? alien to them.

Be it said, meanwhile, that the streets are kept from dirt to an extent that would astonish a Cockney, or even a New-Yorker. This is partly due, of course, to the circumstance that there is comparatively little traffic in the city, and the dirt never has a fair show as against the cleansers. Possibly, since every case has two sides, something might be said in defence of streets which have a strong tendency to get dirty. A street without dirt is like a man without blood—pallid, forlorn, and lacking vigour. Nobody, let us hope, likes unclean streets; but perhaps some people have a secret partiality for streets which demand incessant toil and struggle to keep them pure, and thereby prove their possession of energetic life and powerful vitality. No dead streets should be allowed in this busy world; when they cease to be thronged, they cease to have an excuse for being at all. The same is true of houses, of which many in Dresden are lifeless shells, or nearly so. They look like empty, ugly, overgrown hotels; no human life and bustle informs them. They would seem to have been born insignificant, and subsequently, for no sufficient reason, to have expanded into gawky giantship. In this respect they might be compared with the Saxon people, who possess no qualities to warrant their rising above pigmydom, but whom an ironic freak of destiny has uplifted to a foremost place among nations. They should be taken down and reconstructed upon a smaller and more economic scale.

This, however, is by the way. I wish to remark that there is something peculiar about Dresden cleanliness—I had almost said, something horrible; for though streets, entrance-halls, and stairways are washed, brushed, and put in order with as much careful regularity as if they were race-horses, they are not the less pervaded by a strange and most unwelcome odour, which nothing will eradicate. It arouses the darkest suspicions, though every ocular appearance be calculated to inspire confidence. However spotless the outside may seem to the eye, the nose is not to be beguiled; there must be impurity somewhere. And surely there is something horrible about a thing that looks clean and yet smells badly. What pleases the sight is the more bound to gratify the nostrils. *Noblesse oblige.*

Now, in connection with this circumstance, is to be taken another, the explanation of which will, I think, solve the whole mystery. If we pass from the clean exterior of a Saxon's house to its interior, we shall find his drawing-room somewhat less immaculate than his passage, his dining-room than his drawing-room, his bed-chamber than his dining-room; while he himself is by far the least immaculate of all, tried whether by nose or eye—there is no whited sepulchre about him, at all events. An evil odour is something which only inward cleanliness, working outward, can remove. Men are more apt to desire that their emanations, their works, their expressed and embodied thoughts, should appear pure, than that their proper selves should be so.

Their surroundings, they argue, are more seen than they; and it is their continual delusion that though their actions, having once been acted, are no longer to be concealed, yet it is always easy to hide themselves. The Saxon, consequently, diligently expends his lustrative energies upon his street and stairway, but never thinks of washing his own shirt. Of the omnipresent evil odour he is never conscious, but it is the very essence and betrayal of the whole matter. Dogs are more sagacious; do not trust to ocular appearances; the cloven foot of the devil would not move them; but let them once get to leeward of him, and he stands convicted in a moment. He, in his innocence, would probably be at far greater pains to cover those awkward hoofs of his than to determine the direction of the wind. But it is by oversights such as this that so many honest people get into trouble.

III.

The ancient bridge which joins Haupt Strasse to the Schloss Platz is the only respectable piece of architecture in Dresden. But it seems nearly impossible to make an ugly bridge. Its necessity is to produce an impression of combined lightness and power—of one kind of strength overcoming another—which is the essence of vitality. It requires genius to erect an edifice which shall appear other than dead, but to build a lifeless bridge would need almost as much talent perverted. Man has seldom made anything so flattering at once to the eye and to the self-esteem of his kind. For bridges are fascinating not only at a distance; it is a triumph even greater to stand upon them and watch the baffled current fret vainly below, slipping helpless past the sturdy feet of the piers, and hurrying in confusion away beneath the shadow of the arches. Here is a direct and palpable victory gained over Nature, less exhilarating, no doubt, than a ship's, but more assured. As we saunter across the pavement, firm in mid-air, we mentally exult in our easy superiority to the discomfort and peril from which we are protected. In every step we feel the whole pride of the builders in their accomplished work. Beholding the swirling charge of the river down upon us, we half-consciously identify ourselves with the massive masonry, and share its defiance of the onset.

Yet it behoves our pride not to overween too far, since the immortal river must in the end overcome its stubborn old adversary. Indeed, one pier already succumbed, in days gone by, to the terrific down-rush of a spring flood, armed with huge battering-rams of ice. I have myself often watched great ice-slabs come sweeping on and dash harsh-splintering against the buttresses, and pile themselves suddenly up on one another's hoary shoulders, as if to scale the angry ramparts. But, though seeing, I could never feel the shock, or fancy the bridge endangered. In great freshets, however, when the river boils upwards to the keystone and higher, the push must be like that of a giant's hand. The arches are narrow, so that the stout piers seem to have pressed close to one another for mutual support; they stand foot to foot and shoulder to shoulder, close embattled against their interminable foe. It is sad to think that the successful contest of hundreds of years must issue in ultimate defeat. It will be broken, one day—that rigid phalanx; first one and then another ancient warrior will crumble away, conquered but not subdued, and their stony remains will stand, for centuries longer, in the river bed where they fought; and a future age will dig up their foundation-piles, and out of them build a theory of a city which lay on the river banks some time in the pre-historic past.

The bridge is not a wide one, but the summits of the outstanding piers are furnished with a semicircle of stone bench, which makes them look particularly comfortable on midsummer afternoons. Were Dresden Florence indeed, these recesses would be spread two-deep with lazy *lazzaroni* all day long. But somehow or other (though heaven knows there is little enough briskness or wide-awakeness in them), Saxons never lie about in picturesque attitudes, with their hat-brims drawn over their eyes. Saxons cannot be picturesque, and would only dislocate their joints if they tried to be so. To be picturesque requires an unconscious originality of nature, and disregard of the rules of vulgar conventionalism, or, better still, ignorance of them. But vulgar conventionalism is our Saxon hero's best virtue; when he abandons it he becomes, not picturesque, but brutal. However, tired and shabby people do sometimes sit down on these stone benches, with due heed to the police regulations; so let us not be ungrateful.

The law of keep-to-the-right, which is strictly enforced on this bridge, throws light on some of the traits both of the Government and the governed. The scheme works admirably; there is never any jostling or hindrance; we bowl along with our backs all turned to one another, and entirely relieved from the responsibility of self-guidance. But we pay the penalty of this sweet immunity as soon as we get beyond the law's jurisdiction. We are run into so constantly that it seems as though the world had conspired against us. Everybody appears bent upon button-hole-ing us on particular business. If there be a moderate crowd in the streets, no amount of agility in dodging will enable us to get on fast; either we must shoulder down everyone we meet, or else resign ourselves to a mile and a half per hour. It is useless to blame the Saxons for this—they cannot help it. They are so accustomed to walking through life with the policeman's hand on their coat-collar, that when his grasp is relaxed they stray without helm or compass, and could not get out of the way of the devil, if he happened to be in their path. A fairer mark for criticism is their lack of that American or English sense of humour which alone can compensate for the annoyance of such encounters. To be easily put out or insulted, cannot be said to prove a lofty magnanimity. How we like men who can be amused where most people would get in a passion! Such men are stout-souled and self-respectful; but thin patiences proclaim meagre natures. And a Saxon crowd is deficient not in temper only. There is in the world none to which I would less willingly trust a lady. As I have before had occasion to point out, the Saxons are a strictly logical people; they have sufficient intelligence to understand that woman is the weaker vessel; and if she be unprotected, the syllogism is complete; over she goes into the gutter, and let her thank her stars if no worse befall her.

At night the bridge is lit with a double row of lamps; and, seen from a distance, the dark arches vanish, and the fire-points seem strung upon a thread, and suspended high over the river, which lovingly repeats them. Reflected in water, fire enriches both its mirror and itself—like truth discerned in the shadowy bosom of allegory. But the Saxons are thrifty souls, who do not believe in letting their lights shine before men, after the hour when sober citizens should be a-bed. Accordingly, one half of them are extinguished by eleven o'clock, and the remainder two or three hours later. There is nothing more strongly suggestive of incorrigible death than a street-lamp put out before daylight. It is the more forlorn because it had been so cheerful. No belated traveller needs other companions, if he be provided with an occasional lamp along his way. It shines and wavers, and has in it the marvellous sun-born quality of positive life; it warms and burns, like his own household fire, and is thus a link between his home and him; it brings memories of genial hours, and doubly lights his way. The most natural god of fallen man was Fire; his was an ardent, and withal a poetic and refined religion. Perhaps we should be no worse off were there more men, now-a-days, simple and reverent enough to reinstate his worship. They would possibly be no further from the ultimate truth than were they to evolve God from philosophical mud-pies and Chaos.

IV.

Having crossed the bridge, and walked the length of

a melancholy Droschkey-stand, we reach the Georgen Thor—the triple archway, beneath which entrance is made into Dresden proper—which is the very nucleus of quaint antiquarian interest. Let us therefore pause a moment to admire, before proceeding further.

That the archway is not ornamental must be admitted, but its parent was Necessity, not Art. The way of it was this:—Once upon a time, but for no good reason that I ever heard, a Royal Palace was born into the world, and, as luck would have it, in Dresden. A more awkward, flat-faced, shapeless, insufferable barn of a Royal Palace was never before smeared with yellow plaster. Nevertheless, like other ill weeds, it grew apace, and, before long, had sprawled itself over a good part of the city; but as there happened to be plenty of waste land thereabouts, which people thought might be covered with one kind of rubbish as well as with another, nothing was said, and the Royal Palace went on growing bigger and uglier every day. At length, however, it began to approach the main thoroughfare of the city, and actually seemed to threaten interference with the popular freedom of traffic. Now, indeed, the wiseacres began to shake their heads, and whisper to one another that they should have fenced the Royal Palace in while it was yet young, and have obliged it to agree never to exceed reasonable bounds, and on no account to interfere with the lawful public freedom. But, alas! their wisdom came too late; for what was their consternation, on waking up one morning, at finding that this ugly, good-for-nothing, barefaced Royal Palace had grown clear across their main thoroughfare, and then, to prevent its flank from being turned, it had scrambled hastily down a side street, and made fast its further end to a great sulky block of a building, nearly a quarter of a mile off! All direct access to the marketplace was thus obstructed, and the city lay prone beneath the foot of this intolerable Royal Palace. And so, doubtless, would it have remained to the present day, had it not been for the fairy godmother, Necessity. That redoubtable old personage, who has the valuable quality of always being on hand when she is wanted, was not long in making her appearance; and, seeing how matters lay, with her customary readiness of resource, she thrust three of her long fingers directly through the body of the Royal Palace, thereby opening a way for the people to run to and fro as before. So the people exulted, freedom of traffic was restored, and the lubberly Palace was obliged to put the best possible face upon its discomfiture. This it literally accomplished by setting the royal coat-of-arms over the tunnel, by declaring that it had itself caused the tunnel to be made for the good of the people, and by christening it "George's Gate;" though why not "Limited-Monarchy Gate," or even "Conservative-Republican Gate," I never was able to discover. But it is said that the Royal Palace never grew any more after that deadly thrust given it by Necessity; nay, there are those who maintain that it is beginning to dwindle away, and who cherish hopes of finally getting rid of it altogether. Meanwhile, however, this is the end of the story; and the moral is in the story itself.

Like many seeming misfortunes, this triple tunnel is of more service to Dresden than an unobstructed roadway would have been: it is so delightfully grotesque, mediæval, and mysterious. Its low-browed arches, as our imagination peeps beneath them, lend the city beyond a peculiar flavour of romance. Passing through the dusky groined passage-way, we seem to enter an interior world; we bid farewell to the upper life, and greet the narrow strip of sky, which shows between the high-shouldered roofs of the antique houses, as the first glimpse of a firmament hitherto unknown. That ideal German life—foreshadowed in nursery songs and story-books—is now on the point of realisation; we keep our eyes open, half expecting to encounter a gnome or a good-natured giant at every step; and are not a little indignant at meeting so many people with every-day dresses on. We make the most out of the old-fashioned black and yellow uniforms of the Royal messengers, the scanty petticoats of the bare-legged peasant girls, and the spiked helmets of the soldiery. We rejoice in the narrow gloom of the by-ways, in the gabled unevenness of the houses, in the fantastic enchantment of the shop-windows. And by the time we have traversed Schloss-Strasse and reached the Alt-Markt, we are ready to pronounce Dresden the genuine German Eldorado.

Here, however, the real old city comes to an end, and disenchantment grows upon us at every fresh step: until, having wandered down See Strasse and Prager Strasse, and, from the verge of the railway, cast a glance at the brand-new block of sandstone palaces on the further side, fronting the Reich Strasse and the Bismarck Platz, we discover that the romantic charm wrought upon us by the mysterious old archway has quite worn off, and, alas! is never to be conjured back again. Once more we reiterate it—would that mankind knew where to stop! Dresden, with all its faults, might at least have remained Dresden; but these monstrous outgrowths throw contempt not only upon the quaint simplicity of the original town, but still more upon themselves for pretending to belong to it.

Let us saunter back to the Alt-Markt, which is full of suggestions. On our way we may observe, at the entrance of more than one street, a bit of board nailed to a stick, bearing the announcement, " Strasse Gesperrt." Let no rude hoof approach, no wheel invade. The poor street is diseased, and the surgeons are at work upon it. This warning-off lends a peculiar interest to the forbidden spot; for the first time we feel impelled to make it a visit. Still more remarkable is the fascination attaching to empty-house lots, so soon as they are boarded up preparatory to beginning building. I know no place of public entertainment more sedulously visited. The moment the screen is well up, each knot-hole and crack becomes a prize to be schemed and fought for. Staid citizens, anxious business men, *blasé* men of the world, will pause for half an hour, eagerly scrutinising a bed of slaked lime, a pile of bricks under a shed, a couple of dirty ladders leaning against a maze of scaffolding, half-a-dozen old wheelbarrows, and as many workmen leisurely building a house with a pipe of tobacco and a can of beer each. The fairest *coryphées* of a ballet would be vain of half the attention which these fellows receive. The explanation is to be sought not only in the perverse instinct to see what is not meant to be seen; it is traceable likewise to that universal interest in the process of creation, which is among the most pregnant and significant traits of humanity. Who would not rather witness a house being built, or a book being written, than see either completed? And when the process may be viewed through surreptitious knot-holes, it is enough to captivate a Stoic!

"Strasse Gesperrt" is all too familiar to Dresdeners. The city is for ever undergoing disembowelment; some part of her internal economy is chronically out of kelter. It is the curse of Dresden that she is founded upon a rock: she lies in a granite basin, and can never get rid of her iniquities. So imbued is her soil with impurity, the hero of the Augean stables himself would be baffled by it. Bad as is the disease, however, the remedies do but complicate it. The Dresdeners appear to have an actual mania for hacking at their mothers' entrails, but their unnatural conduct inflicts its own penalty. Her disease is contagious; not earth only is thrown up out of these trenches, but fever and small-pox likewise; whereof many die each year, the rich scarcely less often than the poor. I mention this because I believe it to be little known. The authorities, who are wise in their generation, so manage their reports that even the dying can hardly bring themselves to believe there is really anything the matter with them. The only meliorator, as has been already hinted, is the fierce north wind which at certain seasons, as if out of all patience with the foul atmosphere, sweeps madly through the city, bringing down tiles and chimneys, wrenching off windows, blowing away people's hats, upsetting boats on the river and omnibuses on the bridge. Perhaps a desire to get through with its job as quickly as possible adds impetus to the blast. But the fallacy that Dresden is a healthy residence must be exploded. In addition to its feverish soil, it possesses one of the most trying climates in the world. They say the climate used formerly to be better; which is certainly more credible than that it was ever worse.

V.

A little way down one of the most unsavoury side-streets stands a pump, from which, oddly enough, is obtained the best water in the city. To be sure, that is not saying much; for the best water is quite undrinkable, and cannot be used, even for washing purposes, until after it has been boiled. The pump is made of iron, with ornamental mouldings, has a long curved tail, well polished by the fiction of many hands, and a straight nose, with a single nostril underneath; so that the stream does not issue forth in a sparkling arch, after the graceful old fashion, but gushes straight down at right angles—probably a more convenient arrangement. Although the pump itself may not be up to our ideal in *Faust*, the group of *Dienstmaedchen*, which gathers round it at water-drawing hours, is none the less pleasant to contemplate.

They assemble from far and near, a wooden pitcher in each hand, their heads and arms bare, their skirts tucked up; full of free motion, relaxation, and fun. Ever since Rebecca's time, who has not enjoyed the spectacle of young women at a spring? How graceful and feminine all their movements are, whether standing in good-humoured gossip, awaiting their turn; or stooping to place the pitcher beneath the spout; or lending vigorous strokes to the long pump-handle; or tripping stoutly away with their fresh-sparkling burden, splashing it ever and anon upon the pavement as they go! They seem especially to enjoy themselves at the water-drawing, as though it were an employment peculiarly suited to them. And so it is; men look as awkward at a pump as women graceful. To do the Saxon men justice, they never affront good taste in this matter, if there be a woman anywhere in the neighbourhood to do their pumping for them.

Women have been compared with water as to some of their qualities, but I think the two in many ways complements of each other, and this may be the reason their association produces so complete and satisfying an effect. Sea-born Aphrodite had been less beautiful as a child of earth; and I would rather see a naiad than a hamadryad, for instance. Depend upon it, women are never more dangerous than at a fountain or by the sea-shore, as Cupid's statistics would easily prove: and does not this lend an additional touch of pathos to the thought that women are so apt to drown themselves when love deceives them? They draw bright water from the grimy earth for the purification and refreshment of mankind; and if mankind prove ungrateful, a plunge into the self-same element provides their remedy. Speaking frankly, however, were these Dresden naiads to take an occasional plunge with no more serious purpose than that of cleanliness, the chances against their being driven to a final plunge by disappointed affection would be materially increased.

Midway between the pump and the Schoppen stands the soda-water bottle. The water is manufactured by Dr. Struve, and is a pleasant beverage enough, especially the morning following an overdose of beer. During the summer season it is sold at the Trink-Hallen, which are scattered throughout the town and for a mile or so among the environs. They are neat clap-boarded little boxes, about ten feet square; all made on the same pattern, with an open counter across the front, on which are abundance of flowers in pots, and behind the flowers a young lady, who is not to blame if she happen to be less fair than they. Occasionally a pretty girl will accept the situation; but the service is not so popular as that in the beer saloons; though the one is as sedentary as the other is active. There is no chance for sociability; the hostess has no chair to offer her guest; and the comparative isolation combines with the lack of exercise to produce a gloomy, and even forbidding demeanour strongly in contrast with the smiling freedom of the beer-maidens, not to mention the careless abandon of the nymphs of the pump-handle.

VI.

Along with the new districts which have of late years been added to the city, the Dresdeners have seen fit to provide themselves with a tramway. As an intelligent inhabitant informed me, tramways were first invented about two years ago, and Dresden was one of the first cities to make practical use of them. It commonly happens that we are most proud of those things which we have, as it were, discovered ourselves; and accordingly this honest populace regards its novel experiments with no little satisfaction, not unmixed with wonder, and even awe.

"I was not so fortunate as to be present at the first launching of these extraordinary engines; but about a fortnight later I was attracted by the sight of a large and excited crowd assembled on the corner of Prager and Waisenhaus Strasse. At that time there were rumours of strikes and disaffection among certain of the workmen employed by the Government; and I at once conceived that a disturbance had actually broken out, and that possibly a battle was even then in progress between the infuriated labourers and the police. In vain, however,—having arrived breathless on the ground,—did I look about for the combatants. Nobody seemed to be fighting; no corpses were visible; there was not so much as a drunken man or a woman in a fit. Nevertheless, the crowd was manifestly wrought up to a high pitch of excitement about something; and being too dull to divine the cause, and too proud to inquire it, I resolved patiently to await the issue. By-and-by I noticed that the tramway-rails were laid round this corner, and then methought I began to understand a little.

"The crowd was massed on the sidewalk, and was kept there by two policemen. Some distance beyond the curb, in the hollow of the arc described by the rails in turning the corner, stood a man in official costume, holding a whistle in his lips, upon which he played an irregular and very shrill tune. Occasionally he paused a moment to look down the street; then, turning to the crowd, gesticulated with a red flag in an agitated manner, and blew his whistle more sharply than before. After this had gone on for some time, and every heart was beating high with suspense, a distant rumbling noise was heard, like thunder, or still more like the rolling of the wheels of a tramway car. Along with this sound another of a different description was audible—a sharp, penetrating sound, closely resembling the whistle of a tramway-car-driver. It was answered by the man on the corner with a wild, ear-piercing peal. At the same moment a hoarse voice shouted, 'Es kommt! es kommt!'

"Then began a tumult hard to describe. The cry was taken up and repeated. The crowd surged storm-like, those in front striving to press back out of reach of danger, while those behind seemed madly bent on getting forward. All the time the rumbling grew louder and nearer, the whistling wilder and shriller, the gesticulation of the official on the corner with the red flag more violent and unintelligible. One poor fellow, the warring of whose emotions had been too much for him, entirely forsook his senses at this juncture; and even as wild animals, when driven mad by terror, are said to rush straight into the jaws of danger, did he, eluding the grasp of the now exhausted policeman, dash frantically across the track. Women shrieked, strong men turned pale, and averted their eyes with a shudder. But a special Providence guards the insane. The terrible tramway car was still full thirty paces distant, and he gained the opposite side of the street in safety.

"The next few moments comprise such a sickening

whirl of sights, sounds, and emotions as only a pen of fire could hope to pourtray. Indeed, I have no very distinct recollection of what passed. Something I seem to hear of a clattering of steel-shod hoofs, a panting of straining steeds, a grating of harsh-turning wheels. Something I seem to see of a face, grim-set, with a whistle in its mouth; of a vast moving bulk, which was neither house nor chariot, but a mingling of the essential parts of both, sweeping in majestic grandeur round the iron curve. Something I seem to feel of a pride that was half awe, of an exultation that was mostly fear, of a wonder that was all bewilderment. But I remember no more. When I came to myself, I found that the tramway car had halted a rod or two beyond the turn, and was discharging its pale-faced passengers on the sidewalk. The driver was chatting with one of the policemen, quietly, as if nothing of special importance had happened. The official on the corner had stepped into the neighbouring beer saloon to whet his whistle. But I walked homeward, deep in thought. Come what might, at least I had lived to see a tramway car.

"The conviction forces itself upon me that tramway cars are alive; that, in addition to the destructive qualities of ordinary steam engines, they are endowed with an appalling intelligence all their own, which drivers and guards may be able in some degree to influence, but not wholly to control. To have live engines rushing through our very streets and over our shop doorsteps! Is it not tremendous, and really very alarming? But is it not also grand, and our own invention? The fact that for so many years we have been taught to regard anything in the shape of a railway as the most forbidden of forbidden ground, may explain the consternation wherewith we behold the dreaded rails winding their iron way into our daily walks. Time will, perhaps, accustom us to the innovation, though hardly during the present generation."*

I may be permitted to add that the cars appear exceptionally large to a foreign eye, and are further peculiar in being provided with a second story, attainable by means of a couple of elaborate spiral staircases, one at each end: a sufficiently luxurious arrangement, though perhaps a good steam-lift would be an improvement. Inside they are very comfortable; and no one is allowed to stand up. They do not run singly and at short intervals, but in trains—two or three starting at the same time; and then a prolonged cessation. As for the men with red flags and whistles, who are stationed at short intervals all along the line, it is a question whether they are employed to summon the populace to behold the greatness and majesty of tramway cars, or to warn them out of the way lest

---

* Translated from the Journal of a Saxon acquaintance.

they be run over. Be that as it may, there is never any lack of spectators; and every week or so we hear of some poor creature's having been crushed beneath the Juggernautic wheels.

Collisions with vehicles are frequent. The teamsters and Droschkey drivers have a deadly feud with tramway cars; the latter because the cars injure their business; the former because they make them "turn out." The police always support the new-fangled tramways, and the feud is thereby embittered. Most opprobrious epithets are exchanged, and occasionally matters proceed further yet. Once I saw a lumbering great waggon heavily bumped by a car. The waggoner, an uncouth, stolid-featured fellow, started at the jar as though a new and very ugly soul had suddenly entered into him. He stood up, shaking his fist and his whip, and shrieking out a great volume of abuse and defiance. The car passed on, leaving him to rave his fill. But this did not satisfy him. He presently jumped down from his box and gave chase, whip in hand, his long ragged coat flying out behind him. He caught up with the car, and lashed it with his whip as though it had been a sentient being. The guard was standing on the platform, but it was not until he had said something to the revengeful waggoner, that the latter's whip was aimed at him. The fellow probably thought that since the guard was connected with the car, it would be as well to give him a share of the car's punishment. He sprang on the step, and so plied the unfortunate official with his knotted lash, as soon to force him to retreat inside. The victor then jumped off, fetching the car a parting thwack as he did so, and ran back to his waggon, laughing hysterically, talking incoherently to himself, and tossing up his arms, in the savage glee of satiated vengeance. He ran directly into the arms of an impassive, inexorable, helmeted policeman; and there I left him.

VII.

Dresden abounds in squares or market-places, of great size in comparison with the uniform gloomy narrowness of the streets. It seems as though the streets, ever and anon, got tired of being narrow, and suddenly outstretched their mouths into a portentous yawn. If only a compromise could be effected between the expansion of the market-places and the contraction of the thoroughfares, Dresden would become a more consistent as well as a better ventilated capital. These market-places confine themselves rigidly to business; they are market-places, not parks or pleasure-gardens. Every square foot of them is solidly paved; no enclosed grass-plots, no flower-beds, bushes, or trees are allowed. If you want such things, go where they are to be had; but when you enter the city make up your mind to city and nothing else.

I confess a decided preference for this arrangement over that which prevails in American and English cities—the forcing scraps of country into the midst of every chance gap between the houses. Setting aside the question of hygiene, the effect of such violence done to Nature must be depressing to everyone capable of being depressed. Could there be imagined two more irreconcileable elements than trees and brick walls? unless it were flower-beds and street-pavements? The houses, being in the majority, put out the trees: the trees, so far as they have any efficacy at all, satirise the houses. If we are in the garden, glimpses of the surrounding buildings distract our attention from the foliage; and if we would hear birds sing, it must be to an accompaniment of carriage-wheels and street-cries. Should we contrive to find a more secluded nook, where we might pretend for a moment to forget the city, we are in constant anxiety lest some untoward chance confront us with our hypocrisy. Or if, on the other hand, we stand outside the railings, the case is no way bettered: the poor garden seems to pine like a bird in its cage, and, so far from refreshing us, imposes a heavy tax on our sympathies.

Nature must not be surrounded. Her beauty is not

compatible with shackled limbs; she must be free to extend to the horizon and salute the sky. Caged Nature will not sing, and loses her power to bless. She may hold a city in her bosom, like a jewel, and both she and the jewel will look the prettier; but either her majority must be without limit, or else all comparison should be avoided. Never bring the country into town in larger quantity than may go into a flower-pot. If harmony and hygiene must come into collision here, I am inclined to let hygiene go to the wall, as Dresden does. Let us abolish cities, if we can, but not by throwing small handfuls of green grass and flowers at them.

The Dresden market-place looks dreary enough, say, on a Sunday, when it has been swept severely-clean, and the level expanse of stone is unbroken by so much as a cigar-stump. It needs some audacity to walk across it—the expanse is so large, and the conspicuousness of the walker so complete. The houses on opposite sides stare hopelessly at one another, like hungry guests across an empty dining-table; and it seems as though the table never could be laid. But see what a transformation takes place on Friday morning—market-day throughout Germany. The naked plain, which seemed incurably barren yesterday, has wonderfully brought forth what appears to be a great crop of colossal mushrooms, whereof the smallest stand six feet high. They rise from amidst fertile undergrowths of vegetables and produce of all kinds; and beneath them, in comfortable chairs made out of three-quarters of a barrel, stuffed and padded with old carpeting, sit robust elderly ladies in flannel petticoats and wooden shoes, every one of them knitting a blue stocking, and no less indefatigably soliciting passers-by for their custom. The morning sun slants across the scene, gilding the umbrella-tops, and gloating over the heaps of fresh green vegetables, and everywhere making merry with the warm, omnipresent, stirring, shifting, murmuring life which crowds the market-place from brim to brim.

There is nothing else in Dresden so broadly picturesque and amusing, so rich in antique and piquant characteristics, so redolent of humour and good-humour, as are her markets and out-door fairs. The open sky and kindly sunshine give an air of informality to the ugly business of buying and selling, which renders it charming. Bewitching are the primitive stands improvised by these country dames for the display of their wares. They, too, are bewitching in their way— —a brown and wrinkled tribe, but full of shrewdness, and of broad, ready wit, that is often apt and amusing. There they sit, from early morning till late afternoon, and then the whole establishment is packed into the dog-cart, and trundled away.

Their costume is markedly simple, especially when compared with the fearfully and wonderfully-made head-dresses and sleeves which are the fashion elsewhere on the Continent. They possess, moreover, an admirable talent for making themselves comfortable; never dash our spirits by assuming a miserable and lugubrious demeanour, but, on the contrary, wear the very most prosperous face possible, and address their customers not with an unintelligible whine, but with hearty compliments and clever flatteries, to which the cheerful suggestion that they can furnish the very commodity which alone is needed to give the finishing touch to worldly well-being, appears a purely unpremeditated addition. I owe much to these excellent personages, and rejoice in this opportunity of acknowledging my debt. Had my acquaintance with Dresden never extended beyond the shadow of their big umbrellas, doubtless I had brought away more genial memories of it. As a background to their sturdy figures, the ugly houses, with their plaster faces and hump-back roofs, acquire an undefinable charm. Whoever delineates Saxon life and manners, whether with pen or pencil, should not fail to give the market-place an honourable position in his picture. The sun always shines there.

These Friday-morning market-women must, however, be distinguished from what may be called the every-day class, who have permanent stands at this and that street-corner, rented by the year; who sit, not in three-quarter barrels, but in little wooden sentry-boxes, painted green; who never exert themselves to solicit custom, but let their wares speak their own commendation; who suffer the buyer to depart as he came, instead of throwing after him the affectionate injunction, "Come again, highly-honoured individual! forget not your most devoted servant!" Their permanence, in short, seems to have dried up in them the springs of that *naïve* and piquant humour which their Friday-morning sisters bring in fresh from the fields, along with the turnips and cabbages. They become as stiff and taciturn as the little wooden boxes in which half their lives are passed; and, notwithstanding many luxurious appliances in the way of wraps, cushions, and footstools, which in the course of time they contrive to get together, they never look half so comfortable and contented as my jolly old favourites of the Alt-Markt.

Certainly this market is worth all the enclosed parks and pleasure-gardens in the world. It is the only satisfactory solution of the problem how to bring city and country together. Set them on the honest, if unæsthetic, basis of buy and sell, and the meeting will redound to their mutual credit and profit.

VIII.

But the Alt-Markt, in company with its smaller brethren, is indispensable for even more important purposes than the accommodation of Friday-morning market-women. Three or four times in a year, but notably towards Christmas, does Dresden give symptoms of being in an interesting situation. After a few days' labour, and considerable turmoil and confusion, she is happily delivered of a progeny of ten thousand little booths, more or less, which straightway proceed to arrange themselves as a miniature city within the city, and, in their turn, mysteriously to bring forth an inexhaustible store of every description of merchandize. Meanwhile, a myriad army of buyers and merry-makers has assembled from the surrounding country, and a grand carnival and celebration takes place, known as the Jahr-Markt, or Christmas Fair. It continues for a week or ten days, until, Christmas being fully come, the residue of merchandize is packed away in boxes and baskets, and the little booths, being thus stripped of all their finery, are themselves rapt away to some limbo or other, there to await the time when they shall be born again.

The earliest symptom of approaching festivity, however, is the sudden up-growth, in every quarter of the city, of extensive forests of young fir-trees. They are of all heights, from twelve inches to twenty feet, and there are so many of them, that it seems as if every man, woman, and child in Dresden might take one each, and yet leave half as many more behind. They sprout forth from every nook and corner, and are not at all embarrassed by the necessity they are under of taking up their stand on cold stone pavements. Indeed, they altogether dispense with roots, substituting for them the more convenient arrangement of two billets of wood, mortised together at right angles, with a hole at the intersection, into which the stem of the tree is fitted. The only contingency under which this principle is defective, is when the wind blows. A moderate gust will overturn an entire grove, like a row of cards; and in the event of a persistent breeze, the foresters resign themselves with the best grace they may, not attempting to set their plantation on end again until the elements have calmed down. Their appearance, sitting erect amidst so much prostration, is not a little forlorn; it would seem more appropriate were they to utter a melancholy wail, and fall down likewise. These trees, it need scarce be said, are the property of the good Santa Claus, and are one and all destined to produce a crop of fruit which shall gladden the hearts of heaven knows how many children. In view of so glorious a consummation, no wonder they consent to exchange their comfortable roots for the insecure foothold of a wooden cross; and, after the fruit-bearing season is over, to live on memory in the attic until the period of their second and final coruscation in the kitchen fire. They make friends with all ranks, from peer to peasant; and in the case of any other people than this, would probably create some temporary bond of sympathy between rich and poor. But each individual Saxon walks off with his own tree, and enjoys it in his own way, without troubling his head about his neighbour. As the trade grows brisk, we are continually startled at the singular spectacle of animated fir-trees hastening up and down the streets, and running into us on the corners; careering to and fro through the crowd, as though in anxious search after their owners. It seems almost a pity that so many thousands of beautiful young trees should every year be sacrificed, even to so beneficent a deity as Santa Claus. But, whencesoever they come, the supply never appears to run short; and, perhaps, the brief splendour of these Christmas forests is better than gloomy centuries upon the impassive hills.

Having provided ourselves with a Christmas-tree, we must next repair to the booths for wherewithal to dress it. Ever since I began to take an interest in story-books, the word "booth" has had an inexpressible fascination for me. The spell originated, I think, in a picture of a booth on a certain page of an unforgetable German fairy-volume, called "The Black Aunt;" which, likewise, contained the tragic history of Nutcracker and Sugar-dolly, and the touching romance of Johnnie and Maggie. Most children, I trust, have known the Black Aunt, or some of her kindred; but comparatively few can have been so fortunate as to stumble upon the palpable realisation of her wondrous tales—just at the moment, too, when they were perhaps ready to question her veracity. No less happy a destiny, however, was reserved for me, in wandering through the toy-district of the Christmas Fair; and the sentiment stirred in me by what I saw there was tender to the verge of emotion. I have walked those fairy streets for hours, and not one of the tow-headed little rascals, who were for ever stumbling betwixt my legs, was more captivated or credulous than I.

As for the booths, they are of sufficiently simple construction, being mere sheds of plain boards, which much rain and snow, and a little sunshine, have tinted a rusty black. They vary from six to ten feet in height and breadth, and are open in front, and roughly fitted with half-a-dozen shelves. The counter is generally made of a long plank, supported at each end by a barrel, and the only way for the merchant to get in or out of his shop is to crawl underneath this arrangement. Everything about the establishment is temporary; we feel that, though it is here to-day, to-night may see it taken to pieces, and carted off into oblivion; and this transitoriness is in powerful contrast with the brilliant and warm intensity of its life so long as it endures. Certainly it endows it with a charm unknown to shops, however gorgeous, whose existence is measured by years rather than hours. Charming, too, is the set-off given by these weather-beaten boards to the gaudy colours of the freshly-painted toys, the gilt gingerbread, and the sugar-plums. It is all story-book; and as we gaze, we half listen for the turning of the leaf, or the unwelcome injunction to go to bed, and hear the rest another time.

Most of the booths bear a black placard, whereon is painted in white letters the name of the proprietor, together with his or her condition in life, and native place. "Frau Mellot, Wittwe, aus Tirol:" so we stare at Frau Mellot, who is a comely woman, not too old, and wonder whether her husband met his death hunting chamois; and whether there is not something marked in the regard of yonder stout curly-headed Fritz Wagner, vendor of earthenware from Bohemia, who keeps the booth on the other side of the way. Frau Mellot is doing an excellent business in cheese and sausages. Next year, perhaps, the two establishments will have become one—the earthen pots will have wedded the sausage and cheese. For it is scarcely possible to avoid feeling a lively personal interest in these people; they are all characters in our story-book, and their welfare is essential to the happy development of the narrative. "Hier nur giebt es billige Waaren!" shouts Fritz, with a sly wink at the widow; and she tosses her head, and calls, "Ein Groschen das Stuck, hier! hier ist jedes Stuck nur ein Groschen!" Then she catches my eye, and at once attacks my sensibilities thus:—"Buy something of me, then—you, dear sir! you, who appear so benevolent and so wealthy!" No, no, Frau Mellot, I will not be your cat's-paw, to give honest Fritz the heartache; nay, is he not jealous already? methinks there is something sinister in the way he balances that earthen jug, and glances at my head! Farewell for the present; but next year, if all goes well, I will buy of Mr. and Mrs. Fritz both a round of cheese and a stone jar to keep it in.

IX.

The booths occupy not only the squares, but the streets and alleys likewise, and still there never seems to be half room enough. We cannot hope to inspect them all, and, perhaps, our best plan will be to confine our observations to the Alt-Markt collection, which in itself forms a large town, and may be looked upon as Santa Claus's head-quarters. The shops are arranged with admirable regularity in avenues and cross-streets, the widest barely seven feet in breadth; and, generally speaking, each street is devoted to a separate kind of goods, so that, by the time we have been through them all, we shall have beheld as large a variety of cheap and reasonably worthless commodities as were ever brought together within similar limits since time began. In this quarter, for instance, the whole world seems to have been turned to leather, and so strong is the perfume of tanned hides that, for the moment, we forget that other fundamental odour which reigned here last week, and will resume its ancient sway to-morrow or the day after. Here we turn the corner, and straightway the eye is attacked by an overpowering onset of all the colours of the rainbow, besides a great many which the most charitable rainbow would indignantly repudiate, embodied in hundreds and thousands of rolls of stout coarse flannels, such as the peasant-women make up into petticoats for holiday wear. This district is very popular with the fair sex, though less so than the region of crude ribbons and priceless jewellery further on. The next street epitomises the iron age, and is resonant with pots and kettles, flat-irons and pokers, rakes, spades, and kitchen cutlery; but I think iron should be excluded from fairs, as being too permanent and uncompromising an element where change and the brilliance of a moment are the chief aim and attraction. Pleasanter and more interesting is the place of baskets and wicker work, where we may see the osiers being deftly and swiftly wrought up into an amazing variety of pretty or eccentric forms. Germany is notable for basket-making as well as for pottery—the two most primitive and not least graceful industries known to man.

Manifestly, however, we are not equal to the task of perambulating even the Alt-Markt. We pause on the verge of a wilderness of sparkling glass-ware, and altogether neglect the extensive assortment of dried fish and groceries which monopolise the stalls on the further side of the square. Neither can we hope to do justice to the numberless shows of fat women and strong men, of wild children and tame mice, of conjurors and mountebanks, which swarm here no less than at other fairs. The truth is, I am anxious to spend such time as remains to us in the toy department, which occupies the centre of the Christmas township, and is the nucleus of gaiety into the bargain.

Here, indeed, is rich bewilderment piled ten deep! Every inch of space is used and used again, until we are ready to forget that such a thing as space exists. The vendors are up to their neck in toys; toys are piled on the counters, hung from hooks and along lines, crammed into baskets. Assuredly there are more toys in the world than anything else—toys are the sole reality and business of life, and all else is mere pastime and make-believe. They are all immortal, too; for here are the jumping monkeys and dancing harlequins, the red-roofed villages and the emerald-green poplar-trees, the Noah's Arks, the drums, and the trumpets—all the things of our childhood, which we have loved and smashed to pieces—all as active, as life-like, as brilliant, as new and unstained as when we saw them first so many years ago. Here is the gallant Nutcracker, with his stiff pig-tail, powerful jaw, and staring blue eyes; beside him the sweet and gentle Sugar-dolly, to whose tragic fate I have never been able to resign myself. Yonder is the famous cock who flew to the top of the barn and gave up crowing, but who turns constantly this way and that on one leg, to see whence the wind blows. Near him the squirrel, joint hero with Nutcracker in that never-to-be-forgotten duel of theirs. And here are dear Johnnie and Maggie, grown not a day older; or, if they be the descendants of the historic pair, reproducing the characteristics of their progenitors with a completeness which would make Mr. Galton the happiest man in England. Nor will we forget Hans Christian Andersen's tin soldier, with his shouldered musket, his single leg, and his rigid observance of discipline. It appears he was not melted up after all; and I see the little dancer whom he loved pirouetting not far away. She is a giddy little lady, and military discipline is a serious matter, especially of late years; but I have faith that they will yet live long enough to meet and make each other happy. We human beings are mere toys, who are born, and die, and never come again; but these beings who are not human, and whom we rather look down upon, perhaps, are for ever beginning their existence, and will be the delight of children of future eras when those of ours shall be streaks of sunset cloud!

Verily, this is an enchanted land, unchanging amidst the world's change, undisturbed amidst our wars and factions. Santa Claus has learned the secret of wise government. Here dwells no common sense nor logic —no atomic theory nor doctrine of evolution. The inhabitants of this kingdom know neither Hegel nor Kant, yet theirs is the true philosophy of the unconditioned. The ship of humanity pitches in a heavy sea, but these little people are the ballast that keep her from rolling over. Germany has ever been the home of toys—let her beware lest her ambition move them to emigration! She may conquer Europe and command the seas, but all shall not avail if she let this little Noah's Ark escape her ports. In a few years, more or less, her reign must come to an end; and Bismarck, for all his bluster, is not immortal; but if he lives long enough to drive Nutcracker and Sugar-dolly out of Germany—and it seems probable he may —not the conquest of many Europes would compensate the loss; for when Nutcracker and Sugar-dolly depart, they will take the child-heart with them; men will be born old in the next generation: and we need not pursue our speculations further, because those who have never been children will not be apt to fall into the absurdity of begetting any.

This is no fanciful warning; the seeds of the catastrophe are already sown. At the Christmas fair last year a hateful suspicion possessed me that the children were not quite what they used to be; they clustered round the booths, indeed, and stared at the toys, but some of them seemed half-ashamed of their interest, while others were positively and brutally indifferent. I saw a great peasant, six feet high, stand for ten minutes with his mouth hanging open from pure delight and astonishment at sight of a jumping-jack, which a miserable little rascal, not seven years old, passed by with hardly so much as a glance, I suppose to spend his money on a topographical map of France. As for the countryman, I believe to this day (though I did not see him do it) that he ended by buying the jumping-jack. Unfortunately, however, the small boys will outlive the tall countrymen, and who will buy the jumping-jacks then?

X.

The vein we have fallen into is too sad a one for this blessed season, and we must try to think of something else. The proprietors of the booths are always an interesting study; and seem to be under no restrictions as regards either sex or age. I have seen a candy-booth in charge of a boy so small that he was obliged to mount on a chair to bring his head above the counter; and he could walk out underneath it without stooping. How he could bring himself to sell what should have been to his mind priceless treasures, is beyond my comprehension; not only did he accomplish this feat, however, but he showed an aptitude for business and a shrewdness which might have put many an older practitioner to the blush.

There is a goodly number of grown-up men among the merchants, and the most of them are unusually fat. I suppose a dozen or twenty years of sitting behind a counter in the open air, with no further occupation save eating, smoking, and drinking beer, would go far towards fattening a skeleton. One fellow I remember (at least I remember his head and shoulders: the rest of him—if there were any rest—was so completely hidden behind the heaps of salt herrings and sausages which formed his stock-in-trade as to suggest the idea that he had resolved himself into them so far, and would finish the process by and by) whose physiognomy was overlaid with an amount of padded blubber such as would have made a prime pair of Bath chaps look famished in comparison. It was my fancy that he was a good deal too fat to talk, and, indeed, I never saw him so much as open his mouth. His eyes were very fishy, and there was something of the sausage in the modelling of his nose, and in his mottled complexion.

The majority of the shop-keepers, however, seem to be women of between twenty and forty years old, all of them knitting on the interminable German stocking. The spirits of the women are both depressed and elevated more easily than the men's; at all events, the latter assume an air of phlegmatic indifference under misfortune which few women are able to imitate. In prosperity all grin alike, till one would think fate could never again have the heart to frown upon them. Nor do I suppose she ever does very seriously; a rainy day is the heaviest calamity which she is likely to inflict upon them. To be sure, few things are more uncomfortable and depressing than a rainy day at a fair. The outlying wares must be covered over with ugly black oilcloth, or gathered in out of sight; the water trickles through the cracks of the boards, and drips exasperatingly down upon the empty counter; the crowd of customers sensibly diminishes, and business prospects are gloomy. What if the weather continue in this mood till Christmas, leaving our boxes full and our pockets empty? But when the sun breaks forth once more, and a brisk frost makes all bright and dry again, what a change in these good people's visages! They have shortened an inch or two, and now the booths put forth their leaves again, like flowers in the morning.

After we have become familiar with the daylight aspect of the fair, it is well to visit it after dark, when the flaring lamps fantastically illuminate the long array of sparkling and glowing merchandise, and reveal the multitudinous faces of the shifting crowd; and all is projected against the sable back-ground of night with an effect which is magical indeed, and renders the scene at once more real and more visionary than ever. What London or Paris can boast such streets as these, where the whole house-line is one endless shop-window? where there is no inch of bare wall or vacant pavement? Where else is such a solid wedge of life as here—such bustle and babble—crowding and brilliancy? We are under unceasing pressure of shoulders, backs, and fronts on every side. There are fifty human faces within a radius of five feet from our own; and we seem to tread upon a dense undergrowth of children. A crowd such as this, whereof each individual is intent upon his own private and particular affairs, and is not observant of any one else, is as good as solitude or better. It is only when a mob is more or less inspired by some common sentiment or purpose, that its unpleasant qualities become manifest. I mean, of course, the morally unpleasant ones; the physical drawbacks are not so lightly got rid of. This Saxon crowd has a larger proportion of elderly persons in it, and of those who come on business rather than pleasure, than would be the case with a similar gathering in America or England. But we meet specimens of every class and not a few nationalities of men. Occasionally an American or an Englishman turns up, more rarely with a lady on his arm.

I cherish agreeable recollections of a certain elderly Englishman whom I used to meet every day at the Christmas Fair, some six years ago. He was always hand in hand with a beautiful little girl about ten years old, whose fair skin and long yellow hair were well contrasted with the ruddy geniality which glowed in his complexion and twinkled in his jolly eyes, and with the crisp whiteness of his beard and moustache. His attire was invariably faultless, and he was evidently not unconscious of the nicety of its adaptation to his rather slender figure. A more prosperous-looking old gentleman I have seldom seen; and between him and his fair-haired grandchild there was palpable evidence of a very tender companionship and affection.

There were no two people at the fair who entered with more zest into the spirit of the fun. The sympathy of each enhanced the excitement and enjoyment of the other. Early in the week they selected one of the biggest and straightest trees in the whole Christmas forest, and thenceforward until Christmas Eve they bought such a quantity of toys, bonbons, and knick-knacks as it makes one's heart warm to think of. This pair of youthful personages contributed more than all the rest of the visitors to making the Christmas element of the fair an abiding reality for me. Looking at them, it became impossible to doubt that Christmas was something more than a word. Their preoccupation and unconsciousness of observation were priceless evidence, and argument incontrovertible.

Not that other people fail to have a very good time. Towards evening, the soldiers from the neighbouring barracks get their furlough, and come down in their dark scarlet-trimmed uniforms, with visored caps and sparkling sword-hilts. Here, as elsewhere throughout the world, their sway is supreme over the servant-girl's heart. I never observed these humble lovers say much to each other; but they stand holding each other's hands, and evidently full of an exalted amiability which is preferable to most conversation. The soldiers have one marked advantage over the rest of the

Saxon nation—they are neatly and tidily dressed. The costume of the average non-military man is sadly demoralised. During the winter he unfailingly makes his appearance in a long voluminous garment having sleeves like a coat, but otherwise anomalous. It is lined throughout with fur, and has a fur collar and cuffs, heavy enough to make a polar bear perspire. Yet these Saxons, whose physical warmth appears to be as defective as that of their affections, crawl about in their great fur sacks from November to May: as though with intent to retain the atmosphere of last summer until the summer to come. Again, I find it characteristic of them that they should rather be at pains to prevent cold from getting in than to kindle an inward warmth whereby to repel it. That genial Englishman we spoke of just now, never wore anything heavier than an immaculate velvet walking coat, buttoned over his chest, and slanting down to the pearl-grey perfection of his pantaloons. Even his yellow kid gloves were half the time carried in one hand. But the kindly ardour of his heart—and likewise, doubtless, of the fine old crusted port which he quaffed every day at dinner—not only kept him warm, but made him the cause of warmth in others. . . .

We have lingered so long at this Christmas Fair,

that all opportunity for the sober prosecution of our original programme is lost, and, for my own part, I am glad of it. At best, we can only say of Dresden streets as of the woes of Troy, "*forsitan et hæc olim meminisse juvabit.*" If we praise them, it must be negatively—thus :—The new districts are even more uninteresting than the old, and the old are, if possible, more abominably unsavoury than the new.—Such language, whether flattering or not, is hardly in harmony with the spirit of the season, and we are glad to be spared the use of it.

I feel tempted, on the other hand, to pronounce at this point a eulogistic peroration on the Saxon Christmas; pointing out that insomuch as they (in common with other Teutons) lay more stress on Christmas celebrations than any other people, it logically follows that they are inspired with a larger portion of the Christian spirit, and of that simple charity which gives for pure love of giving. If I do not say this, it is because the Saxons would themselves be the last to comprehend the meaning of such an imputation, and the first to ridicule it when they did. That part of charity which consists in making presents is, with them, but another name for barter. Rochefoucauld has observed (and he must have had Saxony in his eye at the time) that gratitude is a keen sense of favours to come; and he might have added—still making the same tacit application—that generosity is a shrewd calculation of probable returns. A Saxon once told me that he spent more money at Christmas than during all the rest of the year; but added, with touching *naïveté*, that he more than got it back again :—

"Say I have twenty friends: in buying each of them a present I expend my two-hundred thaler, reserved for the purpose. Good. Each, now, gives me a present in return; I appraise their value, and nine times from ten I find myself ten thaler to the good. It is a science, Sir!"

This seems plausible, though it would seem as if some one among the twenty must be a sufferer; but all life is a lottery. And—putting the question of pecuniary profit in the background for a moment—shall we count as nothing all that sweet incense of flattery and compliment which the occasion warrants us in burning beneath one another's noses? I trow not, for only under the circumstances we have supposed do such compliments acquire their full flavour. It is well enough for my friend to call me generous, but half my enjoyment of his recognition is destroyed if I am out of pocket by my generosity. What the world needs is—and it may thank the Saxon nation for the hint—a new set of virtues, guaranteed to do all the work of ordinary virtues, and to receive all their meed of praise; but ensured against being of the slightest risk or inconvenience to their owner. To sit still, and declare that virtue is its own reward, is folly, and weak folly; we must set to work, and make it its own reward—and a good, solid, marketable reward too!

IV.

STONE AND PLASTER.

I.

THERE is a kind of ugliness which is practically invisible. It is not ugliness of the grotesque, fascinating, or forcible order; its characteristics are negative and probably indescribable. It is always tinctured strongly with conventionality, and has a mildly depressing effect rather than an actively exasperating one: it partakes more of the nature of an incubus than of an irritant. It is an ugliness, in short, which, instead of compelling our eyes at the same time that it revolts them, simply causes us not to see it. There are vast numbers of persons in the world,—good, plain persons, with no piquancy or individuality of aspect,—with whom we may converse for hours or years, looking straight at them all the time, yet never actually seeing them. Their image is formed on the physical retina, but the mind's eye refuses to take note of them; and the consequence is an undefined feeling of dejection, expressing itself, perhaps, in a sigh or even an irrepressible yawn.

I think the sombre humour which is apt to settle upon us after a little acquaintance with Dresden may be traceable to the invisible ugliness, I will not say of its people, but of its houses. They curiously elude our observation, even when we strive to fix our regards upon them. We walk street after street, with all our eyes about us (so we fancy), and yet on reaching home we cannot call up the picture of any one among the hundreds of buildings which we have passed. They are featureless, bare, and neutral-tinted, and present no handle for memory to catch them by. They do not make our nerves prick with anguish and our brows flush, as do the palatial residences in New York and elsewhere; a little stimulus of that sort once in a while would be healthful. They deaden us by communication of their own deadness, and it is a mystery how living men built them or can live in them.

The best way to get at them is to put them side by side with houses of our own, and note the differences. These differences all begin from the fundamental difference between the Saxon and the Anglo-Saxon modes of living. They live in layers, we in rows; and when we have analysed all the issues of this variance, we shall have done much towards accounting for things of far greater importance. In some respects the Saxons have the advantage of us. Our city houses are no better than an array of pigeon-holes ranged interminably side by side; the close assemblage of pompous doorways, each with its little flight of steps, its porch, and its twelve feet of area railings, fatigues the eye. There is a constant repetition, but no broad uniformity. Moreover, the fact that the houses are clothed only in front, and are stark naked behind and at the sides, keeps us in a state of constant nervous apprehension. We do our best to see only the brown stone pinafores, and to ignore the bare red brick; but the effort is no less futile than it is wearisome. The bareness haunts us, until the very pinafores seem transparent.

Undoubtedly they manage this matter much better in Dresden. They are as niggard of their doors as though they were made of gold. One door to a frontage of an hundred windows; and instead of a joining together of twenty or more sections of imitation stone cornices of various designs, here we have a single great bulging, rambling, red-tiled roof, covering the whole building; with rank upon rank of dormer-windows and fantastic chimneys figuring against the sky. Whatever its failings, at all events, the house is coherent and conceivable. It has a back, of course, but an honest back, such as we are not ashamed to look at. Three or four of these caravansaries form a block; and there is an absence of fussy detail about them at which the harassed New Yorker may well rejoice. The economy in doors extends itself to door numbers. One would suppose that, let them swell their biggest, these would remain small enough; but they are rigorously decimated by a free application of the alphabet. If the first door in the block is No. 7, the next is not No. 8, but No. 7A, and the third No. 7B, and so on up to G. High numbers are considered vulgar, but letters may be supposed to denote architectural blue blood.

The doorways are flush with the sidewalk; if there are steps, they are within the house-line; and the houses never set back behind a railing as with us. They seem to have grown since they were first put down, and to have filled out all spare room. The larger houses are built round three sides of a court, with which the front door communicates. But houses in Dresden are under no restrictions as regards the ground-plan. Any geometrical figure is good enough for them; and the Royal Palace, already referred to, affords them an example of license in this direction which it would be hard to outdo. The crookedness of the streets abets the eccentricity; and yet the most extravagant sprawler of them all seems more human than our endless repetition of pigeon-holes.

The houses are built of coarse sandstone, quarried from the cliffs of Saxon Switzerland, and brought thence on canal boats. The interior is patched here and there with brick, while to the outside is applied a thick layer of grey or yellow plaster, whose dead surface is sometimes relieved by arabesques and friezes in low relief, or perhaps a statuette or two in a shallow niche. This facade is from time to time oversmeared with a staring coat of paint, causing it to look unnaturally and even violently clean for a month or so, but not improving it from an æsthetic point of view. In the more modern villas, however, which line the approach to the Royal Park, the plaster is generally replaced by a fine kind of stone, dark creamcolour, and better as a building material than our American yellow or brown stone. These villas are four-square, detached, two-storied structures, each in the midst of its garden, and surrounded by an irreproachable iron railing. The roofs are either French or hip, slated and regular; the carriage-drive is smoothly paved with a mosaic of black and white; there is a fountain on the lawn; a handsome porch; and a balcony full of flowers. They more resemble the wooden country seats on the outskirts of American cities than anything in England; there is none of the English passion for seclusion and reserve; no impenetrable hedges, no ivy screens, nor canopy of foliage.

Everything is bare, open, and visible, and seems to invite inspection, like a handsome immodest woman. We can even look through the plate-glass windows and see the painted ceilings and satin-wood doors.

But it is to the city houses that we must look for traits essentially Saxon. Balconies they generally have, fitted to the drawing-room windows of the successive Etages, and supported on stone cantalevers. Not always trustworthily supported, however; for moisture rots the stone, and the balconies occasionally come down, to the destruction of whatever is on them or beneath them. Meanwhile they are a pleasant refuge in summer; we sit chatting, smoking, and sipping beer among the flower-pots as the sun goes down, and long after the stars are out. They may even be used as supper rooms when the day has been very hot, and the company is not too numerous. If we have lived long in Dresden, it will not discompose us that every passer-by in the street may see how our table is furnished.

II.

Twenty families sometimes live under one roof; and the same front door serves for all. Through it must pass alike the Prince on the Bel-etage, the cobbler in the basement, and the seamstress who lives in the attic. This is a state of things which deserves consideration. A house-door, which is common property, which stands agape for any chance wayfarer to peer through—nay, whose threshold is no more sacred than the public kerbstone !—we are democratic in America, but I think the Saxons are in advance of us here. So far as I have observed, New Yorkers and Bostonians are as careful of their doors, and as chary of them as is a pretty young woman of her lips. I would as lief share my parlour with a stranger, as be liable to meet him on my stairway, or to rub shoulders with him over my threshold; especially when his right to be there is as good as mine. There is an indelicacy about it, as if a dozen or twenty people were all to eat and speak through one mouth. The street does not stop outside the house; it eddies into the hall, and forces its dirty current up stairs. True, there is another door within, but after we have given up our outworks, few people will believe in the genuineness of our inner defences. The spell of reserve is broken.

This may be esteemed a fanciful objection to the "Flat" system, which, I see, is gaining favour in America on the score of cheapness and compactness. If we will frankly call such establishments hotels, we may at least escape the evil of growing to believe them homes. Home is no less sacred a word than ever, though, like other English words nowadays, it is getting to be much desecrated in the appliance; and I fear these common doors, standing always ajar, may let escape many delicate beauties and refinements whose value is not fanciful, but inestimable.

To be sure, hall-porters have lately been introduced in the more modern and pretentious houses, whose business it is to keep the door shut, and only to open it when somebody wishes to come in, and not to admit beggars or disreputable persons. Their position is not a sinecure. I made the acquaintance of a Dresden hall-porter, and observed his proceedings for a whole year. He was a small, cringing, hook-nosed man, with thick straight black hair, short black beard, and a ghastly pallor of complexion which no stress of circumstances could ever modify. He cultivated that philosopher's desideratum, a continual smile, and he was full of becks, nods, obeisances, and grimaces. He rose at five in summer, and, I believe, not more than an hour later in winter. Why so early, I know not; there seemed not much to do besides sweeping out the hall, knocking the door-mat against the jamb, and exchanging a morning greeting with the charwoman of the house opposite. But he was a married man, and may have had some household jobs of his own to attend to. He and his wife lived in two rooms adjoining the hall-way, so narrow and close that any respectable house-rat would have turned up his nose at them. The porter followed some small handicraft or other, whereby to eke out his salary; and at odd moments I could see him at the side window, working away, but ever keeping an eye to the sidewalk for visitors. He could lift the door-latch without leaving his seat, by means of a wire pulley, and when a denizen of the house approached, the door would spring open as if to welcome an old friend, before he could lay his hand to the bell handle; but strangers had to ring. In winter, I fear the porter had a sour meagre time of it. Besides the extra work of clearing the ice and snow, there was the cold, which he could not do away with. But in summer he was happier; he wore a striped linen jacket and a long dirty apron, and was very active with his broom, and his street watering-pot. He had a great circle of acquaintances, and his little hall-room had its fill of visitors at all times. He was a very sink of private information, knew all that the housemaids of the various *étages* could tell him, and had understandings with all the tradesmen's boys who brought parcels for members of the household. Whether there was an escape-pipe for this deluge of confidences, must have been a question of some moment to those who were discussed.

All at once a baby was born; it looked as if nothing could prevent its dying instantly; but it lived, and I daresay is alive now. The little porter was as proud of his baby as though there had been the germ of a Goethe in it; he held it constantly in his arms, and clucked at it, and dandled it unweariably. All the gossips admired it, and the people in the house stopped to smile at it as they passed through the hall. I doubt not that various bits of baby-furniture, useful or playful, found their way down-stairs from the upper floors; for babies make even Saxons forget themselves for a moment. No doubt, too, any little deficiency of water in the cisterns, or irregularity in the gas-lighting, or delay in bringing up letters and visiting-cards, was condoned for a time. The porter might reasonably have wished that the baby should be renewed as often as once every four or five months.

Next to the baby, the porter's trump card was a gigantic dog, a cross between a Newfoundland and a Saint Bernard. He was as big as a Shetland pony, and lay majestically about the hall, or stalked lion-like up and down the sidewalk. The chief objection to him was that he was above keeping himself clean, and had no valet to do it for him; and whoever made bold to caress him had reason to remember it for the rest of the day. Nevertheless, this huge beast slept in the porter's room, filling up all the space unoccupied by the porter himself; and, considering that fresh air was rigorously excluded in summer as well as in winter, it was a constant surprise to me to see the porter appear, morning after morning, apparently no worse off than when he went to bed. But I do the dog injustice; it was he who suffered and degenerated; why should he be forced to share his kennel with the porter? There was in him a capacity for better things; for when the porter watered the lawn at the back of the house with the garden hose-pipe, the dog would rush into the line of the stream and take it point-blank on his muzzle, barking and jumping with delight. But the porter never took the hint home to himself, nor understood, I suppose, what pleasure the dog could find in being wetted.

The porter's bearing towards the various inhabitants of the house was accurately graduated in accordance with their elevation above the ground floor. With the waifs of the attic he was hail-fellow-well-met. Pleasantly affable was his demeanour to the respectable families on the third *étage*, whose rent did not exceed £150 a year. The second floor, at £300, commanded his cordial respect and good offices; while speechless, abject reverence, and a blue dress-coat with brass buttons, fail to express his state of mind towards the six-hundred-pounders of the first landing. This behaviour of his was not so much acquired, as an instinct. The personality of its recipients had nothing to do with it; were Agamemnon, on the first *étage*, to change places with Thersites in the attic, our porter would slap the king of men on the back at their next meeting, and hustle him out of the way of Thersites, when the latter came down to his carriage. Moreover, if Agamemnon were a Saxon, he would not dream of getting indignant at this novel treatment.

But hall-porters do not strike at the root of this common-door evil; on the contrary, by pruning away the ranker leaves, they make the ill weed grow the stronger. The door is still open to whomsoever chooses to enter, and would be just as common, were an especial passport from Berlin necessary for every crossing of the threshold. If decency is to be outraged, it is of no real moment whether it be done directly or indirectly. There is a vast moral advantage in the feeling that our home is our own, from the garden-gate to the bed-chamber. Any infringement thereof is a first step towards communism; and I do not believe that a person of refinement can become accustomed to the "Flat" system without undergoing more or less abrasion—or what is worse, hardening—of the moral cuticle. Between vertical and horizontal living there is even more of a difference than of a distinction. To sit between two men—one on the right hand, the other on the left—is endurable; but not so the being sandwiched, prone, over one man and underneath the other. We can neither raise our eyes to heaven, nor set our feet upon the earth; a human body intercepts us in both directions. Surely one door is not enough for so great an escape as is needed here.

III.

In these houses people begin to live beneath the level of the pavement, and thence ascend until scarce a tile intervenes between them and heaven. The basement people must take degraded views of life. They see only feet and legs and dirty petticoats, and their window panes are spattered with mud from the sidewalk. Living up to their necks in earth must considerably impede them in the race, not to speak of the crushing weight of five or six stories overhead. If they were deeper down it would not be so bad, for there is a mystery about the depths of our mother earth—a blind recognition, perhaps, of the interest of buried ages: and we get so much from the earth—everything except our souls, let us say—that what concerns her is our concern also. Miners are a fine symbol of materialism. They live in the earth—earth is beneath their feet, around and above them; no firmament too high to be reached with a ladder; many strange things, but none that may not be handled; a world of facts, wherein they stand self-contained and gloomily serene. As we, sitting indoors, pity the wayfarers exposed to the inclemency without, so do these miners pity and despise us, exposed to the blue and white glare of the bold heavens, stared out of countenance by sun and moon, blown by winds and wet with rain. Who can sympathize with the sky? Yet sooner or later all must revisit the surface, if only to be buried there.

But the grave and taciturn miners, whom we often meet on our walks towards Tharandt, with their odd costume and gruff "Glück auf!" are a very different race from the dwellers in basements. These poor creatures, being half in and half out, can claim neither heaven nor earth, but are exposed to the wrath of both. The feverish damps have entered into their blood, and their sallow faces, as they peer up at us from the underground windows, seem more clay than flesh. I am, however, able to record one cheerful exception, which will help us to take leave of the basements with a pleasant savour in our nostrils. It is on the north-eastern corner of See and Waisenhausstrasse. Here the sidewalk consists partly of a grating, in passing over which a most appetising odour salutes us. We glance downwards through a subterranean window, where behold two or three stalwart cooks in white aprons and paper caps, frying delectable veal cutlets over a glowing range. The window is open at the top, and the spiritual essence of the cutlets rises through the aperture to delight our noses. As we pause to sniff once more, the fattest of the cooks tips back his paper cap and wipes his sweating brow with his warm bare arm. Phew! here, at all events, is more flesh than clay. The fat cook's glance meets ours, and we exchange a sociable grin. He is *chef* of the Victoria Keller, and we know his cutlets of old.

IV.

In the houses which are only dwelling-houses, the next step above the basement is to the Parterre, which is generally raised some four or five feet above the sidewalk level. But the great mass of houses in the city are shops in their lower story, and attain the heights of gentility only after climbing a flight of stairs. There is a subdued mellow splendour about Dresden shops such as I have not seen exactly paralleled anywhere else. Perhaps the gloom of the narrow streets and the musty drab colour of the houses enhance these splendid windows by contrast. But the shopkeepers give much time and thought to the artistic arrangement of their wares; it is a matter which they understand, and into which they can put their whole souls, and the result does them credit. Each window is a picture, with height, depth, breadth, and chiaro-oscuro all complete: and far more attractive pictures, to most people, than those on the walls of the Gallery. Moreover, the details are altered every morning, and at longer intervals there is a re-casting of the entire design; so that the fascination of life is added to the other fascinations. And, finally, the shops are so immediately accessible that it seems rather easier to go into them than not. Our timidity is not daunted by imposing doorways, nor is our inertia discouraged by dignified flights of steps and broad approaches. Within, we take off our hats, say good morning, and feel perfectly at home. However fine the wares may be, we are distracted by no grandeur of architecture; and we are waited on by attendants, not by ladies and gentlemen. We bid adieu at parting, and hardly realize, as we regain the sidewalk, that we have actually been shopping at all.

These are some of the lights of the picture; there are shadows—heavy ones! After some deliberation, however, I think there will be little use in attempting to reproduce them. Those whose lives have been crossed by them will not care to have the experience recalled; while the uninitiated can never be brought to believe in their depth and blackness. Be it merely observed, therefore, that Dresden shopkeepers are sufficiently inspired with a desire to prosper in trade. It may be conjectured that they give their minds to their business; certainly the reproach of discursive attainments can not be brought against them. Their heads, so far as intellectual value is concerned, are about on a par with the silver effigies on the thaler which they cherish. I have somewhere seen it asserted that the German tradesman is notably of a scientific, philosophic,' and æsthetic turn, and that, in the intervals of labour, he snatches up his volume of Rosencranz, Lemcke, Bolzmann, or Goethe, from the perusal of which the very chink of coin will scarcely win him.

So far as my observation goes, this is a cruel and unfounded aspersion upon the character of a guild whose singleness of purpose has profoundly impressed me. They do not know what Science and Philosophy are. They will not read even a novel, nor yet a newspaper, unless it be the *Boerse Zeitung*. They look at the pictures in *Kladdera latsch*, but do not understand the political allusions. Their eyes are dull to the culture and progress of the world, and, to all that is above the world, wholly blind. But they can spy a bargain through a stone wall, and a thievish advantage through the lid of a coffin. Nevertheless, I am of opinion that a wider culture might help them to be even more truly themselves than they are now. Beautiful as is the untutored earnestness of their character to the eye of the psychologist, to the man of the world they seem deficient in the breadth and grasp of mind which would enable them most effectively to carry out their designs. With all the disposition to steal that an ardent Saxon nature can have, they lack the wisdom so to commit their thefts as to secure the largest and most permanent returns. There is a rugged directness in the way they pick our pockets which at first charms us by its *naïveté,* but ends with wounding our feelings and lowering our self-esteem. They take so little trouble to make their lies plausible, that we cannot pretend to believe them without blushing. It is easy to pay a bill of three times the amount of the original charges; but to pay again and again for things which we never had, and which it is not even feigned that we ever had, gets to be almost painfully embarrassing. If I lay my purse upon the counter, it would evince a delicacy of sentiment in the shopkeeper to wait until I had turned away my eyes before taking it. Such a course would be to his advantage, besides; for I could then ignore the theft, and we could continue our relations with the same frankness and cordiality as before, and in due course of time I might let him steal my purse again. But openly to transfer it to his till, while I am looking straight at it, seems to me tantamount to a wanton rupture of our acquaintance. There is originality, there is vigour, there is noble simplicity in the act, if you will; but our effete civilization is apt to forget its beauties in shuddering at its lack of clothing.

This ruggedness is largely fostered, no doubt, by the continual shifting of the foreign population. A customer who is here to-day and gone to-morrow must evidently be robbed without delay; and it makes little difference how, since there will be another to take his place. So demoralising is travel to the places which are travelled through! If a permanent colony of philanthropic English and Americans would establish themselves in Dresden, I question not that, in the course of a few years, the whole mercantile community would be educated into such accomplished thieves that they could steal twice as much as now, without creating a tithe of the awkwardness and misunderstanding which at present exist. Persons in search of a mission would do well to ponder this enterprise.

V.

Passing over, then, the darker shadows appertaining to the Dresden merchant guild, let us revert to the cheery spectacle of the shop windows. The mercers' are the best off for colour; they sometimes look like giant rosettes, with tints sweetly harmonised. There is a bald-headed gentleman on Seestrasse who arranges his silks in a fresh combination every morning, and then steps into the street and contemplates the effect with side-long glances and hands clasped in silent rapture at his shirt-bosom. He forgets that his head is hatless—not to mention its hairlessness; he does not heed the unsympathetic world-stream, hurrying past; the universe is an unstable vision, but his silks are real, are beautiful, are tastefully arranged. We cannot withhold our respect from this man. He is as sincere an enthusiast as Luther or Mahomet, and no less estimable in his degree. Undoubtedly he is a happier man than either, for I never saw him dissatisfied with his work.

But the windows of the stationers' shops are more generally attractive. Here is a world of photographs from life, from still-life, and from art, ancient and modern. There is a sympathy between photographs and travelling; they are mathematical functions of each other. Dresden photographs are remarkable for their softness and delicate tone—qualities which appear to depend in some measure upon the atmosphere, but still more, I fancy, upon the care and skill wherewith they are "finished" in India ink and white. There is a certain Professor Schurig, not the only good man of his name in Dresden, whose profession seems to be to make crayon copies of the more famous pictures in the Gallery; and these crayons are diligently photographed in every gradation of size. The Professor is sometimes very felicitous, but within the last year photographs have been taken from the famous originals; and though they appear rough and stained and obscure, there is always a gleam of divine expression somewhere about them, which transcends the art of the most curious copyist. Besides these, there are a great many of Goupil's French reproductions, and a whole army of female deities, as well of this as of more primitive ages. It is a singular fact that the wholly naked goddesses of ancient mythology look incomparably more modest than do the half-clothed divinities of to-day. The reason may be that the former were never aware that their unconsciousness would one day be photographed; but what a shame that our modern nymphs should labour under so embarrassing a disadvantage!

An artistic fruit more native to Dresden is the china-painting, of which there are many exhibitions in town. It is all copying-work, save for such originality as may belong to an inaccurate imitation. Accuracy, indeed, is not aimed at; for even if attained in the painting, the subsequent baking would warp it wrong again. But the effects produced are marvellously soft, glowing, and pure; and such brilliant falsehoods are generally preferred to the black-and-white truths of photography. Justly so, perhaps, since black-and-white is not the whole truth, and colour is often of more significance than form. A new application of this art is to copying cartes-de-visite, with better success than might be expected. The most satisfactory results are with the faces of old people and young children: in the first the furrows and wrinkles are guiding-lines to the draughtsman; in the others there are few fixed and definite traits in which to err. But the subtle curves and changing, yet expressive, contours of youth make game of the artist's efforts. The best thing to do with paintings of this kind is to inlay them as medallions in ebony and marqueterie cabinets. So placed, they look like great jewels, and any minor inaccuracies are unnoticeable.

As for the Dresden—that is, the Meissen porcelain—it is too delicate a topic for such rough notes as these. I went to Meissen once, and saw it made and painted. I walked up and down long cool corridors, and peeped into oblong rooms, where five hundred sickly young men are always at work, each repeating for ever his especial detail, and never getting a step beyond it. I saw little legs and arms and heads and trunks come out perfect from separate moulds, and presently build themselves into a pigmy man or woman. In another apartment I saw flowers painted so rapidly and well, that they seemed to blossom beneath the painter's fingers. No flower-painting surpasses the best work of these young fellows—for they almost all are young. They apotheosise Watteau, too, making him out a more cunning artist than he was. I am speaking of the flat work; the raised flowers are hideous, indecent, and soulless. It is no small labour to model them, and wonders of skill they are; but what sort of a

Frankenstein must he have been who first conceived and carried out the idea of making them! No flowers grow on his grave, I think; but it would have been poetical justice to bury him in a heap of his own roses.

The little porcelain people are not so objectionable, except when they are made to pose at ease on the precipitous slopes of slippery vases. They are much better before baking than afterwards, however, for they emerge from the fiery furnace with a highly polished surface, which is beautiful in itself, but far too lustrous to be human. . . . I will not moralize here; but on the whole I wish a bull would get into the Messien china-shop and smash everything except the simple flower-painted vases and dishes. There is one vase with a flower-wreath round it, which seems just to have been dropped there, fresh, fragrant, and dewy from some Juliet's garden—a wreath which should immortalize him who created it. "Ja," assents our Saxon conductor, "es ist ja wunderschoen; but here, best sir, here is what far outdoes the nature; behold it, the pride of our manufactory—a porcelain violet, modelled by hand, tinted to the life, baked, glazed, perfect! Verily a masterpiece; and to think that a trumpery, good-for-nothing little violet should have inspired a work of art like that! Strange—oh, wonderful!"

It is strange, indeed. However, we are not in

Meissen. In Dresden is only one legitimate porcelain shop, containing specimens of all the work produced. After the vases, the things best worth studying are a pair of Chinese personages—a lady and gentleman—who squat cross-legged on porcelain cushions, smiling broadly, and hanging their hands as only the Chinese can. We jog them a little, and instantly they become alive—they move! They wag their grinning heads and stick out their pointed red tongues with a jolly, leering, Chinese impropriety impossible to describe. Their hands move up and down in a slow ecstacy of ineffable Mongolian significance. Really it is an impressive sight:—we see them long afterwards, wagging and leering at us, in our dreams. The unanswerable question is, which of the two is the more scandalously fascinating?

Next to this happy pair, I like an epergne, where three charming young women—the Graces, by their costume—embrace a thick column which expands above into a dish. A most comfortable design; for it always appears to me that Aglaia, Thalia, and Euphrosyne have got hold of a round German stove, and are warming their pretty little porcelain stomachs against it. None of the ancient sculptors have represented them doing anything half so cosy and sensible. The notion gives the group just that touch of humour which it requires to be interesting. Beauty, simple and severe, should never be attempted in tinted, melodramatic sculpture such as this: our Saxon artists, though, can in no wise be brought to believe it. They enjoy sentimentality more than fun; and this is one reason why their sentimentality is so sickly.

They succeed better with meerschaum. The goddess Nicotine has a fund of good sense, which prompts her, as a general thing, to put a smile, either broad or latent, into the carving of her pipes and cigar-holders. The material is more beautiful than either marble or porcelain, and is delightful to work in. A man of leisure, education, and refinement might benefit both himself and the world by devoting his whole attention to cutting and polishing meerschaum. There is unlimited field for inventive design, for taste, for humour, for manual skill and delicacy. And how pleasant to reflect that each pipe, over which we thought and laboured our best, will become the bosom friend of some genial, appreciative fellow, who will discover its good points, and be proud of them, and love them. For all good smokers are married to their pipe; are sensitive to its critics, and jealous of its rivals. And when the pipe is worthy of affection, it endears itself ever more and more; and though it be coloured black with nicotine, is tinged yet more deeply with the rich essence of mellow reminiscences and comfortable associations.

The Viennese do their work well, and perhaps have a special knack at it. There was once, in this window which we are now contemplating, a Skye terrier's head, about the size of a clenched fist, with mouth half open and hair on end, which only needed a body to begin barking. It was bought by a Scotchman for twelve pounds, which, if the animal was of the true meerschaum breed, was dog-cheap. This question of genuineness, by the way, is one which every tyro believes he can settle at a glance. There are, he tells you, a few simple and infallible tests, easily learnt and readily applied; he talks about weight, tint, texture, sponginess; and assures you that if you are ever taken in, only your own carelessness is to blame.

It is a fallacy from beginning to end. There is no way of "telling" a meerschaum, except to smoke it for at least a year. We may amuse ourselves with applying tests, if we like, but they will demonstrate only our fatuity. The dealer is as impotent to decide as anybody, so far as judgment by inspection goes, unless he be prompted by the maker. But even the maker will be at a loss between two pipes, the history of whose making he has forgotten. We might go back still farther, and ascribe the only trustworthy knowledge to the Natolian miner, who digs the clay out of the earth. Meerschaum is like a woman's heart—as soft, as light, as brittle, and as enigmatic, and only time and use can prove it true.

Pipes are bought chiefly by foreigners; Germans use meerschaum in the form of cigar-holders—"Spitzen," they call them. Spitzen are economical, but not otherwise desirable; they enable us to smoke our cigar to the bitter end, but they are an unnecessary and troublesome encumbrance. Nevertheless, they are popular, for they colour more evenly and further towards the mouth than pipes do, and they are more striking in appearance. But I scarcely think they insinuate themselves far into their owners' secret affections; a man of sentiment may have vanity enough to wear one in public, but in private he will not be bothered with it. Coarse, hard men, devoid of sentiment, and of the fine quality which can appreciate the quiet charms of a pipe, are precisely fitted to enjoy the ostentation of a Spitze.

Tobacco plays so prominent a *role* in a Saxon's life—so perfumes the air and impregnates the lungs—that we are insensibly led to discuss it at some length. Probably there are not ten righteous men in Dresden who do not smoke or snuff—chewing, luckily, is unknown, though I believe the practice originated hereabouts. I have often met on the street a hundred men in succession, no one without his cigar. Cigar-smoking, it should be observed, is not an expensive habit in

Dresden; it may be indulged in to excess for not more than two pounds sterling a year. Half as much will provide three not intolerable cigars daily. Moreover, it is to be borne in mind that no true-born Saxon ever throws away a cigar, or any part of one. He consumes it in instalments, and his pockets and cupboards are full of pestilent remnants from half an inch to three inches long. A learned Professor, whom I visited occasionally, passed his life at a study-desk, every loophole and cranny of which harboured cigar stumps of various ages and sizes. My first supposition was that here was an eccentric recluse, whose whim it was to rake together this kind of unsavoury relies merely to preserve them. But I presently saw him select the most ancient, stalest stump from its hiding-place in the most cobwebbed cranny, and kindle it into activity with a sulphur match. He preferred such resuscitated corpses—an old tobacco-vulture, with a morbid craving for carrion!

This same people smoke Russian cigarettes—the most ethereal guise under which tobacco presents itself. The variety used is Turkish,—so called Latakia; it is pure and fine; but so pungent that—except hookahs—the cigarette is the only available form for it. Ladies smoke these cigarettes, though only the Poles and Russians do so publicly—they, indeed, smoke cigars quite as readily, and for my own part I much enjoy the spectacle. Not only do they appear admirable as regards their dainty manipulation and osculation of the weed, but their smoking lends an oriental flavour to the scene, whereof the fumes of the tobacco are but the material emblem. When an English or American lady smokes, she simply commits a small impropriety; but in the mouth of a fair foreigner, who has been brought up to know no better, a cigar is a wand to conjure up romantic visions and Eastern fantasies. The gentle reader will understand me aright, nor seek to put me out of countenance by evoking images of coarse, black-pipe-puffing Indian squaws and Irishwomen.

An idiocrasy of Dresden, or perhaps of Germany, is the sausage and smoked-meat shop. It is kept clean as a pin in every part. The dressers are glistening white limestone; the scales and weights of polished yellow brass; there are generally one or two panel-mirrors, very effective. The razor-keenness of the long, bright knives; the clear red and white of the "cuts," and of the complexions of the female attendants; the piquant odour of the smoke-cured flesh, would give a Brahman an appetite. Raw meat is not a pleasant sight except to butchers and medical students; but when refined by the education of salt and smoke, it becomes highly companionable. Of the merits of sausage, it would perhaps be rash in a foreigner to speak; every nation has its pet peculiarity, which no outsider can criticise without offence. Nothing is more peculiarly national than the German sausage, and perhaps the very quality which so endears it to Germans, renders it hard of comprehension by the barbaric mind. The Coat-of-Arms of Dresden has been flippantly described as bearing a sausage in its pocket, with the motto, "Es ist mir Wurst." The people certainly have a way of carrying sausage about with them in their pockets—not always in their coat-pockets either—and pulling it out to gnaw upon it, in moments of abstraction or *ennui*; and if a barbarian expresses annoyance at the spectacle, they shrug their shoulders scornfully and ejaculate, "Es ist mir Wurst!" But the phrase is of very various application, and like the American formula, "It don't pay," is noteworthy only as indicating the bed of the popular current of thought.

There are two or three furniture shops about town, containing plenty of pretty furniture imported from Berlin, and made chiefly after French designs. But in spite of its prettiness, there is nothing sincere or satisfactory in the making of it. The chairs and sofas are never comfortable; the tables, sideboards, and cabinets are never solid, though always warranted to be so. A superficial acquaintance with such furniture predisposes us in its favour; but ripening familiarity

breeds contempt. Our fine friends wear out; their
gay feathers ornament nothing substantial; they are
loose in the joints and warped in the back. In the
day of auction they are found wanting. On the
whole, I think this Dresden or Berlin furniture is
the most worthless that is anywhere manufactured.
Compared with the massive and rich simplicity of the
best American furniture, it shows like a charlatan
beside a gentleman; nor is its case much bettered by
contrast with English work. A Saxon feels none of
the pleasures which we feel in knowing that what
pretends to be ebony, or mahogany, or cloth of gold,
is such, to the backbone. A solid mahogany dining-
table would take away his appetite as often as he sat
down to dinner. It is a fine show from cheap materials
that yields him most unmixed satisfaction; and so the
Saxons are happy in their furniture. What I have
said is in reference only to the best and most expensive
upholstery, such as adorns the villas on the Bürger-
wiese. The ordinary houses are fitted up with a kind
of goods which is, perhaps, preferable; for though to
the full as badly made as the fine sort, it does not so
belie itself by any attempt at outward embellishment.

Some people see a charm in old curiosity-shops,
but they remind me of the artfully constructed cripples
and sufferers from painted ulcers, whose simulated
woe is often obtruded upon innocent travellers. It is

conceivable that a vast deal of antiquated trash should exist, which its owners would gladly be rid of; but that age and worthlessness should enhance value is a circumstance requiring explanation. I never saw a beautiful thing in a Dresden curiosity-shop, and I think the sweepings of two or three old-fashioned attics would outshine and outvalue the richest of them. They are hidden artfully away in gloomy alleys and back streets; their windows are dusty, their ceilings stained, their floors creaky, their corners dark; their rubbish is heaped disorderly together with a coarse attempt at dramatic effect. The dealer is dressed in a correspondingly shabby costume, and cultivates an aspect of dishevelled squalor. I should suppose that the business largely depends for success upon the philosophic principle of the grab-bag at fairs. In such a mass of plunder we cannot help believing in a leaven, however small, of something really valuable; some pearl of price which, by advantage of the dealer's ignorance, we may obtain for next to nothing. But the real lay of the land is quite otherwise. Instead of buying invaluable things cheap, we purchase valueless things dear; and as to the dealer's ignorance—what, in the line of his business, he does not know, is decidedly not worth knowing. The tribe is not peculiar to Dresden; wherever are travelled flies, there likewise spin their webs these curious old spiders.

VI.

But let us rise above shops and shopkeepers and see life upon the first *étage*, where dwell the rich foreigners and the German princes. The staircase which helps us thither is probably very dark, and darker still the passage to which the inner house-door admits us. An artistic stratagem may be intended by this; for, indeed, that were a poor parlour which looked not well after so dusky, not to say evil-smelling an entrance-way. Evil-smelling or not, we must pause to be delivered of an observation before opening the parlour-door. In the Anglo-Saxon mind an entry is associated with the idea of a staircase; without which it seems an anomaly, and we wonder how it manages to dispose of itself. In fact, it sprawls about in an unbraced, vacant-minded manner, with its doors all on one side, and half-strangled by two or three great wardrobes, which also endanger the head and knees of the unwary. This lack of stairs makes itself felt throughout the house, which is comparable to a face without a nose or a land without a mountain. It is insipid. Our houses are rooms grouped round a staircase, and thus gain a flavour and character which distinguish them in the imagination. The different floors, each with its separate sphere in the household economy, are ordered as naturally as are the organs in the human body. But no stairs implies a serious deficiency of moral stimulus. Moreover, we are embarrassed by the loss of handles to an extensive family of remarks. "Go down stairs," "Run up stairs," "Come down to breakfast," "The baby is on the stairs!"—these and many more such expressions must be simply dropped out of existence. It is startling, too, to reflect that the kitchen stands as high as the parlour, and that the parlour is no less out of the way than the bedchamber. We can roll a marble back and forth from one end of the house to the other.

Meantime we will open the parlour-door. Like all German doors, it opens in the middle, the left half being usually bolted to the floor, and only the right opened and shut. There are several advantages over our system in this arrangement. The doors are less obtrusive. They open only with half as much of a sweep and a flourish, and stand ajar without standing in the way. They are the next best things to curtains: for interior doors are all more or less a relic of barbarism, and latches and locks delay the entrance of the millennium. Heaven has its gates, it is true, but those once passed, we shall find none in the heavenly mansions: whereas Hell is doubtless as full of bolted doors as of burglars.

Dresden doors, to tell the truth, are almost too

yielding for this sinful age. They have a strong bent towards warping. The bolts will not shoot, nor the latches catch, and the door is constantly springing open in a generous, free-hearted way, as much as to exclaim, "Look through me, everybody! I have nothing to conceal!" In Heaven, in summer, or in solitude, this vivacity is a charming trait, but at other times it may be annoying. It is partly compensated by the crevice underneath the door being ordinarily so wide that letters and newspapers, and even slender volumes, sometimes, may be slipped through without disturbing the hardly-won attachment of the latch. But in the common event of a sudden gust of wind, all the doors in the house jump open at once, as though a dozen ghostly intruders had forced a preconcerted entrance. The latches, by the way, turn by handles instead of round knobs; a trifle, but one of those which lend a foreign flavour.

The latch gives way, then, and behold the parlour! There is a tall square white stove—a permanent feature in all the rooms—drawn up in one corner like the ghost of a family chimney. In the adjoining angle the centre-table is pinning the stiff-backed sofa against the wall, and four rungless chairs are solemnly watching the operation. There are flower-stands in the slimly curtained windows, and the pallid walls are enriched with half-a-dozen lithographic portraits of the Royal Family, and a large engraving of Schiller at Weimar. In another place there is an eruption of small round black-rimmed daguerreotypes and photographs of dead or departed relatives—a singularly unattractive collection. Neither these nor the larger pictures are hung; they have apparently broken out of the wall in consequence of the diseased condition of the house, and the breaking-out has not taken place in an even or orderly manner; the frames are all more or less awry, and there is no balancing of one against another. Between the windows is a mirror reaching nearly from floor to ceiling; but instead of being one sheet of glass, it consists of three or four sections, the line of junction generally contriving to maintain the same level as our line of sight. The floor is of bare boards painted brownish yellow and polished; or, in the newer houses, it is parqueted, and waxed, so that it reflects the ceiling, and is perilous to walk on. It is seldom left wholly bare, however, unless in the heat of summer; the expanse is tempered with rugs, a large one beneath the table, and smaller satellites in various parts of the room. The banishment of full-grown carpets is by no means an unmitigated blunder. The polished floor communicates a sort of dignity to the legs of the chairs and tables, and puts us in mind of French *genre* pictures. If there is dirt anywhere, it is immediately visible; and the rugs can be thrashed every day without disordering anything. In winter a fox or bear-skin remedies the coldness of bare boards which summer renders a luxury. Our partiality for Aubussons, fitting snug to the wainscot, is perhaps a prejudice; there may be no more reason for them than for tapestry. Nevertheless, the foot naturally loves to be pressed on softness, and requires artificial training to walk on slipperiness. Turf is a good precedent for carpets, and in discarding them we lose in home-comfort what we gain in hygiene and elegance.

The windows open on hinges in the same manner as the doors. It is a pleasant, antique fashion: this is the kind of casements from which the ladies of the Middle Ages were wont to converse with their lovers. They could never have pushed up our modern window, with its uneven grooves and rough-running cords, nor eloped through it with any grace and dignity. Moreover, nothing is less picturesque than an open window of the modern style; whereas the old casement, standing ajar, forms a picture by itself. In winter a supplementary window is fitted outside the original one, with the good effect of excluding noise as well as cold air. When the north winds blow these exterior fixtures are severely shaken, and from street to street, as the gale rises, we hear the slamming together of loose sashes, there being a fine for any window left open during a storm. A praiseworthy regulation, since if the glass be broken and fall into the street, it is liable to shear off people's fingers and noses; and a couple of years ago, as a man was pointing out to another the road to the railway-station, he suddenly found himself without his hand. A piece of window-pane from the third story of a neighbouring house had cleanly amputated it at the wrist.

It is the mark of a civilised people to pay even more attention to their bodily comfort at night than during the day. Sleep is a mystery which still awaits explanation; but we know it to be the condition of visions which sometimes have a vital influence over our lives. In those visions the veil of the freewill is drawn aside, and our naked, unregenerate self stands revealed before our eyes. Pure, upright, and moral though we may be, in sleep we are liable to commit such crimes as the very *Police News* would fear to illustrate.

Surely, then, it were wise to make ourselves as comfortable in bed as possible, for physical unease communicates itself to the spirit, and a cramped position of the legs increases the activity within us of original sin. It is nearly a miracle, from this point of view, that all Germany is not given over to the Evil One. If their beds were a third part so comfortable as an ordinary coffin, there would be comparatively no ground for complaint. But the coffin is better in every respect, and a dead Saxon sleeps vastly easier than a live one. Were men like jack-knives, they might contrive to fit six feet of stature into four feet of bed-room; and, perhaps, to lie unmoved beneath an overgrown feather pillow, which combines in itself the functions of sheet, blanket, and counterpane. It is imponderable, that pillow; a sort of ghost of a mattress, but so hot as to suggest anything but a celestial origin. What are we to think of a people who put up with this sort of thing from year's end to year's end? Can we expect from them gentleness and refinement—an appreciation of fine shadings—a discriminating touch? Can such a people be supposed capable of distinguishing between lying and discretion, between science and quackery, between philosophy and charlatanry, between war and brutality, or even between statesmanship and bullying? They cannot tell why respect is due to women; they are a mingling of the animal with the machine; and I believe the Survival-of-the-fittest Law to be a libel on their Gothic ancestry.

So we merely pass through the bedroom—the most desolate and cheerless spot in the house—and are glad to find ourselves in the passage-way once more. The kitchen-door is ajar, and we may look in if we like; though, except the white china range, there is nothing there describably novel. An English cook might find some difficulty in broiling a steak; but the arrangements are well suited to Saxon needs. To be a thorough German cook requires only a callous conscience, a cold heart, a confused head, coarse hands, and plenty of grease. If, therefore, the other arts and sciences should ever pall upon them, one half the nation might very successfully cater to the palates of the other half. Some of the hotels have French cooks, or German cooks French-trained; but the people accept them as they accept knives and forks to eat with; not because they appreciate them, but because they are the fashion.

The best virtue of these *étages* shows itself when they are thrown open for a ball. The long suite of rooms, merging vista-like into one another, appears palatial. The smooth floors seem made to dance upon. The only dissatisfied people are those who live on the *étage* below; and even they may be conciliated by an invitation. The Saxons are much given to dancing, and may possibly have built their houses so as best to indulge their inclination. It seems a barren use to put a home to, but, on the other hand, it is no bad expedient for disguising the ugly fact of Saxon homelessness.

VII.

There are certain features of the Saxon household, upon which I have no disposition to enlarge, and which I shall pass by in silence. Special diseases should be left to the treatment of special physicians, and let us trust that, in the progress of the water-cure and of the sense of decency, they may be alleviated. Meanwhile we must pass through the second and third Etages, which are poor relations of the first, with nothing original about them,—and take our final observations in the attic.

Unquestionably this is the most attractive part of the house, whether viewed from without or from within. The very inconveniences are an enticement. Here we are next-door neighbours to the clouds; and if we look down from our dormer-window to the street,—we may be so straitened as scarcely to be able to pay our ten pounds of rent, yet cannot we repress a feeling of superiority to those absurd little people crawling to and fro beneath us. By dint of our commanding outlook, we become to a certain extent prophets of the future. We can see the coming event while yet it is afar, and can predict what will happen to a man on his way from his house-door to his office. Prophecy is easy, if only our views of life are lofty enough; and its exercise creates an agreeable glow of power. What can be more pleasing than to watch two persons running along two sides of a corner, and to foresee what they cannot—that there will be a collision at the apex? Courage is easy too, and charity; and in general our moral and intellectual capacity is indefinitely enlarged. We appropriate the stature of the building, and become giants sixty or seventy feet high, able to straddle the Alt Markt and vault the Cathedral. We perceive the littleness and the vanity of man—the not-ourselves which eternally makes for gain. We are broadly critical, and marvel at the narrow-mindedness of people who cannot see through stone walls, nor five minutes ahead. We smile compassionately at yonder stranger, who positively cannot find his way to the American Bank. But shall we, in descending to the street, descend likewise to the level of intelligence of those who walk there? Heaven forbid! Yet if so it be, let us henceforward forswear the staircase, and make our promenades over the roof-tops, with only the crows, the cats, and the chimney-sweeps for company.

I must assume that everybody has felt the fascination of an attic, for it is beyond my skill to reproduce it. It depends in great measure upon the refreshing unconventionality of the ceilings. which do not hesitate to make advances to the walls, and sometimes stoop to acquaintance even with the floors. These eccentricities are a death-blow to the maintenance of any downstairs formality and stiffness; we must be free, good-humoured, and accommodating in our behaviour, nor hold our heads too erect, lest they catch a rap from the rafters. It is strange how soon this sort of restraint and inconvenience impresses itself upon our affections; perhaps on the same principle that we are said to love best those who make the greatest demands upon us. The place is full of makeshifts and compromises, which may be bad things in conduct, but in housekeeping are delightful. The mind and character, being met by constraints upon all sides, leave their counter-impression in the more unmistakeable colours. The room grows human a hundred times faster than if it were square and ten feet high.

Moreover, attic-life is so condensed, that it must needs appears rich and idiomatic. And it is original because it is poor, and poverty cannot afford to be in the fashion. Poets are fabled to live in attics, because they cannot pay for grander lodgings; but I suspect there are better reasons for it; and certainly we often have cause to regret their better fortune; for the songs they sing on the Bel-étage are seldom so sweet and pure as those that sounded above the eaves, though doubtless far more ornate, ponderous, and regularly proportioned.

These Dresden attics are a city by themselves, and

doubtless there is a kind of Freemasonry between the inhabitants. There are often two or three stories above the eaves, and it would hardly be too much to say that half the city population have their homes there. If the rich people knew what was to their advantage, they would gladly exchange lodgings with these Arabs of the roof. It is the roofs that redeem the houses from the charge of nothingness. They are the nonconformists, rich in individuality and warm in colour, uneven as a tarpaulin flung over a pile of luggage, rambling, sloping, cornered, full of lights and shadows. The dormer-windows are of inexhaustible interest, jutting out of the mother-roof like baby houses taking a first look at the world. Doves roost on the little gable, and occasionally perch among the flower-pots on the window-sill. Now comes a young girl, to water the plants and complete the picture—one which Hendschel's pencil has inimitably drawn. She pauses a moment to watch, with a half-smile, the courtship of two pigeons on the eaves-pipe; a blush gradually steals over her lovely face, for that canary, warbling in its little wooden cage at her ear, is perhaps reminding her of a certain maiden love-passage of her own last evening, when her sweet lips made some lucky fellow the happiest man in the world. How tenderly the morning sunshine brightens on her fair hair and virginal figure! How lovingly that green vine droops over head, and how rich is the perfume of that heliotrope!

I should not have ventured upon this outburst but for that sketch of Hendschel's, which stood before me as I wrote. The responsibility is his; I should never dare create such a face as that and call it Saxon. Being ready-created, however, I am well content to believe it true, though the women I have seen in dormer-windows were invariably homely, and engaged in no more poetic occupation than sewing, or hanging out clothes, or screaming something to their gossip in the gable opposite. On rare occasions I have seen a cat steal along the tiles, harassed, meagre, with painfully suspicious eye, pausing ever and anon to peer and snuff and wave her tail. I suppose she was sparrow-hunting; but cats are the very scarcest wild-fowl in Dresden. They are an exponent of another kind of civilisation than any which Saxons will attain. They are pariahs among this people—no one sympathises with them or understands them. The dogs have ousted them perhaps; and certainly there is more of the cur than of the cat in the Saxon character.

Dormer-windows exist in other places besides Saxony, but the eye-windows are, so far as I know, a peculiarly German institution. It shows a grotesque kind of humour to invent such things. They are single panes, about a foot square, standing upright in the body of the roof, which curves over them like a sleepy eyelid, and broadens like a fat cheek below. The life-likeness is often enhanced by various ingenious additions; and a couple of such windows, with a chimney between, give the house a curiously human aspect. The effect is not carried out in the body of the building; but, in fact, all the vitality of the house is concentrated in the top part of it, as if it rose up from below, like oxygen bubbles, and collected beneath the roof. The basement is torpid, the middle floors are stiff and taciturn, but the attics draw the very breath of life.

VIII.

There is a class of citizens in Dresden whose home is even higher than the attics; who dispute the ridgepole with the crows, the pigeons, and the cats; but who, though occupying the most elevated position in the city, above even the heads of the King and his council, are outdone by none in humbleness of demeanour, and sadness of attire. They are clothed from head to foot in jetty black; and, as though this were not enough, they smear their countenances with an application of the same joyless hue. Bare-footed are they, and walk the streets, when they descend thither, with folded arms and downcast eyes, as if their very glance, not to mention their touch, might chance to soil the immaculateness of somebody's shirt-bosom. Nevertheless their complete blackness gives a strange force to their appearance—a condensation of meaning, so to speak, of the very darkest import. They are an embodied lesson to mankind. People of one colour—of one consistent idea, however gloomy—are sure to be more remarked in the world than the gayest of piebalds.

This singular tribe never appears to have any interests or sympathies in common with humanity. Never are they seen conversing with a friend; and as to sweethearts and wives!—the thing is inconceivable. A species of awe invests them; in the most turbulent crowd their persons would be respected, and a pathway would be cleared for them whithersoever they might choose to pursue it. But they are seldom seen on earth: their abode is in the upper air. In the early morning, when most men are asleep, we may see their lonely figures far aloft, silhouetted against the pale tints of the sky, and gilded perchance by the first rays of the day's sunshine. What are they doing there at such an hour? Are they priests of an unknown religion, bound by dark vows to this sable garb and these mysterious rites? Mark yonder crazy anchorite—with what weird agility he clambers to the top of that tall chimney, and stands with the sleeping city at his feet, himself the blackest object in it—a blot against the pure heavens. Does he not look rather like the Devil, setting his foot upon the conquered world? Can it be that, under the impression that they are merely a useful and harmless, albeit personally unprepossessing order of the community, mankind may have been harbouring in its midst a deputation from the kingdom of darkness?

Let us observe that creature on the chimney? He seems to have a rope coiled round his arm; now he unwinds it, and lets it slip rapidly down the chimney's throat, till it must have reached the house's deepest entrails. Is there anything below which he wants to catch? See how he jerks the rope up and down, and how curiously he peers into the sooty hole. His motions remind us vividly of a fisherman bobbing for eels. Is this the devil, bobbing for a human soul? What bait does he use?—not worms, surely: more probably it is a deed of mortgage; or, perhaps, the good name of a young woman. Ah! was not that a bite? yes, he has caught it at last—whatever it is; and, mercy on us! with what an ugly eagerness does he haul his booty up. If only it would come unhooked; and, after the experience of this one mortal peril, have a chance to be wiser for the future! but that is not to be: the black fisherman is even now stooping to grasp his prey. Let us veil our eyes from the ghastly spectacle of its last struggles. Heaven grant that ugly hook never come dangling down into our own fireside circle!

Nay, but this gloomy fantasy is unworthy our common sense; in fact, it was only the last traces of a nightmare from which, at this early hour, our brain had not entirely freed itself. Yonder is no devil, but, as we read him now, some eccentric misanthrope, who vents his spite against the race by plucking defilement from the very flame which makes the household hearth bright—or would do so, were there no china stove in the way. He likewise finds a pleasure in making himself hideous with the soot from other people's chimneys, and thus rendering his aspect a perpetual silent reminder to them of their inward depravity. He takes a grim delight in their avoidance of him—he smiles to see them recoil from the contact of his garments; a little introspection, he thinks, would reveal to them a blackness of their own more foul than that which disfigures him. He may be black-hearted, too,—he does not deny it; but at all events he hesitates not to conform the external to the interior man. Nobody can call him hypocrite. He is proud of his sooty brow, and shares the Indian's contempt for the pale-face.

But, once more, have we yet reached the deepest solution of the problem? May not this questionable shape be a secret benefactor of his species? Is he not a philanthropist of such large charity that he is willing to be loathsome in men's sight for the sake of relieving them of the results of their misdeeds; willing to sacrifice his own good name and social advantages in the attempt to clear a passage of communication between his brethren's homes and heaven? True, he would, in this case, like other philanthropists, lay himself open to misconstruction, if not to ridicule; for persons who take advantage of chimneys to seek the sky are commonly looked upon as anything but proper objects of benevolence. Nevertheless, if our sooty friend be neither philanthropist, misanthropist, nor devil, what, in the name of common sense, is he? Well,—it is not every man who can be mistaken for these personages; and should he, at last, turn out to be nothing more than a chimney-sweep, he may justly console himself with that reflection.

V.

DRESDEN DIVERSIONS.

I.

WE can judge better of a child's character from seeing it at play than at work; and so of men and nations. The Saxons have a marked inclination to amusements; they play like children, with an absence of stiffness and self-consciousness which might surprise those who had been used to regard them only as philosophers. But a shrewder consideration will probably discover in this seeming anomaly but another evidence of the profundity of Saxon wisdom. It takes more good sense than most people possess, properly to alternate study with diversion.

The famous picture-gallery is open every day in the week, in a featureless stone building one-sixth of a mile in length, and two stories high, with an elaborate archway through the centre. To and fro beneath the archway pace for ever a bayoneted rifle and a spiked helmet; the *bas-relief* of Mars on the base of the arch is not more constant in its place. An inner door to the right admits us to the entrance-hall and staircase, where we are met by a gold-laced cocked hat and silver-headed mace, and bidden to exchange our walking-stick or umbrella for a bit of brass with a number stamped upon it. Should we chance to drop this on the marble floor, the sound re-echoes as if we had let fall a brazen buckler. It is curious what an embarrassing responsibility we feel for our actions, when each one bears its echo. It puts me in mind of those stories of scientific marvel-mongers, who would paralyze us by the assertion that the stamp of a foot permanently displaces the whole stellar universe. I always feel oppressed in an echoing apartment; and if I thought much about the stellar universe, I should end either by crushing it, or letting it crush me.

Arrived at the staircase top, we push against a stiff-moving door, and find ourselves in an ante-room; one wall is covered with a huge hideous picture of a Court —ladies and gentlemen in seventeenth century costume, and, down in the right-hand corner, a little corkscrew-tailed cur, which somehow reminds us more of human beings than anything else upon the canvas. The only other object in the room is the catalogue stall, with its bald-headed attendant, who is not only a cynic but a misanthrope. Considering that he passes his life face to face with that Court scene, and never (to my knowledge) sells a catalogue, I am only surprised that he is not a suicide as well.

In this room we already become conscious of the picture-gallery smell—that most peculiar and depressing of odours. It cannot be called offensive—still less, agreeable; but it produces an effect of lassitude and apathy, such as is experienced under no other circumstances. It is an aroma of old canvasses; or we might regard it as the ancient breath expressed from the oily lungs of the innumerable old portraits. It is not fit food for living organisms; it dulls the eye and pales the cheek, and cuts short the temper. The buff beadles who pervade the place have acquired so sour and suspicious an aspect, that it is hard not to feel guilty in their presence. The morbid influence is enhanced by the arrangement of the rooms, which is such as to give the idea of hopelessly interminable extent; and by the style of architecture, which is beyond words monotonous, idealess, soulless, dry, dispiriting, unbeautiful. Our boot squeaks and slips on the parqueted floor, and there is scarcely one chair to a thousand pictures. And as for the pictures—be their merits how great soever—they are still the most tiresome feature of all.

Why are picture-galleries allowed? The best time to visit the Continental ones is on Sunday—the people's day; for then we may find relief from the rabble on the walls in observing the rabble on the floor, which is vastly more amusing and less impertinent. The latter is for ever on the move, and still forming new combinations; whereas the former varies not a hair's breadth from age to age, as if conceitedly conscious that its present attitude must be the very best imaginable. Moreover, even admitting each one of a hundred thousand pictures to be a masterpiece of colour, form, and design, the value of each would be a hundred thousand times less than if it stood alone. Picture-galleries are the greatest æsthetic abuses of our time. They are that saddest chaos which is formed of disordered beauty—like an insane poet's mind. Why has no artistic vigilance-committee arisen to annihilate this insult to good taste and modesty?

We admire the intellectual self-command of a Newton; but it is nothing to the power of mental abstraction necessary to the appreciation of a fine picture on the walls of a gallery. In fact, real appreciation is, under such circumstances, an impossibility. We do not see the picture which the great master painted. We discern only a certain arrangement of lines, and harmony of colours. The painter may have been divine, but he cannot show us his most precious secrets in a crowd. On the contrary, the more subtle and profound he is, the less our chance of apprehending him. It is not too much to say that no great picture, whether in the Dresden gallery or another, has yet been seen by mortal eyes. Good copies—which, to be good, must be a slight improvement on the originals—are out of the question; and therefore these paintings will remain a dead letter until the time comes for mankind not only to acknowledge commonplace truths, but to do them.

Then we shall see picture-galleries built upon a different principle. A picture that is worth anything is worth the devotion of, at least, one room. Of that room it should be the reason, the expression, the key, the consummation. Everything in the room should lead up to it, comment on it, harmonize with it, interpret it, reflect it. Without the picture, the room should appear like a man without his head; and the imagination should be able to predict the precise subject and tone of the painting from the testimony of its accessories.

Upon this principle shall the new gallery be planned—a private city of picture-homes, each work the sole occupant of its own apartments. Any picture not worth a room shall be burned; and of the remainder (which will not be over large) some shall be housed in a single chamber, others in a suite, others again shall have a palace expressly built for them—according to their respective merits. No person shall be permitted to visit more than one picture in one day: at which rate it would take at least three years to see a gallery of any extent; and true picture-lovers would probably confine their attentions to two or three favourites; spending day after day at their houses, not always gazing on the very canvas, but musing upon the fine symbolism of the surroundings, and leisurely accumulating fresh power to see and understand. A year so spent would be culture; but what shall we say of this elbowing and jostling of jaded throngs in barren, bare, unfurnished rooms? What shall we call those persons who sit for five minutes before the Sistine Madonna, and comment in strident whispers, and giggle, and retire as empty as they came?

It is time that they, and other evils of like nature, departed, to return no more.

Meanwhile it may be admitted that the human eye has a wonderful and providential faculty of blindness, which is of great service in picture-galleries as they are now. When, by long subjection to torture, we have learnt the walls by rote, we can sometimes contrive to concentrate our attention upon what we wish to see. But how far from the ideal is this hard-won and imperfect vision! As well compare the tantalization of seeing a glass of Madeira wine to the enjoyment of quaffing it. We know how sweetly we could be intoxicated, if only we could get the goblet to our lips. Nevertheless, unless we have resolution enough to avoid galleries altogether, our next best course is to spend our whole time there. We may thus acquire the faculty of keeping our eyesight somewhat under control, and of being conscious of the outer mass of pictures only as of an ill-digested meal—by a general uneasiness which jaundices our vision, but does not altogether prevent our imagining a better state of things.

II.

There is a fine view of the Theater-Platz from the windows of the gallery, and I have often found relief in watching the building of the new opera-house from that vantage ground. It will be a more pretentious edifice than the old one, but not so unique and impressive. The latter was a sort of infant Coliseum—or dwarf Coliseum, rather; for it was so smoke-blackened and weather-beaten that it looked five hundred years old. The interior was respectably upholstered in the usual red velvet; and though the audience might be somewhat put about for room, the stage was of good size. As regards ventilation, I need not say that every precaution was taken against it which enlightened ingenuity could devise; and with complete success. There were two companies connected with this theatre—one dramatic, the other operatic; and it should be observed that the latter, who were good enough in their line, never could be accused of taking a leaf from the former's book. The orchestra was one of the finest in Germany; it played sacred music in the cathedral on Sunday mornings, and the same evening, at the theatre, would interpret *Figaro* or *Tannhaüser*. Occasionally some grand oratorios would be produced, when the stage would be merged in the orchestra, and the singers wear evening dress,—thereby, it seems to me, laying themselves open to criticism. I heard and saw Haydn's "Creation" thus given, and could not drive away irreverent thoughts. The principal singers had their seats immediately in front of the foot-lights; and were down in the programme as the archangels Gabriel, Raphael, and Uriel; and Adam and Eve. Raphael was a bald-headed, severe-looking gentleman, with eye-glasses; he sat apart, but occasionally leaned over to whisper something to a person whom I at first mistook for Uriel, but who turned out to be Adam. Uriel I afterwards identified with a rather foppish young man on the left. These two archangels, and Adam, were attired in black broadcloth and snowy shirt bosoms and neckties. But Gabriel, who sat next to Uriel, and was manifestly on the best of terms with him, was a handsome young lady in a black satin dress cut low in the body. She had a slight cold, and blew her nose during the lulls in the "Creation." Eve—for whose appearance I looked with some interest—was a staid and decorous personage of some forty summers; she was dressed with strict propriety in a black moire antique, high in the neck; and, as if this were not enough, a lace shawl was superadded. Adam was a tall man with a big voice, a prominent forehead, and a scraggy beard. He was an impulsive man, and his book and his voice were always uplifted simultaneously.

Since I have gone so far, I will add that every one of these exalted individuals consumed a great deal of time in saying very short sentences. Having hit upon a phrase—sublime, certainly, in its original inspired simplicity—they so hung upon it, and stuttered over it, and muttered it, and mouthed it, and shouted it, and then began it again with fresh vigour, and broke off in the middle, and went back again, and picked out a word here and a word there, and juggled and dilly-dallied, that what was grandeur became buffoonery. True, they had to do it—the inexorable music, grinding out behind them, pulled their wires to suit itself, as the music of a street-organ seems to animate the puppets in its show-case. But this is Haydn, not the Bible; it was not thus that the morning stars sang together, and all the sons of God shouted for joy. Am I to be blamed for finding Haydn's "Creation" ludicrous? I think the blame lies elsewhere: I do not find the first chapter of Genesis ludicrous. Either Haydn was not so great a man as Moses, or the "Creation" cannot safely be entrusted to Euterpe.

But there was always compensation in the Royal box. A true democrat must ever be interested to observe a human being who holds himself, or is held, above the ordinary human level. In some moods, the idea pleases the imagination; while at other times, as we gaze upon the Royal faces, it seems irresistibly funny. The apparent difference between them and other people consists in an admirable simplicity and repose of manner, and a full directness of eye, most refreshing after the fussy gestures and evasive glances of plebeianism. The chief use of princes is to preserve a tradition and standard of perfect manners, and a respectable independence of soul—qualities one or the other of which is pretty sure to suffer in the progress of republicanism. But there is a *naïve* innocence about them and their paraphernalia and pretensions which, amidst all the regal pomp, suggests a simplicity more primitive and genuine than Franklin's plain coat at Versailles.

But the plain coats are coming into fashion. A Yankee friend of mine, while at a medical college in Saxony, had the honour, together with fifty or a hundred other students, of being visited by the new King, Albert. His Majesty, in his progress round the room, addressed some conventional remark to the American, who remarked, in answer, unconventionally enough, that Albert was the first King he had ever seen. The seeming artlessness of this observation at first conceals its originality, and this, again, veils its profound subtlety. For in it spoke the prophetic voice of revolution; and it is due to the King to say that he was both startled and impressed; and perhaps he raised his hand to his head, to be sure that his crown was there. When that remark has been made a few times more, there will be no king left to hear it.

III.

The most brilliant performance I ever witnessed at the old opera-house was its burning down, some five years ago. The fire caught in the garret, and a puff of smoke popped hastily out of window, as if to summon assistance. But its appeal was received with sarcastic incredulity. Fifteen minutes elapsed, and then a body of flame burst suddenly through the roof, and the Cassandra-puff was avenged for its rude treatment. It was a magnificent fire, and the Dresden firemen showed their appreciation of its beauty by making no attempt to put it out. There was not a breath of wind; had there been, Dresden would have perished upon the funeral-pyre of its opera-house. Very soon an oval column of flame, seventy feet in diameter, stood straight up, and roared two hundred feet aloft. Above the flame, a dark stem of smoke ascended perpendicularly, so high, that it seemed to impinge against the dull grey cloud which screened the heavens. Here a petulant breeze caught it, and trailed and drifted it hither and thither athwart the sky, until the whole resembled a titanic palm-tree, with a stem a mile in height, whose feathery foliage overshadowed the whole city. And in what a red-hot flower-pot was that palm-tree planted! so hot that the pictures were blistered in the gallery, more than seventy yards distant; and the Madonna descended in haste from the wall, and took refuge at the further side of the building.

Early in the proceedings, the soldiers were called out, and formed in a cordon surrounding the building, and distant from it about fifty paces. All these gallant fellows afterwards fought the French, but not at Gravelotte nor at Sedan was it their destiny to face so hot a fire as this. The thermometer, at this range, marked almost 200° Fahrenheit. Their rifles grew so warm that there was a general disposition to ground arms, and acknowledge that the old opera-house had the best of it. Retreat they could not, for they were hemmed in by a solid wedge of human bodies a quarter of a mile deep on every side save one, and there was the river. The precise reason of their being there at all has always been a mystery to me. Ostensibly it was to prevent the populace from getting into dangerous proximity to the burning buildings, but, inasmuch as it was physically impossible to advance twenty paces nearer without being shrivelled to a cinder, I can hardly suppose this to have been the true cause. Perhaps it was merely to accustom the warriors' souls to stand unmoved in the presence of ruin and devastation. Or, again, it may have been a subtle stroke of policy, to establish the precedent of military intervention in municipal affairs, by thus parading when there was no real occasion for it, and could, therefore, be no possible objection on the municipal part.

There were the usual instances of mental aberration to which fires give rise. A number of men, at the risk of their lives, brought forth from the burning pile a huge load of rusty iron bolts, bars, chains, screws, and pulleys, which had been used in the stage machinery, but they left the splendid wardrobe untouched, either from fear of soiling it in the transportation, or else upon the supposition that its value would cause the flames to respect it. But fire is no respecter of finery, even in Dresden, and the greater part of the actors' clothes and of the musicians' instruments mounted heavenward in flame and smoke, and are perhaps awaiting their owners in some celestial opera-house.

IV.

The German language, as socially spoken, does not sound musical, but the opera-singers so modify the pronunciation as to make it soft and agreeable. I am acquainted with no language, however, which sounds so differently from different lips as does this German. The Saxons are not of true German, but of Wendish origin, and their pronunciation, though by no means the harshest, is the most demoralized of all; and those foreigners who have formed their accent on Saxon models have, humanly speaking, disqualified themselves from ever getting it right. In its perfection, German is eminently a masculine tongue, but Dresden has emasculated it. She clips it, whines it, undulates it, sing-songs it, lubricates it, until it becomes a very eunuch of languages. The hard, clear, deliberate Hanoverian pronunciation compares with hers as chips of ice shaken in a crystal goblet, with lukewarm dish-water filliped in a greasy slop-bowl.

My feeling with regard to the pronunciation of foreign languages is perhaps curious, but observation inclines me to believe that it is not altogether unique. I never imitate the native accent without feeling a little ashamed of myself, and the closer my imitation, the greater my loss of self-respect. On the other hand, an execrable English twang, or still more, a few

English words thrown in here and there, revive my drooping independence like a tonic. I may be as correct in my grammar, and in the placing of my verbs and participles, as my knowledge will admit, without a whisper of self-reproach; but the moment I attempt to disguise my nationality I am degraded.

Moreover, supposing such disguise possible, what is gained by it? Is it so great a triumph to be mistaken for a Saxon, for instance? There is surely nothing intellectual in mimicry, and our best success amounts to nothing higher than that. No; a foreign accent is to be shunned rather than sought. It is as demoralizing as to wear another man's clothes. It cannot be attained without doing violence to the inner nature—to those fine perceptions of modesty and decorum which give character its worth. A person who speaks a foreign language so well as to deceive a native, is rarely a delicate-minded man. He will either be subtle, deceitful, sly, with a talent for intrigue, or else superficial, coarse, and vain. He can seldom possess a sensitive and nicely-balanced individuality. Besides, what is called a broken accent is not displeasing to the native hearer; rather it impresses him as a sort of indirect compliment to the supreme refinement of his tongue. And, at the best, we find ourselves saying things in a foreign language which we should never dream of uttering in our own. We feel it to be a veil over our real selves, and so venture upon unaccustomed liberties; like scurrilous critics who write anonymously. There is a point beyond which cosmopolitanism becomes unwholesome.

V.

If we can once succeed in freeing ourselves from the vulgar prejudice against Sunday amusements, a main obstacle in the way of our Dresden diversions will have been removed. Look upon Sunday as a holiday—it is nothing else, indeed—and theatre-going, dancing, and junketing can hardly appear illegitimate. Live among Saxons for a year or two, or for half-a-dozen years if two be not enough, and Sabbath bells will cease to distract us from enjoyment of the opera-bouffe overture. Walking out, in the clear Sabbath twilight, to meditate upon the immortality of the soul, we shall but meditate the more at the glimpse of heated couples gyrating to a fiddle in yonder dance-hall. And, as we grow wiser and broader-minded, we shall gradually cease to associate Sunday with any thoughts of God, or of a life beyond this world. This point once reached, we may congratulate ourselves, and push onwards hopefully. Is it not, after all, fatal to our appreciation of the world we are in, to keep mingling with it speculations about a world we may never attain? Saxons have emancipated themselves in good measure from such confusion. They recognize religion as a word of four syllables whose meaning is open to discussion. It gives them a holiday once a week, and a pretext for bullying the Pope every day. It is true that the Royal Family are Roman Catholics, and a good part of their subjects also; but that is a matter of detail. There is no personal animosity in the attitude of the rival parties—nothing but political exigency. Except His Holiness and Prince Bismarck, nobody really cares how the cat jumps. Select a Lutheran here and a Catholic there, and confront them with each other as spiritual enemies—they cannot keep straight countenances. The Catholic makes the sign of the cross, the Lutheran hums his "Wein, Weib und Gesang," they link arms and are off to the Sunday masquerade.

Let us be emancipated too, and follow them. These masquerades are a prominent Dresden diversion during the winter. They are widely advertised, not only by the placards which glow forth in crimson, yellow, and blue, from every advertising-post, but still more by the masks which now begin to crowd and grimace in shop-windows. Here is every variety, from the simple false nose to the elaborate head and shoulders, complete both back and front. Here they hang, row above row, grinning, empty things, a curious revelation of what men would make of themselves if flesh change countenance, and we indulge our maddest freaks with entire composure. This were a merry world if no one knew his fellow, nor could find him out. It is lucky for civilization that we cannot so much as black our boots in a manner inconsistent with our past and our prospects.

But the spur of the fun is its necessary briefness. If the masquerade could last a year, we should only have shifted one self to take up another quite as burdensome. Besides, the spice of mystery and novelty is evanescent, and, by-and-by, we cease to laugh at one another's long noses. Why we ever laughed at them is hard to say: perhaps only as an alternative to shuddering or weeping. Children are more frightened than amused by masks of all kinds, which proves them not funny, but monstrous; and our laughter only shows our callousness.

As to these Dresden masquerades, I may observe that the more masked they are the better. The majority of their patrons are in attendance to regale such phases of human nature as are commonly kept in strict concealment. Under such circumstances, a hideous mask is often the best virtue possible: it is, so to say, devilishly appropriate. However hideous it may be, the revelation of the naked face is often yet more revolting; and my chief quarrel with Dresden masquerades is on the ground of their indecency in too often neglecting to keep their indecency veiled.

VI.

At masquerades the Saxon disguises himself in more ways than one. He lays not much stress upon his domino and vizard, but he bewilders us by an unwonted pecuniary extravagance, and himself with too much champagne. Although there are no people that can less truly be considered temperate than the Saxons, we seldom find them helplessly intoxicated; and this precisely because they habitually drink so much. Fortunately, moreover, it is to beer that they chiefly address themselves, as being the cheapest liquor and the most accessible. But when they forsake this honest beverage for more costly and potent ones, they are speedily overcome. And they betray an unwholesome delight in drunkenness. An American or a Frenchman is apt to be very troublesome when intoxicated; an Englishman, more or less brutal; but the Saxon is purely disgusting both in act and aspect. Besides, neither in the prospect nor the retrospect is he at all ashamed of his vinous fermentation, but, rather, proud, as the Bacchantes might have been.

Whoever should attempt—without any definite information, but relying upon his knowledge of Saxon change countenance, and we indulge our maddest freaks with entire composure. This were a merry world if no one knew his fellow, nor could find him out. It is lucky for civilization that we cannot so much as black our boots in a manner inconsistent with our past and our prospects.

But the spur of the fun is its necessary briefness. If the masquerade could last a year, we should only have shifted one self to take up another quite as burdensome. Besides, the spice of mystery and novelty is evanescent, and, by-and-by, we cease to laugh at one another's long noses. Why we ever laughed at them is hard to say: perhaps only as an alternative to shuddering or weeping. Children are more frightened than amused by masks of all kinds, which proves them not funny, but monstrous; and our laughter only shows our callousness.

As to these Dresden masquerades, I may observe that the more masked they are the better. The majority of their patrons are in attendance to regale such phases of human nature as are commonly kept in strict concealment. Under such circumstances, a hideous mask is often the best virtue possible: it is, so to say, devilishly appropriate. However hideous it may be, the revelation of the naked face is often yet more revolting; and my chief quarrel with Dresden masquerades is on the ground of their indecency in too often neglecting to keep their indecency veiled.

VI.

At masquerades the Saxon disguises himself in more ways than one. He lays not much stress upon his domino and vizard, but he bewilders us by an unwonted pecuniary extravagance, and himself with too much champagne. Although there are no people that can less truly be considered temperate than the Saxons, we seldom find them helplessly intoxicated; and this precisely because they habitually drink so much. Fortunately, moreover, it is to beer that they chiefly address themselves, as being the cheapest liquor and the most accessible. But when they forsake this honest beverage for more costly and potent ones, they are speedily overcome. And they betray an unwholesome delight in drunkenness. An American or a Frenchman is apt to be very troublesome when intoxicated; an Englishman, more or less brutal; but the Saxon is purely disgusting both in act and aspect. Besides, neither in the prospect nor the retrospect is he at all ashamed of his vinous fermentation, but, rather, proud, as the Bacchantes might have been.

Whoever should attempt—without any definite information, but relying upon his knowledge of Saxon character and tendencies—to form an idea of what a masquerade in Dresden would be like, could not fail to be taken aback by the reality. The extent and boldness of the advertising is misleading, for how can that to which the whole community is invited be very improper? We are prepared, perhaps, to be a little scandalized, but we certainly count on being amused, and most likely gratified by a gorgeous and imposing spectacle. The carnivals of old, we have heard, were splendid to the eye, however questionable otherwise; and some of us have read Mr. De Quincey's "Masque of Klosterheim," and are ready for all imaginable mystery and grandeur. The very name "masque," "masquerade," possesses an indescribable magnetism of its own.

So we present our ticket at the door, and pass through the dressing-room into the main hall. It is thronged from side to side, full of light, music, human hum and tumult, and occasionally a shriller laugh or call heard above the even din. The orchestra is somewhere overhead; the whole broad floor is given up to the dancers, actual or potential. The latter form a wide, dense ring around the former, whose reeling heads we behold confusedly agitated; now merging exhausted in the ring, anon starting from it with new vigour. The Saxons are clever dancers, one and all, and devoted to the pastime; but I confess I like it less since seeing them enjoy it. They dance with emphasis—with a greedy persistence which is disenchanting. When warmed to their work, the partners face each other, the man's arms round the woman's waist, her hands clutching his shoulders, and so fixed, they spin teetotum-like. But though this arrangement is good for pace, it lacks the artificial grace which is the charm of modern dancing. Since we cannot be veritable nymphs and fauns, it is best to adopt as different a style as possible.

The hall is draped with banners, and the walls glow with various emblazonment. But when we turn to the masqueraders themselves, they seem less fine than their surroundings. Three-fourths of the men are in evening dress or even in ordinary clothes, with nothing better than a half-mask, or a false nose to hide their faces withal, and not a few have dispensed even with these poor disguises. Such nonconformity is discouraging—nay, insulting—as if our host at a banquet should present us our food uncooked. The women are more orthodox; scarce one but wears a mask, generally a silken vizard with a veil for the lower part of the face. Most of them, too, are clad in fancy costume—either a gay domino, or a stage dress more or less elaborate. There are half-a-dozen ballet-dancers, in gauze and silk tights—somewhat dismaying, by their palpable proximity, those whose ideas of such beings have been formed only from behind the foot-lights. Others there are in still more dashing attire, which I will not undertake to describe. But it would be all very well, and in keeping, were it not for those black-coated, barefaced, besotted, masculine intruders, who, like a malignant touchstone, reveal the ugliness beneath the gay outside, and force us to see only a cheat in the prettiest pretences.

Such as it is, however, there is more masquerading in the main hall than in the side rooms, and the discreet visitor will not push his investigations far beyond the sound of the music, lest some sudden Gorgon freeze him to stone. A glass or two of wine beyond the common is, perhaps, a wise prescription at this juncture. Now, let us force our way through the ring, and seize our partner. We need not be ceremonious, and wait for an introduction; nor is such a thing as monopolization of the chosen companion countenanced. To the Saxon, all woman is one. For convenience sake, she is multiplied into fractions; but one is just as good for practical purposes as another. The nearest at hand is the most ours; yet we must not resent having her taken from our arms after the enjoyment of a turn or two. The question is not, With whom did you dance? but, How much?

To launch forth, with a good waltzer, to excellent music, compensates many evils; and, but for collisions, slips, dust, heat, and exhaustion, we should henceforth get on famously. But as the evening advances, such checks increase. The wine makes the floor slippery and the dancers unwieldy. The scene begins to wear a very dilapidated appearance. The noise is greater, but more disorganized; the laughter is wilder; there are sudden screams; and now and then a short struggle, and perhaps a fall. Meanwhile, the music pours on unceasing, infusing a strange harmony into the discord. The policemen—a number of whom have been lurking unobtrusively in shady corners—are now occasionally in requisition; but it must be admitted that they are very lenient; it would need a murder to move them to real severity. They cast reproachful glances; or, in extreme cases, impose a remonstrative hand. But there is no clubbing, no show of arms, no dragging out by the coat-collar. Nor is it needed; the mere sight of the black helmet is ordinarily enough; for beneath it lowers, to the evil-doer's eye, not the inoffensive visage of the individual policeman, but the impending brow, trenchant glance, and aggressive chin of Germany's greatest statesman. Mumbo Jumbo teaches even drunkards to reason and refrain.

Meanwhile, eating and drinking proceed in the ante-rooms, and above-stairs in the galleries and lobbies. But the guests are in a sadly dishevelled state; even the women are now unmasked, and so the last reserve is overthrown. We must have a boisterous appetite to compass a supper at one one of these tables, amid such queer neighbours. Debauchery has no attractions in Saxony beyond its naked self; and those who indulge in it there, must love it for its own unmitigated sake. It is for the gratification of these its children that a paternal Government provides masquerades, and finds them remunerative.

VII.

Far different from this masked iniquity are the balls given by the proprietors of beer-saloons to their customers, and to such friends as the latter may choose to invite. Hither flock minor tradesmen with their wives and daughters, and hotel-waiters, clerks, and such small deer of society. They are all well-behaved; there is nothing of the riot and disturbance which would mark a gathering of the same rank in America. Here is peaceful good-nature, and though joy be unconfined, there is decorum—at least what Saxons understand as such. There is little attempt at dress; the men are in their Sunday coats and light trousers, the women in robes of stout material, not of Parisian design, but prettified about the arms and shoulders with lace and muslin. Gloves are unknown; you receive your partner's hand as nature and exercise have left it. The fun is not confined to the young people; they bring their fathers and mothers with them, and the latter dance as vigorously and enjoyingly as their offspring. Every one is on familiar terms with his neighbour, so that the assembly feels like a family party.

A friend of mine, who, with me, has investigated many curious phases of Saxon life, accompanied me to one of these merry-makings. We had for some weeks past assiduously visited a modest *Restauration* in the Am See, where the beer was brought us by a stalwart maiden named Anna. Our calls being usually made about the middle of the afternoon, Anna had leisure for social converse, and surprised us by the extent of her attainments. Not only could she play on the piano, which prolonged a tuneless existence in one corner of the room, but she could beat us at capping verses from Heine, and even, as we subsequently discovered, could rhyme a very creditable stanza herself. In short, she was a young woman of parts, and I fancy she had ambitions. Her personal attractions are soon enumerated. She was short and broad-shouldered; her arms and cheeks were red-shiny; her wide, good-humoured mouth was always stretching to a smile. Her bright, small grey eyes twinkled in a very contracted cranium, which was surmounted by a swathing of hair so flattened down and polished off that it seemed to be a coating of yellow-brown paint, laid on thick and varnished.

Anna invited us to this ball—we accepted—and she gave us each a card on which were neatly written her own name and ours, her chosen guests. I have seldom received an invitation so genuinely cordial as this. Anna was proud of us, and even a little anxious lest something might prevent our coming. Again and again did she earnestly beseech us not to fail her, and did grin from one honest ear to the other when we affirmed that nothing short of death should detain us.

The ball was at a saloon half-a-mile out of town, and had been going on for an hour or two before our arrival. We discussed a *Schnitt* of beer in the Vorsaal, and then peeped modestly through the ball-room door. A waltz was in progress, and for a while we looked in vain for Anna among the whirling couples. There were near a hundred people present, and all at work; and the evening being rather a warm one, they were pretty thoroughly heated. The Saxon, in this condition, is less attractive than at other times. Perhaps, speaking generally, there are few better ways of distinguishing the aristocrat from the plebeian than to get both in a profuse perspiration. It is as sure a test of physical purity as was the fairy girdle at Guinevere's court of moral cleanliness.

At length we caught sight of Anna's genial countenance, brilliant with heat and pleasure, glowing over the shoulder of a revolving young shopkeeper. She shot a broad smile across the hall, and spinning her partner to a seat, hastened up to us all redolent of hospitality. How pretty she looked! She was really the belle of the evening. She was enveloped as to the upper part of her stout person in white muslin, through which shone mistily her rosy arms and shoulders; below, fell a skirt of some respectable grey fabric, not so long as to incommode her dancing feet. Her ears were splendid with glittering glass pendants; round her neck a yellow glass cross was suspended by a black gutta-percha chain. Is there not pathos in these poor little details of finery, and her manifest delight in them? On her short fingers were three or four broad rings as yellow as gold. At her throat—for even so much magnificence was not enough—Anna wore a brooch as big as the palm of her own fair hand, of tin, artfully moulded to resemble diamonds. As to her hair, it seemed to have grown by the yard since yesterday, and was frizzled in short curls over the forehead. It was plentifully anointed with some glistening unguent, upon which I forbear to dwell. It was the only thing about Anna which we could not admire.

Nothing could be more flattering in its simplicity than the way Anna took my friend's hand, rested her chin upon his shoulder, and, without question asked or expected, danced him off into the steaming tumult of the hall. I watched their devious course, whirling, plunging, staggering, desperately keeping time, now hidden, anon reappearing, and evermore revolving! I marvelled at the pained contraction of his brow, and at the tireless vigour of her flying feet! Finally, either he relented, and gasped in her ear to remember her deserted guest, or it was her own kind heart that brought her whirling back to where I stood, and transferred her from his fortunate arms to mine.

Be that as it may, it was I who, the next moment, breasted with her the dangers of the dance. But I will pass lightly over my own exploits. How long the spell lasted I never knew, but it seemed to me that Anna must be Atalanta in disguise. At length, however, our motion appeared to have ceased, though still the room wheeled and tipped before my eyes. We had eddied into a seat—Anna and I—and it was given me to know that her threefold performance had finally exhausted her.

"Ach! so müde bin Ich," she faltered, and with that she innocently drooped her anointed head and laid it on my shoulder. Being a constitutionally timid man, I confess that, at this juncture, I could not repress a movement of apprehension. The situation was really too tender for long continuance: the fragrant head was uplifted; but I found its imprint on the broadcloth the next morning—"Zum Andenken," as Anna would have said.

At midnight supper was announced, and the response was unanimous. Three long tables were placed on as many sides of a square, while opposite the open end a small one was set apart for the host and his family. We occupied the top of the right-hand table, with Anna between us. We were scarcely well settled in our places when the toasting began. The host's health was first proposed by an orator at the lower table. Amid the consequent enthusiastic uproar, the host filled his goblet, and stepping into the hollow square of tables, touched glasses with all his hundred guests, they meanwhile standing up, or even climbing on their chairs, loudly chanting the "Hoch soll er leben!" which is always an accompaniment of the ceremony.

When the noise had subsided, the host—he was a small, dapper man, with bushy whiskers and a rather nervous manner—made an address of some length. He was cheered throughout, and ended with proposing somebody else's health, which was received in precisely the same manner as his own had been. Thus the ball rolled round the table, every other guest, at least, being called on, and responding with a speech, a song, or an original poem. The ladies took part in the exercises no less than the men; and Anna, after replying to the flattering terms in which her name had been brought forward, recited, with good emphasis and discretion, some three or four easy-flowing verses of her own composition. I think we had but half appreciated our little sponsor, after all.

Well, at last there was a pause, and we wondered what was to happen next. But gradually, as it were by some magnetic attraction, the eyes of all present turned and fastened upon us. Then solemnly the host arose, and began, with formal hints which by degrees grew more and more transparent and complimentary, to call attention to the presence in the assembly of two distinguished strangers—foreigners—in fact Americans. A brief eulogy of that great nation followed; and finally came (the host's version of) our names, and a summons—most heartily supported—to drink us with all the honours.

During the succeeding tumult we held a hurried consultation; and my friend showed himself equal to the occasion. He arose, and in understandable German regretted that his limited acquaintance with that language denied him the pleasure of addressing the company in it; but, for his own sake as well as for his country's, he could not sit down without giving utterance to a few sentiments which would only be the more cordial that they were expressed in American.

And here followed a speech which could not have been better received had the speaker's tongue been a very Goethe's. Indeed, I fancy our Saxon friends felt even more gratified and complimented by a speech which they could not comprehend than had it been otherwise. We immediately became cynosures, and were introduced to everybody—among others, to those two unexceptionable little personages, Anna's father and mother. I think the old lady was pointedly kind to me; we never failed to touch glasses with a smile and a bow before drinking: and afterwards, in the *cotillon*, she bestowed two favours upon me—the Cross of the Legion of Honour and the Cap of Liberty.

It were too long to rehearse in detail a tithe of the events which followed. Anna, unwilling to choose between her two guests, was partner of us both in the ensuing *cotillon;* nay, it seemed that even we could not satisfy her waltzing appetite, for she had three or four relays of young Saxons constantly in waiting for the spare turns. She did not spare herself at all; and we could not help wishing, on more accounts than one, that she had been somewhat less popular. Indefatigable Anna! Her muslin garments clung to her as though she had been immersed in beer.

Till two o'clock we jigged it ceaselessly; then there was a universal pause; each couple sought their chairs, and gradually the lights burnt blue, till we scarce could see across the darkened hall. Presently, however, we were aware of a mysterious apparition— seemingly an incarnation of the gloom—in the shape of a gigantic extinguisher, about seven feet in height. This spectre glided in silence thrice around the room, to slow music, bestowing upon each lady a small roll of paper containing a sugar-plum and an amatory epigram. The last round having been completed, the ghostly extinguisher vanished as mysteriously as it appeared—seemed to put itself out, in fact—and then the lights suddenly resumed their brilliancy. Some people departed after this, and we were of the number, after a melting farewell from Anna. She told us, the next afternoon—and a touch of paleness on her cheek confirmed the tale—that she had danced till six that morning. And then she sat down to the piano, and regretfully touched the chords of Strauss's waltz, "An der schoenen blauen Donau."

"What, Anna!" we exclaimed, "not yet enough of dancing?"

"Ach, bewahr!" she murmured; and with a subtle mixture of tact and coquetry, she hummed with Goethe's "Mignon,"

"Dahin, Dahin, mocht' Ich mit Dir, O mein Geleibter, zieh'n!"

But we could never agree which of us it was she had in mind; and too probably it was neither.

VIII.

There are diversions of war as well as of peace. At all times in history the sight of blood, human or bestial, has been delightful to mankind; symbolic, I suppose, of the cruel scoffing spirit which would rend asunder the holy mysteries of nature, and discover her vital secrets to all eyes rude enough to look upon them. What siren was ever so seductive to entice men to their harm as is the voice of a brother's blood crying to heaven?

We cannot be long in Dresden without meeting about the streets, and at the *cafés* and beer saloons, specimens of a guild which is peculiar to Germany, and not likely to be exported. Their leading traits are tolerably well known, having been diligently described by travellers ever since "Hyperion." They pace the streets, proud, in a striking costume, of which the only invariable features are a pair of high boots, reaching six or seven inches above the knee, which, like snow-shoes, cannot be properly worn without practice; a round cap, four inches in diameter, and an inch and a-half deep, clinging by invisible means to the north-east corner of the head; and a striped ribbon crossing the chest from the shoulder to the hip. They swing a light cane in one hand, stare the passer-by boldly in the eye, puff tobacco-smoke in the ladies' faces, and are very high-spirited and quarrelsome. On cheek and brow are scars from an inch to four inches in length, which it is no part of their religion to conceal. They are inclined to monopolize the sidewalks, and to hector it in the beer-gardens. They are of that undesirable age, between sixteen and twenty-three, through which, as through a miasmal swamp, mankind is condemned to pass on its way to better things.

Yes, these are the University students—or at least, students from the Mining College in Freiberg, a curious old town some twenty miles from Dresden. The strong class spirit of these young fellows, and their superstitious observance of antiquated forms and customs, undeniably makes them an interesting study, the more because it seems unlikely that they can exist many years longer in their pristine quaintness. The vital essence of the "Kneipe" is its vast absurdity; and its attraction to outsiders lies in the startling contrast between its laws and customs, its costumes and its creeds, and those of the present day. We cannot expect it to hold its own in the teeth of modern innovations and refinements, military laws, science, persecutions, and republican despotisms. Its dying aroma is being even now exhaled.

Between the soldiers and the students there has always subsisted a hatred and rivalry, wherein the former have generally the advantage. There is no assignable cause for this feud, unless it be that the students fight with the *Schlaeger* and the officers with the broadsword. In extreme cases, however, both parties use pistols, which put them on more equal footing. A regiment of infantry was formerly quartered at Freiberg, much to the discontent of the thousand or more students residing there. Collisions were frequent; and at length an officer mortally affronted a Bursch, and in the consequent meeting shot his opponent dead. Hereupon an indignation gathering of all the Kneipen; and the next day the officer was the recipient of no less than a thousand distinct summonses to the field of honour— weapons, pistols. Not only, therefore, did he stand a thousand chances to one of being killed, but—supposing him passed through such a hell-fire unscathed— he must bear during life the not entirely enviable reputation of having slaughtered a thousand human beings, and depopulated a college. A council of war was held, resulting in the transmission to the student champions of the apologies of the regiment, and the withdrawal of the latter from Freiberg, which thus vindicated its name.

But such serious affairs as this are very rare. Duelling among the students is regarded as a means of culture and a sign of good breeding; it forms an important part of the routine of University discipline; and a scar or two—or a dozen, if possible—are quite as conducive to the credit of a graduate as his diploma. Duelling meetings are held between rival corps several times a year, and champions are matched against one another, not by reason of personal enmity, but according to their prowess—as we would match two college boys to row a single scull race. A spice of genuine hostility between the duellists is not, however, objected to; and doubtless it is quite as well to fight out petty quarrels and heart-burnings with the *Schlaeger* as to promote their unhealthy growth by a diet of bad language and morbid backbitings. My observation leads me to the conclusion that a sound bout at fisticuffs is better than either; but fisticuffing would soon put an end to the Kneipe system, and to that peculiar code of etiquette, morality, and refinement which it inculcates on the student's mind. We must recollect, moreover, that the sword renders the small fist as dangerous as the big one; and since what is known to Anglo-Saxons as fair play is but dimly apprehended by the German intellect, perhaps this safeguard of the weak against the strong is not unimportant.

It is curious how the periodical shedding of a little blood, organizes and vitalizes these guilds. In all ways, blood is the strongest cement between man and man. Armies would soon thirst to death if blood were denied them; nor are elaborate discipline and forms of behaviour anywhere so rigorously maintained as where the rules are written with a bloody pen. The reason is perhaps not far to seek. Bloodshed, pure and simple, is vulgar, disgusting, and brutal. Nothing else has so strong a natural tendency to degrade and coarsen the nature. And it is the very recognition of this which leads man to spend his best skill in surrounding all its circumstances with the utmost pomp and formality. It seems to be a universal law that those things which have the strongest native tendency to drag mankind to chaos, should become—by virtue of the struggle they compel him to make against their destructive power—his most potent educators. The completest gentleman—the holiest saint—is he who has withstood the strongest temptation to be a charlatan or a devil.

So with these corps-students: there is not much education, one would suppose, in a slit nose, or a cheek laid open. No; but the processes which have led up to it—have we considered them? There is the fencing-school, in which, at all events, the hand and eye are trained to an accuracy and strength to which they had else been strangers. There, too, is the corps etiquette to be learnt and preserved—the recognition of authority and order, and the careful observance of self-respect. Each one is responsible for his conduct to all the rest; and if called upon to defend himself, it is his fault should he fail successfully to withstand his challenger. As to physical courage, I cannot own to any great faith in its development by *Schlaeger* duels. It is true that the duellists soon cease to fear the "cuts" and even learn to enjoy them. But then, they are never mortal, and seldom very serious. And I have no reason to believe that the most inveterate *Schlaeger* duellist is any braver before a pistol than other men might be. Special pleadings on questions of this kind are, however, misleading; since, however well the theory may be supported, the practice always belies it more or less. The best that can be affirmed with regard to corps-students is, that we are not obliged to make so many allowances for them as for the unmitigated barbarians.

IX.

Perhaps the reader would like to be present at one of these duel-meetings, and form his own judgment upon the matter?—We turn down a narrow side-street, whip under a gloomy archway, enter by a glass-panelled door, and find ourselves in a dismal beer-saloon. Passing through this, we arrive at an inner apartment, to which a peculiar knock gives us admittance. This is the Kneipe-room, where the corps is to rendezvous before proceeding to the field of honour. It is narrow, dark, and smoky, blearing out through its one grimy window into a back yard. The floor is strewn with a little white sand; a rough wooden table, bearing marks of age and hard usage, extends the length of the room: wooden benches to match, and unpretending chairs. The walls are adorned with the coat-of-arms of the corps, emblazoned in gold and colours; round it are arranged a score of old *Schlaeger*, like rays of a central sun. Elsewhere are hung up enormous drinking-horns, such as King Olaf might have used, with inscriptions on their silver mountings. Here are trophies of all sorts; pictures, too, representing famous duels; and photographs of past and present members, taken singly or in groups. Traditions are jealously preserved among the Burschen, and some of the societies are of very great antiquity; so that the Bursch of to-day may see upon the wall the sword with which his great-grandfather fought, and drink himself seas-over out of the ancestral *Schoppen*.

Has the reader ever held a *Schlaeger* in his hand, and examined it? It has a large basket-hilt, guarding the hand completely: the blade is straight, and about three feet in length—a thin, narrow strip of soft steel, pliant but not elastic. It is a light weapon, easily wielded; were it heavy as the ordinary broadsword, the muscles of an average Bursch would soon tire beneath its weight, for the attitude in fighting is an excessively wearisome one at best. Its deficiencies in heaviness and stiffness are fully compensated by the razor-keenness of the blade; the soft steel taking a marvellously fine edge. The point is rounded, and the edge extends sixteen inches down the front of the blade, and half as far down the back. Both blade and hilt are gallantly scarred and hacked; from these the bloodstains have been wiped away; but the "armour" shows enough of such to sate the most sanguinary warrior. The gore of hundreds—ay, of thousands, is encrusted on these breast-plates and cuishes, and presents a spectacle really ghastly, and calculated, one would suppose, to dampen the courage of a virgin duellist. A pig-sticker's apron would be more reassuring. For this armour, excellent in other respects, can never be cleansed; it consists of stout buckskin pads, protecting the throat, right arm, and the whole right side of the body to the knee. Iron armour would speedily destroy the fine edge of the *Schlaeger;* though I doubt whether it would be found any heavier than these enormous pads, and stiffer or more awkward it certainly could not be. The pads detract much from the aspect of the contest; a polished cuirass and glittering arms would be more inspiring, and the blood would seem more noble when shed on steel than when absorbed and stiffened in dirty leather. There is another objection. The rattle of a sword against a steel breast-plate is a martial sound; it kindles the imagination and inspires the courage; but the "flap" of the blade against the buckskin pad reminds us of nothing more dignified than carpet-beating. If we close our eyes upon the bloody scene, and only listen to the fray, we are transported to the back-yard of our childhood's home, where John and Bridget are knocking clouds of dust out of the parlour carpet. The illusion is heightened by the fact that the warriors, like John and Bridget, deliver their blows alternately, in rapid and measured succession. "Flap—flap!—flap—flap!" It is carpet-beating, for all the world! However, we must not carp and criticize so much. Use is itself a beauty; and since the leathern pad answers its special purpose better than anything else could, it must appear beautiful to the unprejudiced observer.

Besides the furniture and ornaments, the room contains a dozen or more young men, high-booted, round-capped, and ribboned. Some of them are to be the heroes of the coming tournament, though we might not learn as much from the Indian stoicism of their countenances. Probably the signs of battle will be plainer after it is over than beforehand. The students are not all Germans; there are Hungarians,

Poles, Turks, an American, and a couple of Russians. One of the latter is vice-president of the corps—a tall, burly fellow, with a rough face and small grey eyes; but when he speaks—and he does so in four languages—we perceive an unexpected courtesy and refinement in his manner. His familiarity with the English tongue is astonishing: he has even caught the colloquialisms of the day.

"Do we fear the spectacle of blood?" he asks us; "does it nauseate us? he should say:" and he proceeds to tells us a gory tale or two, by way of gentle initiation into the horrors we are soon to witness. Once he was present at a notable duel between two renowned fencers; and for a long time the advantage was on neither side. No cut had been given; it was feared that their skill would prove too perfect—that there would be no blood. Just then, however, Fritz appeared suddenly to grow an inch taller; his wrist extended itself admirably—ah! Karl was hit. So true and swift was the blow that Karl himself knew not, at first, that he was overcome; only when he went to speak, and the blood poured into his mouth, did he become aware of it. A sponge was brought; the blood wiped away; when lo! Karl had no end of his nose. Du lieber Gott! where is then the nose which Karl had lost? All search for it—it is still in vain—the nose—the nose had disappeared! Then cries out all of a sudden Fritz—"The dog! the dog! Potz tausend Donnerwetter! look once at the dog." One sees the dog make like a cough, with something in mouth. One runs to him, catch him, pound him on the back, lift him by the tail and shake. Ach! lo! at last the nose, the poor nose, the end of the nose which Karl has lost. Then Karl takes that end and sticks it to his face—to the root, you see."

"Yes; well, did it grow on again?"

"But surely yes. For seven days it is held continually on; then is the bandage removed, and the nose is once more whole. But alas! an unlooked-for misfall has occurred."

"How so?"

"In the haste of replacing that lost end, the poor Karl has it upside down applied! It is now too late to alter—so grows it to this day. Karl was before a handsome man: he has still the *Geist*—the vivacity; but the profile—one finds it irregular."

I should not have ventured to repeat this story at length, had I not the best of reasons for believing it true. I heard it not long afterwards from the lips of the redoubtable Karl himself, and when, at the conclusion, he turned his head pensively aside, the "irregularity" was unmistakeable.

This was by no means the only tale of blood unfolded by our courteous Russian; but I cannot undertake the responsibility of any more of them. It was not without a touch of pride that he recounted the exploit of a countryman of his own, who, it would appear, was possessed of more fortitude than skill. In the first bout his adversary's point caught in the corner of Snipitoff's mouth, and created a permanent grin on that side three inches in length, laying bare all the teeth in the right jaw. Snipitoff, however, was no way discouraged, but intimated his resolve to fight it out. The contest was therefore resumed; and Snipitoff's adversary, who seems to have been gifted with an almost unreasonable eye for symmetry, next inserted his blade in the left corner of the gallant Russian's mouth, and brought it out at the ear. This terminated an affair which was considered to reflect equal credit on both sides. The mouth—which now measured from corner to corner a trifle over nine inches—was sewed up, with the exception of about three inches in the middle; and unconquerable Snipitoff then called for beer, and drank until—to use the forcible expression of our courteous informant—" his back teeth were under water," for three days. The practice of drinking heavily after receiving a cut is universal among the duellists, and is indulged in by way of delaying the healing of the wound, and thus perpetuating the glorious scar.

While such tales are telling, we are otherwise regaled with beer, bread and cheese, and sausage, whereof the long table has a plentiful load. Perhaps, however, after such fare as our imagination has been treated to, we care not so much for the nourishment of the flesh. In that case, the announcement that the hour for setting forth has arrived will be not unwelcome; we gladly issue from our dark and musty quarters, and are soon threading the outskirts of the city. The "field of honour" is some two miles off, and is only metaphorically a field; literally it is an old Gasthaus, deserted at this Lenten season, but hired by the Kneipen for the occasion. There is, by-the-by, a prohibitory law against the blood-drinking in which these young savages would indulge, and its influence is no less remarkable than is that of analogous legislation among us in New England. The unnatural thirst is augmented, and the ingenuity requisite to its gratification adds a moral and mental delight to the merely palatal enjoyment; encouraging the dipsomaniac to drink a gallon where he would otherwise be satisfied with a gill. The law is also serviceable, as a species of persecution, in consolidating the Kneipen, and riveting the union of its members. The State desires the permanence of the guild; and as if the cement of blood were not bond secure enough, doubles its strength by making its use unlawful. There is much subtle wisdom concealed beneath the plain outside of Saxon law.

X.

The Gasthaus is a forlorn and dilapidated old pile, overgrown of bulk, with countless melancholy windows, and streaks of greenish damp meandering down its plaster walls from eaves to basement. Within, we climb an aged winding staircase, and presently find ourselves in a large upper room, of great length in proportion to its breadth, wainscoated, with tarnished chandeliers depending from the ceiling, and an iron stove warming its further extremity. The tables and most of the chairs have been removed. The floor, especially at that spot where blood is to be shed, is strewn with sawdust. A crowd of upwards of a hundred students are standing about in knots, discussing the instant fray. They are not a physically noble race; many faces are marked with disease latent or developed, and the figures are ill-hung, awkward, or weakly. No other land, perhaps, could show so large an assemblage of young men with so small a leaven of physical manliness. Half of these wear—not the sportive eye-glass—but the sober earnestness of spectacles. There is a fortune for oculists in Saxony; and I should not wonder if a good part of the current belief in the national learning might be traced to the sage and studious aspect bestowed by these semi-universal spectacles. As a matter of fact, however, their genesis is from bad diet, and perhaps from some quality in the atmosphere. Most foreigners who have lived long in Saxony will have found their eyesight more or less impaired.

We glance with some curiosity at the champions who are to win their laurels to-day, or add to them. The two youngest—boys of about sixteen—look a little pale; and we may observe a trifling nervousness beneath the gaiety of that young American, who is destined to flesh his maiden sword this morning. But as for the rest, old duellists all, their faces are quite impenetrable. None of them are in what we call fighting condition; the Saxon makes it a point of etiquette to live loosely for some weeks before and after his duel; and if he be a trifle beery even at the hour of engagement, it is set down to his credit. Blood is the thing wanted, and scars that will not fade away; and he is most properly in condition whose veins are most plethoric, and whose flesh is least apt to heal.

Well, the hour has struck. The landlord, a stout, short-winded personage, of demeanour at once servile and exciteable, trots in for the last time to see that all is as the gentlemen wish; and then the door is closed, and the company gathers in a wide ring about the battle-field. Those two pale boys, who are to open the proceedings, are arming with the assistance of their seconds; and most curious is the contrast between their bloodless and pathetically inoffensive faces, and the horrid arms, stiff with ancient gore, in which they stand pilloried. Besides the system of leather pads which we have already examined, they wear a kind of spectacles, or iron guards, for the eyes; and these lend an indescribably gaunt and demoniac quality to their expression.

Are the champions prepared? Let them enter the lists—a space between two chalk lines twelve feet apart. Within this space, they must confine their struggle. Here they stand, the sword arm supported by the seconds, lest the weight of the armour should needlessly fatigue it. The president now steps forward, inquires the names and designations of the combatants, and is informed thereof by the seconds— all in conventional phrases. The president then states the rules which must govern the contest; and finally the orders are given in a sharp peremptory tone:—

" Auf die Mensur!"

The warriors accordingly toe the scratch.

" Los!"

And the carpet-beating begins.

The position is a peculiar one, owing to the circumstance that the head is the only part attacked. The right arm, pads and all, is arched above and a little in front of the head: the *Schlaeger*, its point tending downwards, continues the arch of the arm. The arm is not moved at any time during the bout; the cuts being made by a rapid and elastic turn of the wrist, whereby the blade is swung over or under the adversary's guard. The parrying is all done with the padded right arm, which comes in contact with the flat of the attacking sword: and the safety of the duellists' heads depends entirely on the true position of this guard arm. An inch too low or too high, and lo! a bleeding cheek or forehead.

Meanwhile our young heroes are at work, flapping away manfully, but doing no execution. Each makes his cut alternately with the other, and the "recover" is instantaneous. After every few strokes the seconds interpose their swords, and take charge of their principals' right arms for a score of seconds' rest; the swords are straightened, and if their edges be turned, they are replaced with fresh ones from a great bundle of them lying in yonder chair. The heads of the combatants are, moreover, carefully searched for cuts; with a knowing gravity of manner which reminds us of certain transactions in the monkeys' cage at the zoological gardens. There is no find, however, and work is resumed with fresh vigour. "Flap-flap! flap-flap!"

But this duel is destined to be a failure. The spectators become first apprehensive, then depressed. The heads are examined with a plaintive anxiety. The fifteen minutes—beyond which no duel may extend—have elapsed. There is no blood. The unfortunate duellists drop their swords, kiss each other as the law commands, and are hurried away by their seconds to disarm. No scars for them.

But the next combat is truly a refreshing exhibition. Our young American is matched against a full-blooded Saxon. It is gratifying to have this palpable assurance that our barbarous countrymen are capable—after due transplantation and training—of rivalling the culture of the philosophic Germans. May his good genius procure him a scar so deep that the next fifty years—should he live so long—shall fail to obliterate it.

The combat begins with the same formalities as before: but ere the "flap-flap!" has lasted five minutes, a lock of wiry brown hair is seen to jump suddenly from the American's head, and immediately a stream of scarlet blood rushes out of doors, painting one side of his face and dripping on his gorget. He looks surprised and rather relieved. So, this is being cut, is it? Well, it doesn't hurt so much, after all; no more than to hack one's self shaving. He is seated in a chair and sponged off, though the blood continues to flow rapidly, giving him a very grim aspect. Will he continue? Oh, certainly: just beginning to feel like it. So the two stand up to each other once more. The ring of spectators draws closer; they have tasted blood—we may know it by the dilation of their eyes, and their eager parted lips. Blood, brothers! stand ready, we shall have another draught immediately. Be it Saxon or American, what difference? Either is sweet to the taste of the philosopher. Oh, blood!

This time the aspect of probabilities is somewhat changed. The American's blood is not only out, but up, whereas the Saxon appears somewhat out of sorts; being, perhaps, sickened at the gory locks and red-dripping cheek of his adversary. He indulges, it may be, in a flitting imagination of himself in like condition. In that moment his guard wavers a trifle from its right position; over comes the sharp blade, catches him beneath the nostril, and slices open his cheek to the temple. The seconds strike up the swords. How the man bleeds! already there is a pool on the floor. The surgeon sponges and examines, and announces a cut four and a-half inches in length. Happy Saxon! Just at present, however, the abundance of his good fortune a little overcomes him. He sinks back in his chair with a dingy pallor in his face, sharply contrasting with the dark blood which issues from it. He will not be able to continue the duel: he cannot even rise to salute his opponent, who must therefore kiss him where he sits. Did ever two more unlovely countenances exchange such a token of affection? It is an odd sight, and we cannot help wishing they had restrained their ardours until somebody had washed their faces.

There are six duels still to come off; and, though one is pretty much like another, we undoubtedly would like to stand by and see all the twelve heads carved to ribbons. But just as the next pair are got to work, and our eyes are following each blow with silent expectation, there is heard a scurrying and a scrambling up the stairs outside. The door bursts open, and in flies the landlord, his eyes far out of their sockets.

"Polizei-mein'-Herren! Polizei-mein-Gott-in-Himmel! Ach! Polizei-ist-da!"

The police! In an instant, the ring has vanished; there is turning this way and that, voices and counter-voices. Off run the wounded, their tell-tale wounds but half sewed up, and have vanished through a back entrance. A loud crash of glass causes many a bold heart to throb—pshaw! it is only that bundle of *Schlaeger*, which some thoughtful person has sent flying through the window. Now a hasty tub of sawdust veils the guilty floor. Tables start up as if by magic, with glasses of beer upon them, and peaceful students quaffing the same. This is not a tournament, but a quiet picnic in country solitudes: here is no blood, save such as flows in decorous pulsations through its proper channels. Enter, O police! we receive you with the frankness of innocence.

Well—but the police do not enter. How long is this suspense to last? can our worthy landlord have been mistaken? or was he speculating for the price of a few score glasses of beer? At all events, it was a false alarm; no rude preservers of the peace are here to offer us violence, and the games may proceed.

But, for our own private parts, either the fright, or the reaction, or some more hidden cause, has dulled our appetite for further feasting in this kind. We have seen blood; and were we to remain to the very end, they could not shew us anything more interesting. Let us, therefore, depart, and strive to introduce *Schlaeger* fighting into the colleges of our own land, in place of boating, base-ball, cricket, and such like unmeaning diversions.

There are other amusements in Dresden; but after this, to treat of them would be an anticlimax. We must leave the skating-pond, and the boating, and the horse-races, and the minor theatres—yes, and the American and English clubs, which, however, are quite as much of a business as of an amusement—we must leave these to future historians or to silence. As to chronicling the movements of the fashionable foreign and native society, the magnitude of the theme daunts us. But blood will tell, and must be told about; and let us hope the moral of the tale will not be disregarded.

s

VI.

TYPES CIVIL AND UNCIVIL.

I.

THAT the German army is the finest in the world; and of that army, that the Saxon division is the most commendable, is a fact very generally admitted. The world is ancient; there have been many ages and races of men; but of all, the Saxon soldier is the flower. It were rash to affirm that the future may not produce a warrior better yet than he; the automatic theory holds out high hopes of possible progress in this direction. When we shall have disembarrassed ourselves of the notion that we live as we please, a rigid system of discipline will become our dearest comfort; for it will tend most strongly to put us out of the way of fancying our actions self-willed. The new gospel shall be the manual of drill and tactics. What a humiliation to man's conceit—the thought that soldiers are nearer the eternal verities than any other bodies! Let the fools of sentiment hasten to range themselves on the winning side. But, whatever our haste, the Saxons are still ahead of us. Though they may not, as yet, have put in words the truth of automatism, they have nevertheless done more to verify it in nature and conduct than have the philosophers who set the theory going.

It must not be forgotten, however, that their pre-eminence is owing quite as much to the age they live in as to their intrinsic quality. In short, we are called on to admire an exquisite harmony of times and traits. These sons of the drill-book would scarcely have suited the days when personal prowess was an essential soldierly requirement. Their best recommendation to the modern, and still more to the future, recruiting-sergeant, must be their unlikeness to the old Greek and Roman giants of sword and spear. Not hot blood and youthful fervour is wanted; rather a thin, colourless, meek, mechanical habit. What has been called soul and individuality is to be got rid of: an unbounded stomach for discipline is the desideratum. We may look forward to the time when the best soldier will be the least man—I speak to consenting ears, and need not, therefore, pause to explain the paradox—and already Napoleons and Hannibals are at a discount, and the cry is for Moltkes. As for

Prince Bismarck, he is still too much himself to be put in charge of the army.

It was observed the other day, in regard to the boat-race, that such was the minuteness and accuracy wherewith the result was foretold, there was really little use in rowing it; it was won and lost long before it started; and will, a while hereafter, be calculated before an intellectual audience on the blackboard, instead of being uncomfortably proved a foregone conclusion on the river. Thitherward, likewise, tends war. When the soldiers have become unmitigated puppets, and so afford as secure a base for calculation as other mechanical material; when the officers have grown to be incarnations of subtle scientific foresight, fed on statistics; shall we not be beyond the folly of shedding blood and burning towns otherwise than on paper? It may take a little more time to write a campaign than to fight it; but after one side has mathematically proved the superiority of its potentialities, the other will find it all the easier to pay its indemnity. In fine, the incubus from which it is our destiny to emancipate ourselves is action—vulgar, physical action. Brahma shall be the one true God, and Saxony his chosen Israel. Far off his coming shines—very far, perhaps; but prognostics favour him.

Meanwhile, I take pleasure in repeating that Saxon soldiers are the best in the world. They can swallow most discipline. They submit to so much stuffing with rules and regulations, great and small, that little of the original creature is left save organic life and uniform. They are a docile sort of Frankensteins. This is well, so long as they remain in the service; but picture the sad plight of a being thus drained of its proper entrails, and inspired solely by the breath of Mars, when Mars no longer needs him! Mars re-creates men showily enough; but he lacks the constancy of an original maker, and by-and-by leaves his re-creatures dismally in the lurch. Even the uniform is bereft them. Let who becomes a soldier reflect that he enlists for life; and whether he be killed in his first battle, or honourably discharged after half-a-dozen campaigns, his life still ceases with his soldiership.

It would be edifying to contrast Saxon soldiers with other nations', point by point, and so arrive at a practical comprehension of their superiority. Much is signified in the fact that their captains address them as "children," while we Americans and our English friends, try to inspire our warriors by appeals to their "manhood." Men, forsooth! Such is the fruit of illogical sentiment. But persist in calling a person child, and treating him so, and presently he will share our view of the matter, and thus become fit for the camp. But my business is not so much with comparisons as with the incomparable Saxon soldier himself.

II.

Even his uniform is admirable, and, after the shoppy productions worn by our Seventh Regiments, and still more by English Guards and Grenadiers, truly refreshing. It is mainly dark, the darkness enhanced by narrow lines of red adown the leg and round the throat and wrist. His headgear, though called helmet for lack of a better name, is not imposing, but eminently practical; while as to his cap, it is positively made and worn to cover the head, and scarcely inclines more to one ear than to the other. What a pregnant subject for analysis, by the way, is that matter of wearing the hat aslant instead of upright! Some seer, one of these days, will draw a deep moral from it.—The head itself is not propped fiercely up in unrelenting collar, but sits as easily as the heads of ordinary men. We look in vain for the stiff-kneedness, out-chestedness, square-elbowedness, high-mightiness, which we are accustomed to associate with the thoughts of things military. This model child of battle seems so comfortable in his uniform, he might have been born in it. He can stoop, kneel down, run, or vault a fence, without bursting a button. His belt is leathern—no pipeclay on his conscience. He can be very dirty without much showing it. Padding and lacing are unknown—

at least to the private. His short sword seems as natural an appanage as a monkey's tail; he would look maimed without it. He walks the streets—with measured tread, indeed, for he is drilled to the marrow, but—with an infantile self-unconsciousness subversive of all precedent. He looks of a race distinct from the civilian, it is true, but quite at home in his distinction.

Soberness of uniform is so far from being a trifling matter (things being as they are) that, should the English be beaten in the next war, they may safely lay the blame on their own red coats. In the time of Marlborough or of Wellington these may have had their use; but nowadays, scarlet, added to the vicious my-soul's-my-own doctrine which even yet obtains but too widely, gives the private soldier too much of an opinion of himself. He esteems himself too grand a being to be cuffed by corporals, and unceremoniously bidden to right-about-face and present arms. Moreover, his ruddy splendours attract the feminine eye and heart, and women are not wholesome for modern warriors. Such individual inspiration as they may once have given is not needed in battles fought out in sight of the enemy. That army will be found most efficient whose uniform is least seductive to the female mind. I am far from asserting that the Saxon uniform is perfect in this respect. No; it has a dapper appearance, a snug neatness, a sparkle of helmet-spike and sword-hilt greatly to be deplored. Still there is none homelier, so far as I am aware; and we may cheerfully trust to the natural instincts of the Saxon mind to make it uglier yet.

To be rid of woman, however, we must take thought not of the uniform only; there is the traditional heroism of the soldier to be done away with. Women persist in loving those who make a business of getting killed, more fondly than those who get killed in the way of business. Such preference is not only irrational—it was always that—it is now foundationless. When will our wives and daughters learn to believe that he who, with unfaltering resolution, takes the train to the city every morning, or calmly spends the day in his confined study, and trembles not at the dinner-bell, is more valiant than the man who leads a healthy life in camps, and goes to battle with a telescopic rifle once in twenty years? But no, to her mind the soldier is engaged in daily hand-to-hand encounters; his life is ever next door to a violent end; there is something heroic and perilous to himself in his own sword and gun. I am compelled to admit that even Saxon soldiers have their sweethearts, who lavish upon the lucky dogs such looks as the poor Kellner or shop-tender can never hope to obtain; and the necessity of being in barracks by a certain hour adds a romance to the daily parting which makes it worth a dozen optional ones.

The infantry are all uniformed more or less alike, but the cavalry are more gaudily attired in light blue and white, and the lancers are the dandies of the army—greatly bedizened in front, with knowing little helmets cocked on one side. This is perhaps not wholly inadvisable; lances and sabres suggest close fighting or nothing, and a man on horseback is not liable to so much bullying from the drill-master as is his comrade on foot. The horse helps him, makes him more respectable and respected, and the cavalry is in higher consideration than the infantry, though the artillery, I believe, ranks higher than either. A little self-esteem is not amiss with a man who may be called on to use muscles and courage of his own in attack and defence; and it will take a long time to make ideal soldiers out of horsemen. It may be observed, meanwhile, that the Saxon cavalry, though superbly mounted, are inferior in horsemanship and individual efficiency to either Sheridan's troopers or the English Horse Guards, which can be taken as a sign that the knightly element in the coming army will gradually be refined away, unless we succeed in starting a breed of scientific horses, on the principle of hobbies.

But the real efficient Saxon uniform is the uniformity of the men themselves. Of a regiment, one man can scarcely be told from another; it is one man a thousandfold multiplied. Height, breadth, features, wonderfully correspond. There are few men either so well or so badly made as many in our own and English regiments; but such as they are, they are alike. They have none of the ruddy freshness of aspect which one sees in the best English soldiers, and little of the compact briskness of their French friends; they are coarse-skinned, pallid, big-boned, inelegant, almost undersized; but—as I have been assured, and never either doubted or denied—they have shewn themselves equal to all demands made upon them in the late wars; and I will add of my own motion, that, were a given number of Saxon troops to encounter an equal body of picked French, English, or Americans, the former would dispose of the latter with a facility which would leave nothing to be desired—or everything. They are the best soldiers in the world, this year; and unless the farm-women break down sooner than is expected, they may be so in years to come.

III.

When I say that I have observed these war-children a good deal, I am only intimating that I kept my eyes open. Every third man, every other woman, is a soldier! Fortunately they are not the least agreeable part of the population to look at. Once used to them, their uniformity soon makes them our old friends; they pleasantly fill all gaps and pauses; we do not exactly see them after a while, but we should greatly miss them, were they absent. They never call for a new thought, the same old thought does for all. There is no extravagance in their look or behaviour. They seem quite serene and undemonstrative, and yet there is a fantastic skeleton underlying this outward calm.

This may be seen any morning by repairing to the barracks and watching the drill. It looks absurd enough, but it is tremendous, and it works wonders. Not a drop of the man's blood, not an ounce of his flesh, not a breath of his body, but feels the impress of the manual. What a stretch of the leg was that! and now what sharp angles, short corners, starts, jerks, dead pauses, sudden veerings, dashes, halts, thumpings, clankings! The man is beside himself, and that grotesque caperer is some puppet whose strings the sergeant is pulling. This periodical fit or seizure—they may call it drill, but in fact it is possession of seven devils, recurring at a certain hour every morning, lasting a fixed while, and then the devils depart, and presently the victim appears, rehabilitated: but we know his secret now, and all his quietness fails to impose on us: we discern his mad-pranks ill concealed beneath the most innocent actions. The mark is on him; the Seven will rend him again to-morrow. Skeletons are seldom attractive spectacles; but this skeleton of Drill, once seen, is not lightly forgotten. The discovery of so grisly a substructure to the pomp and circumstance of war is impressive in its way. It is kept discreetly secluded within the barrack walls, only venturing thence in the guise of commonplace marching and rifle exercise. To the barracks, too, are confined the more flagrant tyrannies of the drill-master, whose cuffs, shoves, and beratings make the on-looker's blood to boil, and him to marvel at the silent, unretaliating meekness of the berated one. It is odd to see that one of mankind whose avowed business in life is retaliation, thus outdoing the forbearance of the mildest country clergyman. But a soldier's spirit is bound strictly to the rules of the manual: when not required in the way of business, it must remain prostrate in the mire. Soldiers are generally credited with elasticity of spirits, and from this point of view it is no wonder. But in many cases, I fancy, the spirits are broken betimes, and what afterwards passes as such is merely a kind of galvanization produced by fear. Doubtless galvanism is better than courage, being mechanical, and a safer factor in calculations.

Besides their elemental training, the men are taken

off on daily morning tramps of eight or twelve miles, often in heavy marching order. They issue forth from the barrack gates with an outstreaming rhythmic undulation, curve steadily aside, and proceed with rustling tramp along the centre of the street, seeming to move more slowly than they do. Their bayoneted rifles gleam aslant in serried evenness, each helmet glistens alike, the brass spikes swaying aligned. Every hand and red-bound coat-cuff swings parallel, every knee crooks with one impulse, every empty scabbard wavers in similar arcs. There is an onward impetus, not swift, but so strong that it seems as if houses and stone walls must move aside to let them pass—the impetus of hundreds of men moving as one. The complete unison of physical and spiritual movement, in vast numbers of human beings, is awful to contemplate; or, if we let ourselves be swept with it, it hurries off our heads as a hurricane would our hats. But the unison is everything, and it is this which makes the march of Saxon soldiers more impressive than that of troops less perfectly drilled. Their gait is as good as it can be—a long, elastic, measured shamble, as easy at the end of twenty miles as at the beginning; and the accuracy with which they keep to straight lines, whether in march or drill, is as satisfactory as a theorem in Euclid.

The division, which thus issues from the barracks several hundred strong, soon begins to separate into detachments that switch off on different roads, and in their turn split up, till the whole is parted into squads of ten or a dozen men each. Having got beyond the outskirts of the town and the chance of stray officers the severity of the discipline is somewhat relaxed, the men are allowed to carry their rifles and to march as they please, and to chat with one another as they go. Of all these privileges they gladly avail themselves and try to be disorderly; but the attempt only shows how intimately their training has entered into them. What is ease to other men has ceased to be so to them. The rigour of the march tires them less than irregularity. Behind their most careless laxity one sees the iron method and precision which makes the squad like a machine, out of gear for the time, but evidently needing only the turn of a crank to fall in order once more. On they tramp, dusty, muddy, heated, tired perhaps, but the pace never slackens; and when, two or three hours later, they pass again beneath the barrack gates, rifles and helmets, line and step, are as even and accurate as before.

After labour, play. At mid-day the crowd which has been collecting for the last half-hour in front of the Neustadt barracks beholds come forth a goodly detachment, clad in its newest uniform, and headed by a military band in full triumphant blast. Band, detachment, and crowd set out in gleeful array towards the bridge, every foot within range of the music keeping time to it. A halt is made opposite the old black guard-house, and here some of the music remains, disposes itself in a ring, and discourses away heartily for half an hour, the echoes coming finely back from the tall ungainly buildings that shut in the square. Now the market-women are enviable, sitting comfortably at their stalls: and our old friend Werthmann, if it be summer, plants tables and chairs under the oleanders outside his hospitable doors, and finds plenty of customers. Every neighbouring window has its head or two, passers-by loiter or stop, the soldiers in the guard-house are gradually drawn forth to lounge and listen in the great dark portico, the perpendicular sun pours a jolly warmth over everything, and only Augustus, mounted aloft on his brazen steed, and carrying on his immemorial flirtation with the weatherworn water-nymph on the corner of Haupt Strasse, seems wholly indifferent to the melody ringing in his brazen ears.

Meanwhile another and larger assemblage is enjoying a similar concert in a corner of the Schloss-Platz on the other side of the river. The bands are the same which play in the afternoons at the Grosse Wirthschaft or other beer-gardens, and the music, excellent in itself, is enhanced by its quasi-incidental conditions. There is a rich spontaneity of flavour about it which is apt to escape the malice-prepense performances.

IV.

Of the barrack-life of the soldier not much is visible to the outsider. Passing along the sidewalk, we may glance in at the lower windows and exchange a stare with the inmates, but we gain little wisdom thereby. Often there are pots of flowers on the sill, and sometimes the *carte-de-visite* of a relative or sweetheart pinned to the wall. But the warriors themselves do not appear to advantage in undress. Neatness and sweetness in a Saxon private's barrack-room (or any other private's for that matter) are hardly to be expected. They wear their dirty canvas jackets, and lie about half asleep or drowsily gossiping together. There seems nothing but the lazy body of them left. It takes a sergeant or a sweetheart to enliven them.

When they obtain leave of absence after four o'clock, and come out in brave attire to drink a glass of beer, and take Gretchen's rough, affectionate paw in theirs, they are perhaps at their best. Some of the Freiwilligers, who belong to the better order of people, attend lectures at the Government schools and colleges during the intervals of their military duties; but the multitude are of the reasonable opinion that a day's drill is work enough, and that a taste of love and malt liquor is only fair compensation. Accordingly they form a good part of the guests at every saloon and concert-room, and at some of the dance-halls they have a monopoly. They are almost always the quietest and most decorous persons present; drunkenness is not for them, nor loud talking, nor insolence; they are a kind of children that do credit to their bringing up, and forget not the voice of the instructor even when out of his presence. But can these mild, smug fellows be successors of the shaggy, brutal, fierce, gigantic Suevi who roamed the Hyrcanian forests scarce two thousand years ago? and is it not funny that a chemical discovery or two and a smattering of mechanics should render these small inoffensive-looking moderns a hundred times as formidable in battle as those savage ancients?

One of the most touching sights in connection with military matters which I have happened to notice is that of the newly enlisted men roaming the streets during the day or two of grace allowed them before donning the uniform and beginning the long, weary servitude of powder and ball. They are permitted a license of behaviour quite extraordinary either to soldier or citizen; they are on the neutral ground between, and may have their fling, for once. Police-

T

men are blind to their escapades; officers ignore them; people in general smile good-naturedly, and pick them up when they fall down. For it almost invariably happens that the first thing these unborn war-babes do is to get drunk: it is the traditional way of passing the solemn period of incubation, and appears to commend itself anew to each successive brood. They wear green ribbons in their button-holes, and stagger along arm in arm, crooning discordant lays, laughing or crying, and committing much harmless, foolish, and piteous uproar. Many of them bring smooth, inexperienced faces from unknown country villages; others are already coarse and stolid; a few bear traces of culture, but Gambrinus lays all alike in the gutter. Occasionally, indeed, from the midst of this beery bedlam, a sane and sober pair of eyes meets our own, making us marvel how they came there. Perhaps the drunkards are the wiser; the prospect is too sorry a one for sober contemplation; it requires all the enchantment that malt and hops can cast over it to make it tolerable. But what a rueful scene must to-morrow morning's drill be, with its *Katzenjammer*, its helpless ignorance, and its savage sergeant!

V.

Sentries represent, to my mind, the most interesting phase of army life. Something of poetic sentiment still attaches to them. A solitary figure, with gleaming weapon and watchful eye, moving to and fro with measured tread on the beleaguered ramparts, or along the snow-bound limits of the night encampment,— such is the sentry of the imagination. His suggestiveness is fascinating, and renders him impressive. How much is confided to him, and what power is his! He is the waking eye and thought and strength of the army, which slumbers defenceless but for him. A signal from him, and a thousand men spring to arms; or, if he choose to play the traitor, they are massacred without remedy. So great a responsibility so faithfully borne seems a remnant of the heroic age; and to see commonplace men of to-day, with small intelligence and infirm principles, so trusted and vindicated, is beyond all question encouraging. And in all ages of the world, sentries have maintained their good repute; the veriest scamp rises above himself when left alone on his beat, with the enemy at hand; so much depends upon his honour, that the sentiment he had fancied extinct is recreated in his breast. Generous thoughts renew a long-interrupted acquaintance with him, and when the relief-guard comes round, they perhaps find another and better man than was placed here three hours ago.

But we are venturing rash lengths, hardly borne out by our Dresden sentries in time of peace. With these our main quarrel is that they are too numerous —the poetic loneliness is wanting. Where one would suffice are two, and one where none is necessary. Moreover, they are used for mere display, and are set to watch over nothing more precious than their own sentry-boxes; it is hard to be enthusiastic about such a peril, such a responsibility as that. Again, the crowded streets belittle them; and finally, they are mere lay figures; if we brush past them, they do not challenge us, and if we ask them a question, they cannot answer it. To put so noble an instrument to such paltry uses is like cutting bread and cheese with Excalibur.

The chief business of city sentries—the only thing that gives a fillip to the lethargy of their plight—is saluting. This affords them a constant supply of mild excitement, varying in degree according as their man is a second lieutenant or the King. They are always on the look-out, like hunters for their game; and that were a soft-footed officer indeed who should catch one of them napping.

The whole idea of saluting is graceful; it is pleasant to see men paying one another mutual deference, even when it is based on so trifling a matter as the fashion of an epaulette, and the cut of a coat. It seems to declare a human sympathy and brotherhood outgrowing the bounds of mere private acquaintance. It is a pity that all men should not adopt so good a custom; we all wear the uniform of flesh and blood, and our common nature is perhaps respectable enough for us to touch our hats to it. Only, the respect we pay, to preserve its integrity, must be impersonal; I am Quaker enough to think that there exists no man who, in his private capacity, is entitled to the cap or knee of anybody. Into these subtleties, however, the simple soldier entereth not; it is enough for him that he sees his officer and knows his duty. The officer must salute in return, and since he is greatly in the minority, he is sometimes kept at it pretty steadily. When, for instance, hundreds of soldiers are streaming across the bridge to their evening diversion, whatever pair of epaulettes is unlucky enough to be going the other way has to run the gauntlet of them all. The men glue their hands to their caps, straighten their shoulders, and will not be denied. No doubt they enjoy forcing his acknowlegdment—the confession, as it were, that despite his grave dignity he is but their fellow soldier, after all. Sometimes the soldier has both hands occupied, and then he only bends a respectful glance, while the officer must still touch his cap, with however arrogant a dab. The messenger, with his despatches in his breast and his rifle on his shoulder, is likewise privileged to a certain extent; his mission elevates him for the moment above ordinary regulations. But it is odd that so fraternal and catholic a practice should obtain only, and of all places, in the army; it is like the honey in the carcase of Samson's lion.

To return to our sentry, who has just discerned his quarry approaching up the street. In consideration of the spasmodic rigidity which always fastens upon sentinels when under the eye of their superiors in rank, the latter, one might suppose, must get queer notions of them: what is this fixed, convulsed object, gorgonized at my glance in so ungainly an attitude? Does it live? has it intelligence? As for the King, he probably thinks of his soldiers as of so many wooden toys, quaintly postured; and only by a determined effort realizes that they may have moved in a natural manner before he laid eyes on them, and will be likely to do so again hereafter. But kings are unfortunate in never being able to steal a march upon nature: in the attempt to express her sense of their divine rights, she becomes unnatural; and the more ineffable their majesty, the more fantastic her grimace.

Meanwhile, hither comes the officer, self-contained, leisurely, dignified: his gloved hand on his sword-hilt, his iron cross on his breast. If he be a colonel, the sentry begins to be spasmodic while the great man is yet half a block distant, and "presents arms" at a time when, unless the colonel's arm were sixty or seventy feet in length, he could not possibly avail himself of the offer. A lieutenant, on the other hand, succeeds in stiffening his man only within a range of six paces, and even then the rifle is but "ordered." But in any case, the inferior is anxious, tense, electrified; the superior serene, indifferent, haughty; he affects to be unsuspicious of the brewing of the salute, and acknowledges it at the last moment by a lazy uplifting of the forefinger. Gesture nor expression could better express aristocracy's contemptuous recognition of the plebeian's existence. But should the plebeian fail to discharge his whole debt of reverence, the aristocrat wakes up. I saw an overgrown captain whose rank the sentry had mistaken, keep the fellow at the "present" fifteen minutes; till the sweat ran down the poor devil's scared face, and the heavy rifle trembled in his tired grasp as though it shared his apprehensions. These are not insignificant details; they are the lifeblood of the army.

When the King or any member of the royal household comes by, the sentry is full of hysteric bustle and excitement. He runs to the bell-pull, jerks it, and back to his place, now craning his head forwards to see how near Majesty is, now twisting it back over his shoulder to see whether the guard has turned out and the drummer is ready. Now passes the outrider, high jouncing on his hard-trotting, blindered horse; now follows the smooth-rolling carriage, Majesty within; the drum beats, the guard is transfixed, the sentry a motionless bundle of right angles. A few breathless moments, and all is over: the guard relaxes and stacks arms, the sentry comes to life and shoulders his rifle; the drummer puts up his drumsticks and disappears. Majesty has been saluted by man, and we may breathe again.

VI.

We continually encounter squads of men uniformed from head to foot in dirty canvas, marching hastily along the streets in military order, and in charge of a corporal. But though evidently connected with the army, they are always weaponless, and they pass their brethren of whatever rank unsaluted and unsaluting. Sometimes they carry spades, hatchets, brooms, or other agricultural and menial implements; and if we follow them up we shall find them sweeping the streets, digging gardens, chopping firewood, or otherwise making themselves sullenly useful: while the corporal looks on with folded arms; and, perhaps, when the weather is cold, wishes that military etiquette allowed him to bear a hand. These men are generally of a gloomy and dejected aspect, never laugh or sing over their labour, and converse, if at all, in a growling undertone. When their work is done, they are not allowed to go and play, but must shoulder their implements and march to barracks. They never have leave of absence, and must never stray beyond the corporal's reach. Their week seems to be full of Fridays.

These melancholy drudges are the *Bestrafene*—soldiers who have outraged discipline in one way or another, and have therefore incurred the penalty of deprivation of all soldierly privileges, and subjection to all refuse employments. All the more irksome burdens are put on their shoulders, and they get no thanks for bearing them. Nothing could be less exhilarating than their position: they are hopeless of bettering themselves, though any indiscretion will surely sink them yet deeper. They are prisoners bereft of the prisoner's right to fetters and stone walls; for certainly it were better to be dungeoned outright, and, by dint of never beholding human freedom and natural beauty, grow to forget that such things exist, than thus daily to be flouted by the sight and contact of blessings which they may not share. The lot of the common soldier is not, under any circumstances, the kindest in the world; and the sting of his punishments is the fact that they are inflicted for offences intrinsically so trivial. The army is so portentously abnormal an institution, that its code of right and wrong must needs be exaggerated to match, and the strangest consequences ensue. Soldiers—and especially, it seems to me, Saxon soldiers—are constantly subjected to burning provocations, none the easier to bear because they are part of inevitable discipline. Nevertheless, any symptom of restiveness is treated as a flagrant crime—and properly so, if armies are to exist. But what intolerable wrongs may not be thus facilitated! Even Saxon soldiers, it appears, can lose their complaisance at last; and if an officer has a grudge against a private, it is evident that the private is doomed; either his life is made a bane to him by constant insult and oppression, or his forbearance yields for a moment, and he incurs perhaps twenty years' *Bestrafung*. There are thousands of *Bestrafene* in Dresden; and since they have all rebelled with a full knowledge of the consequences, we may partly estimate the severity of Saxon discipline.

Their terms of punishment vary from a few months to life, according to the offence. One cannot help being surprised that the crime for which they do penance is not always murder. And indeed, if the question is of moral accountability, were it not less sin to have slain a tyrant in one fiery instant, than impotently to curse him in cold blood every day for twenty years?

It must often happen, moreover, that the *Bestrafene* who are thus laid on the shelf so far as any manly use is concerned, had it in them to be the very flower of the army. It was the pith and force of the man that got him into trouble. Had he been a little more white-livered, he would have escaped. But he was convicted of a flickering of manly spirit, a spark of independence, a heat of temper; and for these unwarrior-like qualities he is extinguished. Is there no help for it? no allowance to be made for provocations and possibilities? By no means: discipline must be true to itself, or die. There is no flaw in the logic of the army. If mankind to-day really loved fighting as much as they seem to have done of yore, they would not stop to do it scientifically; the main expense of a campaign would be for grave-diggers; while peace could afford to be something more honest than a gatherer-together of expensive brickbats against the next contest. To shoot at a man is not to fight him; but get at him with your fists, or with a club, or dirk at most, and immediately you have satisfaction; you feel that you have measured yourself against that man; if you kill him, it is with the serene assurance that your superior personal prowess was the sole cause of victory; if he kill you, you are spared the annoyance of succumbing to some sleight-of-hand trick or mechanical hocus-pocus. Rifles, cannon, and military manœuvres are among the Will-o'-the-wisps of the age. They seem to give us that which they rob us of.

Since they came in vogue there have been no battles— no defeats nor victories. Unless we can slay our enemy as Cain slew Abel, and perhaps eat him up afterwards, we would better let him alone. "Civilized warfare" is the very most dangerous device of the devil, worth all his other investments put together

I scrutinized the faces of these canvas-backed fellows with morbid interest. There is not a cheerful one among them: many have acquired a sinister expression; some are sullen-brutal, some sullen-obstinate, some sullen-fierce. Only a few have the passive stolidity of despair, for hope is more obstinate than most misery. Some wear a hang-dog look; others stare us defiantly in the face. All this is what might be expected, but I was not prepared to find so many well-built heads and able countenances. I do not mean to say that there are any Liebigs or Goethes among them; but only that their intellectual promise outdoes that of their unpariah-ed comrades—no difficult feat, heaven knows. Brains, of a certain kind, are desirable in the leaders of the army, but not in the army itself. The analogy with man is strict. He must not allow his arms and legs, his liver and stomach, to be intellectual; the head is the place for cerebration, and any other member that presumes to do anything in that line ought to be licked into shape without delay.

The unlucky wretches sometimes try to escape, but only succeed when they accept the faithful co-operation of death. All plans for freedom to which that venerable friend of man is not made privy are sure to fail. The whole country rises and greedily hunts them down; and—such is human frailty—the fugitives generally suffer themselves to be caught alive. Occasionally they adopt other methods. Not very long ago a squad of *Bestrafene* were at work on some job in the Grosser Garten, when Albert (at that time Crown Prince) came riding by, unattended, except by the groom some distance behind him. Suddenly one of the men left his work and rushed up to the royal soldier — the head of the army, to whom all power was given to pardon, promote, or condemn.

Here I pricked up my ears, thinking I was going to hear something worth hearing. What! had this man's misery risen to so tragic a height as to nerve him to lift a revengeful hand against the Prince? I have done injustice to the strength and colour of the Saxon nature!

"Before he could be stopped," continued my informant, "he had thrown himself on his knees in the bridal path, and had seized the royal stirrup. He besought the Prince to remit some years of his sentence. He had been condemned to five-and-twenty years—ten had already elapsed. By this time assistance arrived; the groom rode the impudent fellow down, and his comrades dragged him off."

"But the Prince was gracious, of course?"

"Most gracious! he kept his eyes all the time averted; had he once looked at the man, it would have been a life-imprisonment! but he affected to be not aware of him. Thereafter he called to him the corporal, and graciously commanded that the man's term should be not at all increased."

"I should think he might have pardoned him a year or two," I said.

"Pardon! God forbid! where then would be discipline—the army?"

The gentleman who told me this was not a military person, but a simple Saxon citizen, a doctor of philology, and an excellent man. On consideration, his view of the incident rather relieved than otherwise my injured sensibilities. If he, the most humane of Saxons, could thus utterly ignore the down-trodden petitioner's side of the question, might it not be justly inferred that the petitioner himself, being a Saxon as well as the doctor, and presumably of duller perceptions, was less affected by his misfortunes than I had rashly supposed? It has been recently established, I believe, that the beetle which we tread upon suffers very little corporal anguish after all. Why should not the analogy be applied to these *Bestrafene?* Our sympathy has been thrown away upon them; they do not half mind being put out of the sunshine of existence. Whoever attempts to apply to Saxons the moral, mental, or emotional standards of other peoples, may succeed in discovering himself, but not them.

VII.

The Saxon officers are a fine-looking body of men. They are taller, on the average, than the common soldiers, and possess symmetrical figures. Their uniforms are kept scrupulously neat, their bearing is not devoid of conventional grace, and, though not invariably remarkable for general culture, they are thoroughly competent to their duties in the field, and by no means ignorant of the arts of bowing, dancing, and uttering smiling compliments to pretty young foreigners, whose appreciation thereof is enhanced by the consideration that the complimenter, besides being an officer, is almost always either a Count or a Baron.

The army is, of course, the first profession in Saxony; all the young sprigs of nobility crowd to the cadet-schools, and are thence commissioned to the various branches of the service: there is little fun and less profit to be got by staying under the paternal roof-tree. The profession is no sinecure, however; these dapper captains and lieutenants must work like Irish labourers every day; from four in the morning till four in the afternoon they are sometimes kept in the field; while such pay as they get would hardly keep an American gentleman in cigars. In view of this fact, their immaculate coats and white kid gloves and snug boots are doubly admirable. Such genius for economy, combined with such capacity for labour, would seem to argue just the men with whom love in a cottage could be made at once pleasant and profitable; and yet these Spartans never happen to fall in love with the penniless young ladies. This may be in part due to the fact that army benedicts, high or low, must pay into the exchequer a fine equivalent, I believe, to a third or more of the capital whose interest is their pay. It generally needs a full-fledged heiress to make this possible; and hence the law is a sinister bar to the marriage—or a bar-sinister in the escutcheon—of the great majority of Saxon warriors.

Well—but they are amusing and good-natured, and really the life of American and English parties. They have a child-like theatricality of manner which is highly entertaining; and their courteous extravagances are charming to women used to the cold attentions of English and American men. The French do it better, perhaps, but we cannot always be in

Paris. It is something to have one's hand kissed without being obliged to consider it the first step towards a declaration. If only the Saxon officers would learn discretion at table, they would be the darlings of the foreign circle in Dresden; and I understand that they have considerably reformed in this respect. Still, the table is their weak point, and they might sin far more grievously in other directions without incurring half the reproach which this peccadillo brings upon them. I will not attempt to describe their manner of putting food into their mouths; it would lose colour in description; but in this connection a characteristic trait or two should not be omitted. They had a habit, when supper was announced at the entertainments given by their English or American friends, of stopping neither for host nor partner; but forming in an impenetrable phalanx round the table, whence they budged not either for man or woman until the time came when they could eat no more. They would then retire in good order to catch their breath, while the civilians of the party would seize the opportunity to help the ladies, and, it is to be hoped, to snatch a bite for themselves afterwards. It is true that the ordinary rations of a Saxon officer are neither rich nor varied, and that such repasts as these must have offered extraordinary allurements: nevertheless, with a little more tact, they might surely have contrived to satisfy the demands of both breeding and appetite, and thus have removed the sole stain from their social escutcheon.

VIII.

The Lodging-house keeper, the Droschkey-driver and the Dienstman, however slight their apparent resemblance to one another, do nevertheless come under one and the same category. They are all three consequences of that widespread social disease—the indisposition to do our own work. They exist to indulge the slipshod caprices of an enervated civilisation. They are a species of moral vermin, generated by the sloth of the age. The cleanest and nicest of us permit ourselves to be infested with them, and are fain to think them a convenience: but can that rightly be styled convenient, whose tendency is to stunt our faculties? To look closely into the matter —to realise how intimate is our dependence upon unsavoury and unsympathetic strangers—would be perilous to our self-respect: but by the mercy of Providence, we seldom do look closely, and at the worst refuse to believe a tithe of what our analysis declares is truth.

This is a mechanical era, and we are all aiming at a state wherein nothing shall interfere with continuous intellectual exaltation. Accordingly, instead of running on our own errands, we hail a Dienstman. The bargain between us is, that in consideration of from one to five groschen paid to him, he is to engraft upon himself a certain portion of our life—to enact our character, according to his conception of it. As a guarantee of good faith (for even in such transactions the cant of respectability is retained) he gives us a slip of paper, inscribed with a name and a number; and thereupon we go our several ways. We, who have voluntarily docked ourselves of part of our rightful existence and office in the world, depart with light step and jaunty air: and like the tailless fox in the fable, would argue ourselves in better case than before. We perceive no indelicacy—still less absurdity—in the contract. We reflect not that we have adulterated our God-given personality,—that instead of decently limiting ourselves, as nature meant we should, to the confines of our own skin and bones, we have divided in pieces, as some insects do, and are partly masquerading about the streets in the ignoble guise of the canaille, exposed to all coarse association and vicious interpretation. We have admitted this rude, infragrant fellow, with his soiled blouse and heavy boots, to a share in our conduct of life, and in so far we have given him influence over our destiny and reputation. Do we expect him, for the sake of sixpence, to appreciate the delicacy of our mutual relation, or try to do justice to it? A private body-servant, used to our humours and bound to us by every tie of interest and gratitude, is still a questionable commodity enough: but the Dienstman—the public footman and scullion—who is at the beck of a hundred masters in the course of each day—there cannot be much question about him!

Men who serve ignoble ends are seldom among the chosen of the race, to begin with, and at all events, the nature of the employment must have an evil influence upon them. The Dresdeners complain that the Dienstmen are fallen from their original goodness, having been corrupted by the American practice of overpayment and bribery. But loth as I am to see a flaw in aught Saxon, I fear these fellow-mortals were always an ill-conditioned lot—stupid, clumsy, untrustworthy, and prone to insolence. They come from the lowest ranks of the community, and in spite of their "receipts" are practically irresponsible, so far as foreigners are concerned. In short, they are an unceasing protest against the depraved social conditions which brought them forth; and the best I can wish them is, that they should ultimately protest themselves out of existence. Meanwhile, objectively considered, they form an entertaining and instructive feature of the population. They are very numerous, standing in knots of three to a dozen at the street corners and in the squares and market-places, bloused and belted in summer, and in winter mounting a coffee-coloured top-coat; always provided with a coil of rope, and cognisant of a small hand-cart not far off. They constantly smoke a pale brown brand of cigars, which can be obtained in the shops at the rate of about one shilling the hundred. They will undertake any job, from delivering a billet-doux or packing porcelain, to sawing wood or moving house-furniture. But it is somewhat odd that although essentially a labouring guild, they should yet contrive to produce the impression of being among the most indolent people in the city. They wait for the job with an air as if the job itself were waiting : but no sooner do they fall to work, than they appear abnormal and out of place, and we long to see them with their hands in their pockets once more. The reason must be that though their leisure is their own, their labour is always borrowed from some one else, and thus sits more or less awkwardly upon them. They have no personal interest in their work, nor can it be either regular or homogeneous. For them, therefore, work must evidently be demoralizing: and the only alternative being idleness, it follows that the honorablest deed for Dienstmen is to do nothing,—a conclusion to which no one will assent more readily than their sometime employer.

IX.

As for the Droschkey-drivers, they appear to be broken down Dienstmen, who prolong life solely to nourish their implacable resentment against mankind. They are an elderly set, of furrowed and malignant visage, and a complexion which weather-beating outside and hard-drinking inside has wrought up to an extraordinary pitch of inflammation. They wear cobalt-coats and caps, trimmed with vermilion, and their vehicle is upholstered to match. In cold or rainy weather they wrap themselves in an anomalous, voluminous, dingy garment—caped, skirted, wadded and belted, and put on a broad brimmed, platter-shaped hat of coarse black felt. They sit on their box-like excrescences—a new species of centaur; looking as if nothing short of a surgical operation could detach them from it. Dull-eyed, round-shouldered, with chin on breast; evil-tempered, foul-mouthed, thievish—these men are among the curiosities of human nature. I was fascinated by them, and begot for them at length a horrible sort of affection. There was a fearful joy in putting one of them through his paces—in leading him on to demand (as was demanded once of me) nine times his lawful fare; and then witnessing the grisly fever of his wrath at being forced back to the confines of sober truth and justice. A tremendous experience, indeed; but such as no man of ordinary nerve would care to sustain more than once or twice a year at the utmost. Here, at last, we have the Saxon character in its most unredeemed phase; and I repeat, there is a hideous charm about it.

Why are cabbies all over the world (Parisian, cabbies are perhaps an exception) so cross-grained, misanthropic and cynical? Is it because they are always sitting down, and thus never get a chance to work off their ill humours? There is certainly potent virtue in a man's leg; and were he anchored to a single spot, like a vegetable, it is odds but he would be a poisonous one. Cabbies, moreover, live in an atmosphere of petty exasperation. The state of the weather, and of their horses; the perverseness and stinginess of their customers; envy of their rivals on the stand; anger against Providence and the world for having given them nothing better to do—these and numberless other flouts of fortune come in for their daily quota of grumbled curses. The degree of a cabby's interest in his fellow-beings varies as their probable need of his cab; and he searches their faces only for the signs of ignorance or weakness which may enable him to get the best of the bargain. He begins each day sullenly; ten minutes sooner, and he might have found an early worm; and ends it with anathema, because ten minutes longer might have found him a belated one. Go where he will, his surroundings never vary; his steed plods ever before him, his four wheels rumble behind, his whip stands at his right hand, his toes still stub against the self-same old dashboard. He naps on his box—but even in his dreams is cabby still; his nightmare is a just fare, his vision of bliss an exorbitant one. What has he to look forward to in life? and after death how does he expect to manage about his Droschkey, which seems to have become an organic and spiritual part of him? It is ill-adapted to ascending straight and narrow paths, but exhibits a pestilent readiness to run down hill; and although furnished with a brake, which the driver is morbidly careful to apply at each suspicion of a slope, yet some slopes are steeper than brakes are strong, and wheels will be wheels.

The horses, though they jog along at an easy rate, compare favourably with the London breed. The Droschkeys are all of one pattern,—closed cabs in winter, open in summer. To the back of the forward seat is affixed a large square card, showing the tariff of prices and distances, and the name of the driver—which is always a treble-barrelled name, and, oddly enough, the middle barrel is almost always either Gottlieb or Gottfried. Can it be that the burden of so great titles overpowers that which it is meant to sustain, and lands the would-be protégé of Providence, a friendless Droschkey-driver? When on stand, the Droschkeys are ranged side by side instead of end to end, as though Dresden were broader than it is long; and the one which has stood the longest has precedence over the rest in answering a call; so that you cannot make your own choice of a vehicle, but must respect the rule of succession.

For some reason or other, the clatter of wheels and hoofs in Dresden is more jarring and disconcerting than in any other city I am acquainted with. Allowing for the clumsy construction of the carriages and the cobbley pavements, I believe the explanation to be that there is never enough traffic in the streets to create a continuous and coherent roar; you hear each individual rattle, and the volume of sound is only sufficient to rack your ears without dulling them. The effect on the senses is somewhat similar to that produced by a review of the driver's characteristics on the mind—they are harsh and ugly enough to exasperate and revolt us, but fall short of that plenitude of evil which might relieve by paralysing our moral sensitiveness.

X.

Lodging-house keepers, like Jews and Gypsies, seem to have existed from time immemorial: like them, also, they are solicitous anent profit and loss, and have the outside of poverty, if not the thing itself. But from this point begins a difference. I never heard of lodging-house keepers intermarrying—the heart knoweth too well its own bitterness. There are seldom any handsome women among them, nor can the race be said to possess a distinctive type of physiognomy. As to their religion, whatever may be its ostensible character, I fancy there are passages in its creed which have never received the sanction of an Ecumenic Council.

The profession is very largely followed on the Continent. The people seem unable to fill their own rooms, or averse from doing so. They desire to coin money out of their homes,—to prostitute their board and hearthstone to the highest bidder. A person who will do this must have contrived to disembarrass himself, consciously or otherwise, of a good many prejudices. From a merely sentimental point of view, he might be credited with a degree of philosophical elevation not far removed from spiritual uncleanliness. But it may be doubted whether the majority of the present generation—especially the Saxon part of it—have bethought themselves what a home is; and it would therefore be unjust to tax them with polluting its sanctities. For some people, the only safe preservative against sin is an absence of moral responsibility; and Heaven may have seen fit to create lodging-house keepers without the home instinct, as the only practicable way of keeping them from violating it. However, we who let ourselves be accommodated by the system are in a glass-house, and must conduct ourselves accordingly. Were each traveller now-a-days to set up his own vine and fig-tree wherever he passed the night, travel would soon become unfashionable: the edge of personal and national individuality would remain unblunted, and the thousands of small people who now try to swallow the great world would respect the limits of their own horizon, and take the faults of foreigners for granted. But if, as seems probable, the current of life continues to set towards cosmopolitanism, the time will come when the lodging-house keeper will have it all his own way, and no houses except lodging-houses will exist. In that day we may look forward to a universal speaking of one another's language, wearing of one another's clothes, minding of one another's business, drinking (Saxons do it already) out of one another's beer-mugs, making love to one another's sweethearts, and so forth. The broad enlightenment of the species will dazzle into invisibility the petty distinctions of *meum* and *tuum*, us and our neighbours, and we shall be able to declare with our transcendental Philosopher, " The soul knows no persons."

In our present comparatively unilluminated condition, however, the advantages of lodging-houses still lack full recognition. Some reminiscences of the old-fashioned laws of hospitality embarrass us: we have heard or read of the romantic and delicate relations of guest and entertainer, and are perhaps conscious of a certain awkwardness in the attempt to reconcile these with the straightforward modern plan of adjusting mutual courtesies by an appeal to cash, having previously ensured their observance by signing a contract. Nothing can be more hospitable than the Dresden lodging-house keeper (to take an example) when we first encounter him—and indeed at all times, if we do but consent to adopt his views on whatever questions may arise between us. He is cordial, full of smiles, compliments, and graceful attentions, presses you to come in, to sit down, to remain, to make his dwelling your permanent abode. To throw cold water on such advances would be churlish; and yet—why does he love you at such short notice, and why wanders his eye over the contour of your pocket? Your desire to feel flattered is defeated by the suspicion that under guise of studying your welfare, he is on the scent of his own profit. In the teeth of his smiles you must be cold, critical and distrustful. He conducts you from room to room, pointing out luxuries at every step, with touching confidence in your appreciation: but, whether really pleased or not, principle requires you to grumble and find fault, and turn up your nose the higher, the faster he talks. All the while, those troublesome old reminiscences are hanging about, making you feel mean and humiliated. There comes an impulse (which you resist) to be gracious and chivalrous if it doubles your rent!—a fancy that, cost what it would, you would be the better for in the end. Cynicism and a critical spirit, indulged in their proper place, agreeably tickle the self-esteem, but carry no satisfaction here. Though you malign the world with Diogenes or Apemantius, it is not from their intellectual or philosophic standpoint, but only because you are dealing with a lodging-house keeper. You are shocked at what seems a parody and degradation of heretofore sacred rights, and distressed to find the evil influence reacting upon yourself, and weighing you down to its own level.

But this is all a mistake, due to confusing parody with progress. Hospitality is antiquated: it has lived too long, and no longer accords with the spirit of the age: let it die out of the world and out of mankind's recollection at once. The lodging-house is its legitimate successor, suited to our present condition and requirements. Out of deference to our human weakness, it still masquerades in the wardrobe of its ancestor; but will ere long don its own garments, and frankly assume the throne. Dresden lodging-house keepers have been accused of avarice, dishonesty, and I know not how many other vices and crimes; whereas they are all honourable men and full of humanity, if you treat them in the right way. Let one example stand for a thousand similar cases.—The wife of a friend of mine was lying at the crisis of a fever, her life depending on absolute quiet and repose. As luck would have it, the landlord discovered, at this juncture, a defect in one of the water-pipes in the *étage* overhead, and very properly set the plumbers at work to repair it. It so happened that the defect in question was at a point in the floor directly above the sick woman's bed, and all the hammering, sawing, racket and clatter beat straight down into her brain. Her husband, without stopping to think whether or not he were taking a liberty, ran up stairs, represented to the landlord that his wife was wavering between life and death, that this noise would be fatal to her, and must therefore stop at once. To this the landlord replied that he was surprised, that he was sorry, that he could not believe madame would be seriously incommoded, and that all at events he had hired the workmen for the day, and could not afford to dismiss them. The husband offered to pay the workmen's bill on the spot; but the landlord explained good-naturedly that the flooring had already been torn up, and that it would never do to leave matters in confusion on so slight a pretext. The husband, unable to hold his own with the phlegmatic Saxon, here lost his temper, and renewed his demand in the most peremptory manner. The landlord rejoined with spirit that the Herr was not in America but in Dresden; that in Dresden there were laws; and that Dresden citizens might do what they pleased with their own water-pipes. The husband, driven to his wits' end, resorted to threats; he told the landlord, with an impressive grimness of tone and manner, that, if the noise continued, and his wife's illness ended fatally, he (the husband) would, in defiance of all laws, American, Saxon or Divine, shoot the landlord dead. This put an end to the dispute and to the noise at once. The landlord, profoundly touched, dismissed his plumbers without another word. It is the richest characters that must be probed most deeply ere they betray their wealth. This worthy Saxon, to a less persistent and searching analyst than my friend, might have appeared selfish, inconsiderate, almost unfeeling. Yet mark, when the right chord was touched, how swift and full was the response! how the tender Saxon heart of him throbbed and surrendered! Believe it, Dresden holds many a soul like his—slow to succumb to empty representations and barren argument, but electric in its recognition of an appeal to the vital interests which it shares with all mankind. I cannot justify my American friend, especially since his wife recovered; but he must be credited with having shed light upon an episode of human nature which the world should not willingly let die.

XI.

I have left myself scarce a pigeon-hole in which to put the policemen, and the letter-carriers, men of honest and respectable professions, for whom, in spite of the inconvenience and anxiety to which the course of their duty often compels them to put us, no one can help feeling a regard. To be a letter-carrier must, I should fancy, be a fascinating occupation. You hold in your hand, like destiny, the joy, sorrow, good luck and bad luck of hundreds of people, high and low; and they cannot but associate you with the chequered light and shadow which you bring. It were difficult to speak too romantically on this subject. Before the war, Dresden letter-carriers wore canary-coloured coats and azure trowsers—a uniform distinguishable at any distance, and as grotesque as could be imagined. But not the wearer of the finest uniform in the world was ever watched by so many anxious and eager eyes,—his pace and bearing so commented on,—his turns, pauses and deflections so canvassed. Bless the old blue-legged canaries! what sad and happy moments they have brought me. I cannot forgive Prussia for stripping them of their blue and yellow feathers, and condemning them to hop about in indistinguishable indigo. These letter-carriers must not be confounded with other Saxon post-office employés and officials, in whom the insolence and red-tape of office is flagrant; and, what is more serious, who labour under suspicion of habitual tampering with the mails. Whether this be explainable on grounds of governmental and political exigency, or of mere private enterprise, I know not. But during the latter two years of my stay in Dresden, I lost more letters than in all the rest of my letter-experience put together; and though, in many cases, every possible enquiry and exertion was made towards their recovery, it was in no instance successful. On one occasion the missing article was a small packet containing a jewel of some value; this was formally registered at the Dresden post-office, and a description of the jewel entered in a book. There stands the entry to this day, unless some patriotic Saxon has torn the leaf out; but the jewel has vanished as utterly as Cleopatra's pearl; and no one could be found responsible for its disappearance. I should not recall an incident giving rise to such unwelcome suggestions as does this, had not a somewhat extended enquiry established the fact that my post-office fortunes, such as they were, were very far indeed from being exceptional.

The police are certainly superior in most respects both to our own and to the English force—I speak only of the rank and file—the heads of departments are scarcely up to the average. The men are not brawny giants; their physique is rather slight than otherwise; but then no one (save now and then a recalcitrant American or Englishman) ever dreams of resisting their authority. They are uniformly corteous, low-voiced, long-suffering, imperturbable, and densely stupid, aside from the black and white of their instructions. Discipline, their awful godfather, has so filled them with the voice of his commands, that all such innate and peculiar mental action as they may originally have been capable of, is forced to the wall. They pace to and fro with a mild, emasculated sobriety of demeanour, oblivious of their personal selves, and alive only with a spectral, official life, inspired by Government. They have on white gloves, and carry their hands peacefully clasped behind their backs. But why they, of all men, should be made to wear helmets and swords, is hard to imagine. The swords, of course, are tied into their sheaths by an insoluble white knot about their hilts; the helmets are furnished with a curved Greek crest—a tempting handle to wrench them off by! These accoutrements are purely symbolic; but what puzzles me is, how they first came into use. Was there once a time when they had a practical significance? It is startling even to dream of such an epoch of devastation and bloodshed; but either that, or are we to adopt the yet more appalling theory that something of the kind is in prospect? Should that day come, however, I doubt whether the police will be to the fore; the soldiers will transact the business. Indeed, there can be little doubt that it is the monstrous overgrowth of the military element which has robbed the civic guardians of their virility. In bygone years the latter may have been a very truculent and hectoring set of fellows, with their helmets cocked on their ears and their weapons loose in the sheath; but the bayonet and the pickelhaube have changed all that. When the policeman has laid down his club, 'tis vanity to gird himself with steel. His proper arms thenceforth are the pen and the inkhorn. There is a variety of the Dresden policeman known as Nacht-Waechter; they appear after dark, armed with bunches of keys, and hush up all noisy persons,—belated students and such like; but there is no more of the true beak about them than about their daylight brethren. There is no Five Points in the capital of Saxony, nor Seven Dials either.

XII.

Once, in the first months of my Saxon sojourn, I was hurrying down See Strasse, when I found my way blocked by three leisurely persons—two gentlemen with a lady between them—who monopolised the entire breadth of the side-walk. They were proceeding in the same direction as myself, so I could see only their backs. The outside gentleman, and the lady, appeared to be elderly people, and toddled somewhat infirmly onward arm-in-arm. The inside gentleman was stout, and fashionably dressed, and in the prime of life; and seemed acquainted with everybody, for he was continually lifting his hat and nodding to this one and that, and receiving polite obeisances in return.

I was in haste, and the gutter was muddy, for it had been raining; so I touched the elderly gentleman on the shoulder, and as he moved a little aside, I thanked him and slipped by. At the same moment I caught a glimpse of his face, and had the mortification of finding myself in the attitude of disputing his own sidewalk with King John of Saxony. The mild old man only smiled and toddled on, and his Queen was no less lenient than he; but the punctilious attendant who did their saluting for the Royal couple, gorgonised me from head to foot, and would have cut my ears off two hundred years ago.

But for the misfortune of their royalty, this historic family would be as desirable acquaintances as any in the kingdom. They are quiet, courteous, educated and refined, and what speaks yet more highly in their favour, they have the name of being rather unpopular with their people. Nor are they mere pallid bundles of etiquette and accomplishment, devoid of personal character and individuality; they possess distinct, recognisable human traits; indeed the present King, Albert, is a man of more than average pith, who makes himself soundly felt within his domains, and outside of them also, to a good degree.

About a year before the old king's death, he celebrated his golden wedding. The festivities lasted four or five days, beneath a solemn but unraining November cloud, which afforded an artistic background to the fluttering miles of painted bunting which gaudily draped the sombre town. The newspapers announced the programme some time in advance, albeit in such courtly polysyllabic language as was undecipherable to foreign understandings save through the dictionary. Endless good society, including the Emperor of Germany, was promised us; and beside the grand wedding-service in the palace, there were to be receptions, music, banquets, theatrical performances, two great balls, constant illumination of the city by night, and bell-ringing night and day; the whole to wind up with a colossal torchlight procession I know not how many miles long. It is only fair to say that the performance of this fine programme even outdid its promise.

Banners forty feet long streamed fourfold from every tower and dome top. The main thoroughfare dazzled with flags, festoons, medallions and mottoes; enormous garlands hung clear across the narrow street, supporting shields emblazoned with allegoric devices. Each shop window displayed its busts of the royal Jubel-Paar, egregiously flattered, and swathed in patriotic colours. Small brass and tin Fest-Medallions were hawked about by the ten thousand. Gorgeous military gentlemen of various nationalities thronged the dense side-walks, their white plumes and gilded helmets emerging above the crowd. In the Schloss-Platz, opposite the bridge, were erected two canvas obelisks, all scarlet, blue and gold, fifty feet in height, surmounted with golden crowns, and supported at the base by four allegoric statues, of meditative aspect, as if overwhelmed by their own significance. The bridge beyond pursued the narrow directness of its way through a gorgeous storm of many-hued flaglets. In short, dim old Dresden was transfigured; the good Haroun Al-Raschid would have found himself much at home there. I could not avoid comparing this coherent splendour of artistic adornment with the hysteric dowdiness of my own New York and Boston during the height of a political celebration. But for the chaste integrity of the politics themselves, the contrast might have led me to despair of the Republic.

On Saturday I stood in one of the largest, densest and best-behaved crowds I ever beheld, to see Kaiser Wilhelm drive into town. A narrow carriage-way was kept clear from the Georgen Thor to the bridge. Near my standpoint was a policeman, whose duty consisted in compelling the narrow stream of people who were on their way across the bridge, to keep moving. He was a man of men. He had reduced his profession to a science. He regarded the human race not in the light of a vicious animal with a head to be broken; he divided them into classes, as the timid, the tractable, the polite, the reasonable, the quick, the pliant, the obstinate, the sluggish, the stupid, the defiant,—and was never at a loss to manage any. He would entreat, request, enjoin, urge, argue, expostulate, command, cajole, condole, reproach, wheedle, denounce and threaten; always fitting his appeal to the case with rare tact and wisdom, and invariably carrying his point without a hair's breadth to spare either way. The effect of his pill was uniform,—to move on,—but the methods of administering it were innumerable.

Meanwhile carriages after carriages, coachmaned and footmaned with yellow liveries and irreproachable calves, were passing over the bridge on their way to meet the Emperor at the Neustadt station. One unpretending little *coupé* had the King in it, in general's uniform, touching his cap and smiling in his amiable way, but looking old—in fact, senile. As time went on, the already solid crowd got yet solider. On the opposite side of the carriage-way stood a large, inert young woman, absolutely impassive and impervious, her face round, smooth and smiling—who, while undergoing a fierce shoving, wrenching, punching and pinching from a meagre, red-faced, angry-eyebrowed harridan behind her, did not for one instant forego the serene beatitude of her expression. Another young person, in squeezing through a place too narrow for her, got through indeed, but, terrible to relate, left her petticoats behind her. There was a general broad smile at this mishap.

Suddenly came a stir and a hum—their Royal and Imperial Highnesses were approaching. A golden coachman, golden footmen, prancing horses, four elderly gentlemen in bestarred uniforms, cocked hats, white plumes—driving at full speed—"Der Kaiser!" cried some one. Men cheered and threw up their hats, women shook handkerchiefs and screamed, a wave of enthusiasm surged through the crowd, and every one's toes were trodden on. A few sharp-sighted persons smiled secretly, having perceived that it was not the great German Emperor at all, but only a couple of brace of his creatures, preparing the way for him.

This mistake so mortified and depressed the profane vulgar, that there was no demonstration left for Wilhelm when he actually appeared. He was in an open carriage alone with the King, two outriders in advance, bouncing on the hardest-trotting of horses as only royal and imperial outriders can bounce. The King, bent, dark, wrinkled, skinny, with sunken mouth and elderly smile, was in sharp contrast with the erect, square-chested, sunburnt Emperor. The latter's face was firm and vigorous, his eyes intolerant and haughty even in smiling, his white moustache curled upward. He was a finer and sturdier man than I was prepared to see—looked not sixty, though he was then seventy-five, and four years the King's senior. But his expression is not pleasant—too arrogant for mere flesh and blood. I wonder how he gets over the humiliating fact that he is fashioned after no better a model than mankind in general—the model, namely, of the Creator? Perhaps the speculation is ill-natured, but human charity is scarce lofty enough to deal on equal terms with rulers of nations.

The golden ceremony took place at ten o'clock the

following morning. Seldom does one see collected together so many high-bred, high-conditioned, thoroughly *clean* persons! for certainly there is a world of difference between those who habitually pay scrupulous attention to their toilets, and those who only do so intermittently. Few of the women were beautiful, but they were so delightfully dignified and composed! Every lady above the rank of countess had a high, delicate nose: the higher the rank, the higher the nose, generally. It is the badge of female aristocracy, but does not hold good with the men. I was especially pleased with the pages—smooth-faced, red-cheeked boys, wholesome as milk and roses, dressed in scarlet and gold-lace, with white satin knee-breeches and silk stockings. There was a stately little princess, ten years old, who took charge of the old Queen's enormous train. The Queen, in spite of her moire-antique, golden myrtle-wreath, jewels, diamonds and lace, was not a cheering spectacle. Golden weddings, after all, are more repulsive than pathetic. It is beautiful to dream of two souls faithful to each other through fifty years—but to see the worn and withered carcases in which those souls are confined, grotesquely rehearsing the holy ceremony that united their youth, is not beautiful, nor in good taste, methinks.

At twelve I was in the streets once more, watching

the carriagefulls of aristocracy drive homewards. Some carriages contained men only, with grave and indifferent visages; where ladies were alone, all was animated conversation and laughter; while a mixture of both sexes produced formal smiles and stilted remarks. Such is human nature. I must pass over the remaining festivities; though the illumination was more brilliantly extensive and intense than was ever seen before—the streets, inches deep in mud, being rendered as dry as lava shortly after the thing was set going, while the sky overhead glowed dull red, as though lit up by a volcano. As for the torchlight procession, it was the occasion of the nearest approach to a riot that happened throughout the celebration. The night fell so dark and gloomy that all the gorgeous memories to be conjured up could scarce enlighten it. Next morning, however, on looking out of my window, I saw that graceful Nature had draped the earth in snow. It glistened crisp and sparkling over all the city: and the re-married King and Queen might take the first steps of their further life over its spotless expanse.

XIII.

Since I have gone so far with good King John, I will follow him to the grave, and then take leave of him and of Dresden for ever.

Never was heard such a bell-ringing! Had bells not existed before our time, we should not have had genius to invent them. They are the outcome of an age when people's hearts vibrated readily and harmoniously, and emotions were grandly and sonorously outspoken. The popular joy and sorrow then found fitting utterance in them. Now, though the bells are as well made as ever, the general heart has cracks in it and does not vibrate soundly: and so we sometimes feel that our bells are more moved than we are. Pull away, however, worthy ringers! It is as well, perhaps, that we wag our iron tongues after our fleshly ones have ceased to bear them out. They put us on our mettle, and make us feel better than we are.

The principle upon which Dresden bell-ringing is carried on seems a little obscure. In event of fire, a slow, measured ding-dong arises, better calculated, I should fancy, to put the firemen asleep than to summon them to the scene of disaster. But let there be a funeral, and the steeples send forth an uproar such as might fitly welcome the millennium, or wake the dead, but can scarcely soothe the latter to their last rest. As regards this particular funeral, however, it may not have been so inappropriate. Royalty is less solid than it used to be—indeed, the suspicion grows that it is hollow, and that its voice is big in proportion as it feels itself shaken. Viewed in this light, there was a subtle propriety in giving the bell-ringers a prominent part in the last rites above the poor old monarch's grave.

Some of the circumstances attending his decease were such as might gratify a cynic. For a fortnight before his death it was known that die he must—any moment might bring the fatal tidings: and it was also known that during six weeks following the fatal announcement, all amusement, public or private, must be intermitted. Why was it that, from the first intimation of danger to the night of the king's death, there was an unprecedented succession of gaieties in the fore-doomed capital? Had the old gentleman been able to hold his own at death's door for six months, he would have made the fortune of every amusement-monger in Dresden. I myself walked two miles on a cold, damp night, to see the performance at an American circus, for the sole reason, so far as I know, that he died thirty-six hours afterwards. No—in spite of craped banners and badges, black-edged newspapers and lugubrious proclamations, his people never mourned him. They mourned because they must hear no music and see no Vorstellungen for six weeks. These forms and shows of grief were good when kings were the state; but now it is a mockery to prop up the poor old royal clay upon a gaudy bier, and paint the ghastly cheeks with the hues of life, and call it honouring the dead.

For the very reason, however, that these things are felt to be mere formalities, they must not be dispensed with. We must sacrifice to our hypocrisy—not to do so were scandalous. Perhaps, indeed, did we not rely upon bells, guns and torchlight-proceedings to do our mourning for us in the most orthodox and respectable manner, we might try our hand at mourning ourselves once in a while. Were we to be scandalously negligent of social proprieties for a time, we might develope a new code of morals and etiquette, more true and wholesome, if less mawkishly sentimental than is the present one.

When the King celebrated his golden wedding, busts and photographs of him crowded every shop-window; the same re-appeared now that he was dead. Again were the streets crowded with people—staring at the mourning decorations and pleased with novelty. Again the bridge and wharf were thronged, to witness the arrival of the vessel that bore the royal corpse. The night was damp and dismal, and vantage points were bought by speculators and sold at a premium—a window in the Bruelschen Concert Hall bringing ten thalers. The King had died at Pillnitz—six miles up the river; the steamer which brought him thence was draped in black crape: around the coffin stood pages, each bearing a torch; while a hundred liveried retainers, also with torches, lined the bulwarks. Along the banks of the river were ranged thousands of children, uplifting their small voices, as the sable craft swept by, in funeral hymns—a graceful fancy, if we question not too closely what must have been the children's condition when they got home again. As the vessel neared the landing amidst the silence of the vast black crowd, every one of whom (for the arrival was hours later than was announced) was sick or sullen with cold and fatigue, the first cannon thundered across the river, and all the towers of Dresden sprang into clamorous life. For an hour, while the funeral procession was passing from the landing to the cathedral, the peal of bells and cannon slackened not.

Twenty-four officers of the royal army bore the coffin ashore, and slowly up the slope to the cathedral square. The way was lined with the Saxon infantry and cavalry, who must take oaths of fealty to the new King, Albert, to-morrow. The procession flared with torches, to which the blackness of earth and sky gave full effect. The only music was the beat of muffled drums—a strange sound—the soldier who invented it must have been a poet as well. So the doors of the cathedral were reached, and doubtless the chilled and muddy-footed populace would fain have followed the coffin inside: but this was to be the privilege of few.

The great interior looked like a fairy palace—full of soft light, incense, and sweet music; while the high altar sparkled with gold and precious stones. The blackness of the funeral train, crawling up the central aisle, contrasted solemnly with the ecclesiastical magnificence through which it moved. The difference between the scene here and that which had just passed outside, was wide indeed. There, the vastness and dark uncertainty of the surroundings had dwarfed the pageant—here the pageant gloomed the surroundings. Without, there was compassion at this last appearance among his people of the mortal sovereign; within, the emotion was awe; the shadow of death lurked behind the marble columns and concentrated beneath the funeral pall. A more impressive spectacle than a royal funeral in a Roman Catholic cathedral is seldom met with. In addition to what is actually beheld, we must needs bend beneath the weight of all the moralising upon the vanities of earthly greatness that has been done since kings began; and however lightly we may smile at our emotion next morning, it was none the less a reality last night.

VII.

MOUNTAINEERING IN MINIATURE.

I.

I PACKED my portmanteau full of silent hurrahs, and set off, with a lightsome step, for the Boehmische Bahnhof. It was a divine June day, and Dresden looked so bright that I could almost have disbelieved its evil odour. The club balcony, on Victoria Strasse, had got its afternoon shadow, and never looked more inviting; but there was a train to catch, and I might not pause even there. Prager Strasse, gay and crowded, wooed me to loiter; but I had cast off, for good and all, the lazy leisure which a Dresden residence begets, and felt that time was precious once more. In a few minutes, I reached the broad, open space in front of the Bahnhof, passed through the serried droschkeys on stand there side by side, bought a ticket to Krippen, and took my seat in a third-class carriage.

I have often done the journey on foot; the highway from Dresden to Saxon Switzerland—about five-and-twenty miles—being itself excellent, while its situation is more or less picturesque throughout. The main objection to it is its openness, and the circumstance that Kœnigstein and Lilienstein—the twin rocky giants that sentinel the entrance to the mountainous region—are visible from the outset of the walk, and are a long while in getting to look nearer. For the rest, the road traverses seven or eight tiny villages and two towns—Pirna and Kœnigstein—as quaint, crooked, and narrow-streeted as heart could desire. For many miles it skirts the river-bank; after Pirna, climbs a steep hill, has an up-and-down time of it as far as Kœnigstein fortress, and then plunges headlong down a straight incline, stone-paved and ridged for the behoof of clambering waggons, into Kœnigstein town. Steep and long as is the ascent, it is pleasanter than the going down; the grade being such that running is dangerous, and walking almost impossible. Kœnigstein passed, highway and railway run cheek by jowl along the precipitous river-bank, onward through the heart of the country. The road is level, and parasolled with trees; but the squat, nine-pin-shaped steeple of Schandau church, on the opposite side of the river, now takes its turn in making the walk wearisome by its unintermittent visibility. The scene, however, is really very pretty: and were it not that his five-and-twenty miles beneath a summer sun may have rendered the pedestrian a trifle captious, doubtless he might swallow the incessant steeple with more than toleration.

But it was not my cue to foot it on the present occasion. Frequent pilgrimages to and fro had taken all novelty out of the enterprise—not to mention that my portmanteau did, strictly speaking, have some heavier things than hurrahs in it. So, for the nonce, I chose the railway-carriage; the noisiest, ugliest, tiresomest, most unprivacied mode of conveyance extant; but not wholly deficient, even in Saxony, in the exhilaration of speed, and never lacking in broad variety of human interest. And, to the end of ensuring, while I was about it, the full flavour of the experience, I took a third-class ticket—an unfailing passport to whatever human interest might happen to be in the way. First-class carriages are empty, in every sense of the word; the seats may be softly cushioned, the guard may salute whenever he catches my eye, and request the favour of my ticket with such sweet cajolery that I feel, in giving it up, as if I were making him happier than it is right or lawful for man to be; nevertheless, the noise and weariness remain, and there is nothing better than my own dignity to distract my attention therefrom. As for the second-class, it can be endurable only to penitents and to second-class people; the guard (whose behaviour admirably gauges the travellers' social estimation throughout) now chats with me on terms of friendly equality; while my neighbours are hopelessly unpicturesque and ordinary, yet of such pretensions that I am dejected by a doubt whether they are not as good as I am after all. No: the moral and mental depression brought on by second-class outweighs the pecuniary outlay of first and third combined.

But the third—the third is romantic! It piques my imagination, and gives the observation scope. I fancy myself a peasant: I think of my farmyard, my oxen, my Frau, my geese, my children; of that bargain got out of Mueller; of that paltry advantage gained by Schultze over me. My breath savours of sauer Kraut; in my pocket is a half-eaten sausage; at supper I will devour Limburger Kaese, and quaff einfaches Bier. At the same time I am an observer, a notary-public of humorous traits, a diviner of relations, destinies, and antecedents. My fellow-pilgrims are infragrant, familiar, talkative, and over-numerous; the bench we sit on is hard, and the ticket-collector is brusque and overbearing; nevertheless, if there must be a human element at all, let it be as thick and as strong as possible, and let me get as near it as I decently may. In the long run, I prefer my men and women with the crust off.

II.

Saxon third-class vans, like some English ones, are tranversely divided into five open compartments, each holding ten or twelve persons. In my box, on this trip, was a young married couple of the lower middle-class, who had not yet stopped being lovers. They were in the full tide of that amorous joyance which only lower middle-class newly-married young couples can know. The girl was not uncomely—clear-eyed and complexioned, and smoothly curved; the young husband was stout and earthy, with broad face, little twinkling eyes, and defective chin. The two sat opposite one another, her knees clasped between his, and hand in hand. They showed a paradisaical indifference to stranger eyes, which was either coarse or touching as the observer pleased. When one looked out of window, so would the other; and each rejoiced in the new sensation of seeing the world double, finding it vastly bettered thereby. Such was their mutual pre-occupation, that the guard had to demand their tickets twice before they could bring themselves to comprehend him. Truly, what should two young lovers, lately wed, have to do with such utilitarian absurdities as railway-tickets? Ostensibly, indeed, they might be booked for Bodenbach or Prag; but their real destination had no station on this or any other earthly railway. Meanwhile, the husband was puffing an unutterably villanous cigar, and blowing the smoke of it right down his wife's pretty throat. She —dear little soul—flinched not a jot, but swallowed it all with a perfect love and admiration, such as only women are (or ever can or ought to be) capable of.

My *vis-à-vis*, at the other end of the compartment, was an under-sized Russian—a black-haired, bristle-bearded, brown-eyed, round-nosed, swarthy, dirty-shirted little monster, who turned out to be a travelling agent for some cigarette-manufacturing company. The attrition of the world had rubbed off whatever reserve he may originally have possessed, and he was inclined to be sociable. He began by requesting a light from my cigar, and proceeded to have the honour to inquire whether I were of Russian extraction, observing that my features were of the Russian type. He meant it as a compliment, of course; but it is odd that a German, a Frenchman, and an Englishman should severally, and in like manner, have claimed countrymanship with me on the testimony of my visage. The explanation is to be found, I take it, in nothing more nor less than my affability, which I can neither disguise nor palliate. Why else, from a streetful of people, should I invariably be the one picked out by the stranger to tell him his way? It is not because I look as if I knew—

and, in fact, I never do know—but he feels convinced, as soon as he claps eyes on me, that whether I know or not, at all events he will get an affable answer from me. Or why else, in third-class carriages and elsewhere, am I the one to whom every smoker applies for a light? It is not because my light is better than other people's, but because they perceive in me a lack of gall to make their oppression bitter. Yet, but for this experience, I should have supposed the cast and predominant expression of my countenance to be especially grave and forbidding; which goes to prove that the world knows its individuals better than they know themselves.

Intellect plays but a subordinate part in the divination of character. It is your emotional, impressible person who finds you out most surely and soon: hence women are so apt to pass their verdict at sight, and (prejudice apart) are so seldom entirely mistaken. They cannot say, categorically, what you are—the faculty of formulating impressions being no necessary part of their gift—but they can tell what you are not, and description by negatives is often very good description. Of course, they are easily led to alter, or at least ignore their first judgment; and their second thought is never worth much. It is here that the intellect steps in, confirming and marshalling the emotional insight; and with both at their best, out comes Shakespeare.

If, in these days of committees, we could have a committee on geniuses—those whose works captivate all ages—I think the most of them would turn out soft-fibred persons, of no assertative individuality: egotists, no doubt, but with a foolish personal—not lofty moral and intellectual—egotism; yielding, sensitive natures, albeit finely balanced, and with an innate perception of truth and proportion, sufficient to prevent them being forced permanently out of shape. Were they other than this, they would be always tripping up their inspiration (meaning thereby the power of so foregoing oneself as to reflect directly the inner truth and beauty of moral and physical creation). Obstinate, prognathous geniuses must have a hard time of it: inspiration is not easily come at, upon any terms: how, then, when breathless and sweating from a tussle with one's own personality.

III.

"But you have lived in Russia. At the least you speak the language?" No. I was obliged to confess that I had not. The little agent looked hard at me, debating within himself whether he should ask me outright where I did come from; he decided against it, and applied himself to staring out of the window, and ever and anon spitting towards any part of the prospect that attracted his interest. As there was a strong draught setting inwards, I moved further up the seat. Presently, a thought of his personal appearance visited him, and he pulled from an inner pocket a little greasy box, having a tiny mirror set within the lid, and containing four inches of comb. With these appliances, the Russian went through the forms of the toilet, replacing his box, when he had finished, with a pathetic air of self-complacency, such as I have observed in a frowsy dog who has just scratched his ear and shaken a little dirt from his coat. This human being had an untrained, unintellectual, repulsive aspect enough, but he looked good-natured, and I have no doubt his odour was the worst part of him.

Sitting beside me was a lean, elderly man, of pleasant and respectable appearance, and seemingly well-educated and gentlemanlike. He had a guide-book, which he consulted very diligently, and was continually peering out of the windows on either side, in hasty search for the objects of interest which the book told about. He referred to me repeatedly, with a blandly-courteous air, for information regarding the towns and scenes through which we passed, and, by-and-by, he produced the stump of a cigar, and asked me for a light, which I gave him. At Pirna he was painfully divided between the new bridge then in course of building, the rock-mounted castle, now used as an insane asylum, and the perpendicular brown cliffs on the other side of the river—the beginning of the peculiar formation which makes the Saxon Switzerland. While poking his head out of the Russian's window, he fell into talk with him, and whether they turned out to be compatriots or not I cannot tell, but, at all events, my lean friend spoke my frowzy friend's language: they sat down opposite one another—a pendant to the two lovers at the other side—and emptied themselves into one another's mouths, so to speak, during the rest of the journey. The guidebook and the scenery were alike forgotten—such is the superior fascination of a human over a natural interest. They more cared to peep into the dark interiors of each other's minds than gaze at the sunlit trees and river, and rocks, and sky outside. What is this mysterious, irresistible magnet in all men, compelling them to attend first of all to one another? Is it smitten into them from the infinite creative magnet? I find it most generally sensitive in men of small cultivation, and in women, who, on the other hand, seldom take much genuine interest in grand natural scenery. The conversation of my two friends, so far as I could make it out, was confined mainly to cigarettes and matters thereto related. They fraternized completely; the Russian worked himself into paroxysms of genial excitement, and gesticulated with much freedom. Shortly before our arrival at Krippen, he took out a pocket-case of cigarettes, and shared its contents with his new acquaintance, and the two likewise exchanged names and addresses. Every man searches for something of himself in those he meets, and is hugely tickled if he discovers it.

The remaining occupant of our compartment was a poor, meagre little fellow, pale and peaked, with dirty-white hands, and imperfect nails, and dingy genteel attire. He was chilly, though the day was warm and generous, and kept rubbing his pithless hands together in the vain attempt to get up circulation. He was altogether squalid and dyspeptic, and smoked a squalid cigar, and said nothing, save in answer to some question put to him by his Russian neighbour. Even the endearments of the lovers availed not to bring lustre to his pallid eyes; and when his cigar went out he put it in his pocket, without asking for a light. Some unwholesome city clerkship was his, I suppose, in a street where the sun never shone and the drainage was bad.

The fortress of Kœnigstein reeled dizzily above us, perched indefinite hundreds of feet in air, on its breakneck precipice, shelving towards the base, and shawled in verdure. But the first sight of Lilienstein, as we sweep around the curve, is perhaps, more impressive. The rock, like most in this region, is of an irregular oval plan; its wooded base sloping conically upwards to within two hundred feet or so of the top, at which point the rock itself appears, hurtling straight aloft with black, naked crags. Seen from the river level, its altitude is increased by the height of the bank—at least one hundred feet more; and presenting itself end-on, it bears a striking resemblance to the dismantled hull of some Titanic frigate, wrecked on the tall summit of a hill. The gloomy weather-beaten bows rise in slow grandeur against the sky: there are the shattered bulwarks—bowsprit and masts are gone. Ages have passed since the giant vessel was stranded there, and the prehistoric ocean which hurled it to its place has rolled into oblivion. But still looms the barren hulk over that old ocean bed, now green with trees and crops, dotted with tiny villages, and alive with pigmy men. What mighty captain commanded her on her last voyage?—whose hand swayed her tiller and hauled her ropes?—what enormous exploits are recorded in her log-book? But for some foolish historic and geographic scruples I should christen her The Ark, manned by Noah and his sons, and freighted, long ago, with the hopes of humanity. On second thoughts, however, that could not be, for if there is any truth in measurements, Lilienstein might have swung the ark from her stern davits, and never felt the difference.

IV.

Some of these canal boats, however, would have made her stagger; it seems impossible that anything so ponderous should float. Looking down at them from above they appear to be of about the tonnage of an ordinary London street. Their masts are in proportion, but their sails (which they ostentatiously spread to the lightest breath of air) are exasperatingly insufficient, and help them along about as much as its wings do a penguin. Nevertheless, fleets of them are continually passing up and down, and seem to get to their destinations ultimately. Horses are harnessed to the mast, and tug away along the rounded stone levées, the long rope brushing the willows and bushes which grow beside the banks. One mariner dreams over the tiller, another occasionally slumbers in the bows, upwards of a hundred yards away. Such leisurely voyaging can hardly be supposed to keep pace with the fleet foot of time, and traditions linger hereabouts of boats that have left Dresden early in the spring, and losing four months on the passage, have only arrived at Bodenbach by the end of the previous autumn. Can this be true?

We arrived at Krippen just as a soft grey cloud was poising itself above the valley, and sending down a misty message of raindrops; the sun, however, peeped beneath, and translated it into a rainbow. I hastened down the steps to the ferry-boat—a flat-bottomed skiff about twenty feet long—and sat down there along with a dozen other passengers. Charon took his pole (oars are unknown in this kind of craft) and poked us across; the boat, which was loaded down to the gunwale, rocking alarmingly, and the people ejaculating and protesting. At landing we were beswarmed by porters, but I knew the coast, and escaping from them, took my way along the pretty winding path towards the old Badehaus, which reposes at the upper end of the desultory village of Schandau. Schandau proper, indeed, is comprised in the little garden patch of red-roofed houses huddled in the mouth of the valley where it opens on the river; but its "Bad" reputation has generated a long progeny of stuccoed villas, standing in a row beneath the opposite sides of the gradually narrowing cañon. The pine-clad hillsides rear up within arm's reach of their back windows, and as steep as their roofs. For about half-a-mile up, the valley averages scarce a hundred yards in breadth, while its sides are at least as high as that, and look much higher. Down the centre flows a brook, dammed once or twice to turn saw-mills, and bordered with strips of grassy meadow. The main road, unnecessarily tortured with round cobble stones, and miserable in a width of some ten feet, crawls along beneath the house-row on the northern side; but the southern is the aristocratic quarter—the houses are villas, and have balconies and awnings, overlooking a smooth gravel path densely shaded with trees—the fashionable morning and evening promenade, untrodden by hoof of horse, and familiar to the wheels of children's perambulators only. Very charming is all this, and after the clatter, glare, and poison of the city, unspeakably soothing and grateful.

As I walked along, fragments of the rainbow shower occasionally found their way to me through the leafy roof overhead, while children toddled across my path, escaping from white-aproned nurses; and villa-people —girls in coquettish white hats, and gentlemen indolent with cigars—stared at me from the vantage-ground of their shaded windows. At the garden restaurant were beer-drinkers, merry in the summer-houses, and great running to and fro of Kellner and Kellnerinnen. The dust was laid—the trees were painted a livelier green—the grass and flowers held themselves straighter and taller—the air lay cool and still on the sweet earth, or moved faintly under the influence of a doubtful breeze—the brook gurgled unseen, and the noise of the saw-mill, a moderate distance off, sounded like the busy hum of some gigantic grasshopper.

Where the Badehaus stands, the hill-ridges verge towards each other, till a stone could be thrown from one summit to the other. In the square court on which the hotel faces, the aristocratic pathway finds its end, and thenceforward the road, relieved of its cobbles, and otherwise improved, takes up the tale alone. The brook washes the Badehaus wall, and in the earlier part of its course cleaves to the southern side of the narrow gorge. The Badehaus places itself transversely across the valley, looking down village-wards, and giving the brook and the road scarcely room to turn its northern wing. Its southern end, meanwhile, thrusts right into the hillside, and even digs a cellar out of it, to cool provisions in. The front court, when I entered it, was noisy with multitudinous children, and the daily brass band was on the point of striking up in the open pagoda. The audience were preparing their minds for the entertainment with plentiful meat and drink, and the three Kellner employed by Herr Boettcher had, as usual, three times too much to do. Herr Boettcher (who looks like a mild Yankee until he opens his mouth) and his pale-haired helpmate received me with many smiles, and ushered me into a small scantily-furnished chamber, overlooking the brook and the road, and likewise commanding a view of a small villa crowded close against the hillside opposite.

V.

I ordered supper, and then sat down at my window. The brook, which flowed directly beneath it, was somewhat cloudy of current, and disfigured as to its bed by indistinct glimpses of broken crockery and bottles scattered there. A short distance down, it was crossed by a bridge communicating with the Badehaus court. Some slender-stemmed young trees were trying to make themselves useful along the road side; and there, likewise, were ranged three rectangular piles of stone, awaiting the hammer of the stone-breaker; and a wedge-shaped mud-heap, hard and solid now, but telling of wet days and dirty walking in times gone by. A weather-beaten picket fence, interlarded at intervals with white-washed stone posts, inclosed a garden, devoted partly to cabbages and potatoes, and partly to apple-trees. At one end of this enclosure stood the villa; at the other, a large tree, with a swing attached to it; several small people were making free with this plaything, subject to an occasional reproving female voice from the direction of the house, and the fitful barking of a self-important little cur. I could also see the lower half of a white skirt, squired by a pair of black broadcloth legs, moving up and down beneath the low-extending branches of the apple-trees.

The villa, whose red-tiled roof was pleasantly relieved against a dark-green back-ground of pines, was provided with an astonishing number of windows. I counted no less than fifteen, besides a door, in the hither end of it alone. Over the front door was a balcony, thickly draped with woodbine; and here sat two ladies, in blue dresses, dividing their time between the feminine diversions of sewing, reading, gossiping, and watching the passers-by. Small or large parties were continually strolling up the road towards the Schützenhaus—the women, mostly attired in white, with white hats, and white or buff parasols; and all chatting and laughing with great volubility and good humour. One pretty girl, walking a little in the rear of her companions, happened to glance up at my window and catch my eye; and all at once it became necessary for her to cross the road, which being rather dirty, she was compelled to lift her crisp skirts an inch or two above a shapely pair of little boots. What happy land first received the imprint of those small feet? Could it have been Saxony? They soon walked beyond my field of vision, which was limited by the sash. Here, however, came into play a species of ocular illusion, made possible in Germany by the habit windows have of opening inwards on hinges. The upper stretch of road to its curve round the bold spur of the hill, a bit of dilapidated bridge, and one or two new villas half clad in trees,—all this pretty picture was mirrored and framed in the pane of glass at my left hand. A few moments, therefore, after the owner of the boots had vanished from actual sight, she stepped daintily into this phantom world, and proceeded on her way as demurely as though no such astonishing phenomenon had occurred. She was, to be sure, unaware of it; and we all live in blind serenity amidst marvels as strange. Perhaps, when our time comes, we shall take our first walk beyond the grave with no less unconscious self-possession than attended the march of those little boots across my window-pane.

As the afternoon wore on, waggons and droschkeys, full of returning excursionists, began to lumber by, with much cracking of whips, singing, and jollity. Many of the men wore monstrous hats, roughly plaited of white reeds, quantities of which were on sale in the village for a groschen or so each, being meant to last only a day. They were bound with bands of scarlet ribbon, and lent their wearers a sort of tropical aspect. Every vehicle was overcrowded, and everybody was in high spirits except the horses, which, however, were well whipped to make up for it. Meanwhile, the band in the pagoda round the corner had long been in full blast, and odds and ends of melody came floating past my window. In the pauses of the music I could hear two babies bemoaning themselves in the adjoining room. A small child, with red face and white hair, made itself disagreeable by walking nonchalantly backwards and forwards over an impromptu plank bridge without railings, escaping accident so tantalizingly that I could almost rather have seen it tumble in once for all, and done with it. At last, when the miracle had become threadbare, the bath-girl appeared and took the infant Blondin away; and at the same moment a waiter knocked at my door, and told me supper was ready.

VI.

Supper was set out on a little table under the trees in the front court. The musicians had departed, leaving a skeleton growth of chairs and music-rests in the pagoda; and most of the late audience had assembled at the long dining tables in the Speise-Saal, where I could see them through the open windows paying vigorous attention to the meal.

Several young ladies, however, under the leadership of a plump, brisk little personage, whom I cannot better describe than by calling her a snub-nosed Jewess, had got up a game of croquet, which they played with much coquettish ostentation; but in other respects ill. They were in pronounced evening costume; and my waiter—a small, fat boy, smuggled into a man's swallow-tail—said there was going to be a ball. The Tanz-Saal faced me on the other side of the court; being connected at right angles with the hotel, corner to corner. It was a white stuccoed building, about on an architectural par with a deal candle-box. A double flight of steps mounted to the door, over which were inscribed, in shaky lettering, some lines of doggrel, composed by Herr Boettcher himself in praise of his medicinal spring. The hall inside may have been sixty feet in length, with a raised platform at one end for the accommodation of the musicians.

It was lighted by two candelabra; but these eventually proving inadequate, a secret raid was made upon the kerosene lamps in the guests' rooms, and every one of them was carried off. I retired early that night, and having discovered my loss and rung the bell, an attendant did finally appear, in the shape of the bath-girl. To make a short story of it, no light, except starlight, was to be had. It is a hardship to have to go to bed in Saxony at all in. You know not, from hour to hour, whether you are too hot or too cold, but are convinced, before morning, that you are three or four feet too long. But the Badehaus beds are a caricature rather than a fair example of Saxon beds; and to go to bed not only in Saxony but in the Badehaus, and not only in the Badehaus but in the dark, was for me a memorable exploit. I have reason to believe, however, that three-fourths of the hotel guests had to do the same thing; for my wakefulness, up to three o'clock in the morning, was partly due to the noisy demands and expostulations wherewith they made known and emphasized their dissatisfaction.

But I am anticipating. By the time I had finished supper it was growing dark, and the dancers were arriving in numbers. The dresses were mostly white and gauzy, though here and there were glimpses of pink and blue satins, and one young woman had divided herself equally between red and green. My pretty vision with the shapely feet was not among them. As evening came on, the hall filled, and I could see the heads of the company moving to and fro within; and some were already stationary at the windows. Meanwhile the whole domestic brigade appertaining to the hotel, including Herr Boettcher himself, were busied in carrying chairs from the court yard to the hall, to be used in the cotillon. The least active agents in this job were the two head waiters; the most strenuous and hard-working were the bath-girl and the chamber-maid. Finally, the only chairs left were my own, and one occupied by a huge, fat Russian, at a table not far from mine; and from these the united blandishments of the entire Boettcher establishment availed not to stir either of us

Darkness fell upon the valley—the stars came out above the lofty brow of the impending hillside—the trees stood black and motionless in the still air: all light, life, and sound were concentrated behind the glowing windows of the Tanz-Saal. The musicians had struck up amain, and the heads were now moving in couples, bobbing, swooping, and whirling in harmony with the rhythm of the tune. Now and then an exhausted pair would reel to a window, where the lady would fan herself and pant, and the gentleman (in three cases out of five an officer) would wipe his forehead with his handkerchief and pass his forefinger round inside the upright collar of his military jacket. Then both would gaze out on the darkness, and, seeing nothing, would turn to each other, and launch themselves into the dance once more. Between the pauses I could distinguish Herr Boettcher's brown curly pate hastening busily backwards and forwards, and began to remark an increase of illumination in the hall; but was, of course, without suspicion of the cost to myself at which it was being obtained.

The huge Russian and I were the only voluntary non-combatants; for the half-score of forlorn creatures (among them the chamber-maid and the bath-girl) who had climbed on the railing of the steps, and were stretching their necks to see what they could see, would gladly have taken part if it had been permitted them. It was too dark for me to do more than roughly guess at the outline of my stout neighbour; but I could hear him occasionally take a gulp from his beer-glass, sigh heavily, and anon inhale a whiff of cigarette-smoke. I also had drunk a glass of beer; but it now occurred to me to try the possibility of getting something else. I called the waiter, and bade him bring me a lemon, some sugar, some hot water, and one or two other things—from which I concocted a mixture unknown to Saxon palates, but which proved none the less grateful on that account to my own. The cordial aroma must, I think, have been wafted by some friendly breeze to the Russian's nostrils; for, after an interval, he, too, summoned the waiter and categorically repeated my own order.

Meanwhile the music surged and beat, and the ball went seething on. It is much pleasanter, as well as wiser, thought I, to sit here quiet and cool beneath the stars, with a good cigar and a fragrant glass of punch for company, than to dance myself hot and tired in yonder close, glaring room. Then, somehow or other, the recollection of that pretty figure with the white parasol and the small arched feet, which had marched so daintily across my window-pane that afternoon, entered my mind; and I was glad to think that she was not one of the red-faced, promiscuous throng. She belonged to a higher caste than any there; or, at all events, there was in her an innate nicety and refinement, which would suffice to keep her from mixing in such an assemblage. The more I reflected upon the matter, the less could I believe that she was a Saxon. I had contracted, it may be, a prejudice against the Saxons, and was slow to give them credit for exceptional elegance of form or bearing. That graceful *tournure*—that high-bred manner—no, no! why might not she be a Spaniard—nay, why not even an American? And here I entered upon the latter half of my glass of punch.

The waiter returned, bearing the Russian's hot water and so forth on a tray, and, having set them before him, hastened off to his post at the ball-room door. The soft glock-glock of liquids, and the subdued tinkle of tumbler and spoon, now became audible from the womb of night, accompanied by occasional labouring sighs and tentative smackings of the lips—tokens that my heavy neighbour was making what, for him, was probably a novel experiment. I became gradually convinced, moreover, that it was not altogether a successful one; and I was more pleased than surprised when I heard him, after a little hesitation, push back his chair, and advance upon me out of the darkness, entreating me, in the gentlest tone imaginable, to favour him with a light for his cigarette.

This having been done, he stood silent for a

moment, and then observed, engagingly, that he had been informed the gentleman was an American: that the relations of Russia and America had always been cordial: that the fame of the American punch was known to him, but not, alas! the exact method of preparing it: that——

I here ventured to interrupt him, begging that he would bring his glass and his chair to my table, and suffer me to improve the opportunity, so kindly afforded, of introducing him to a national institution, peculiarly adapted to increase the *entente cordiale* to which he had so pleasantly alluded. He accepted my invitation as frankly as it was given; and in five minutes we were hobnobbing in the friendliest manner in the world. Like all educated Russians, he had a fair understanding of English; and I was anticipating an evening of social enjoyment, when the following incident occurred:—

The first part of the ball was over, and an intermission of ten minutes was announced before the beginning of the cotillon. The hall doors were thrown open, and among the couples that came out upon the steps was one which attracted my attention. The lady, who was dressed in white, after a moment sent back her partner for a shawl; and during his absence she stood in such a position that the light from within fell directly upon her face. The man—

he was not an officer—returned with the shawl, and folded it round her pretty shoulders with an air that was not to be mistaken. They descended the steps arm in arm, and came forward, groping their way and laughing, in our direction. They stumbled upon a table only three or four yards from ours, and sat down to it. After a short confabulation the man called out "Karl!" and the waiter came.

"Karl, two glasses of beer; but quick!"

"And a portion of raw ham thereto, Karl," said the lady, in the unmistakable Saxon accent: "I am so frightfully hungry!"

"Two glass beer, one portion ham," recited Karl, and hurried off.

The man pulled a cigar from his pocket, and lit it with a match. I had recognized him before: he kept a small cigar-shop on See Strasse, in Dresden. He threw the lighted match on the ground, and it burnt there until the lady put out a small, arched foot, neatly booted, and daintily extinguished it. She was a pretty girl for a Saxon, especially a Saxon in her humble rank of life.

"Herr Kombustikoff," said I to my Russian friend, "I must leave you. I am very sorry—but I have received a great shock! Good night!" and I was gone before Karl returned with the raw ham and the beer; and thus it happened that I went to bed so early that night. I rested ill; but it would have fared yet worse with me had I known then what I discovered next morning—that my too courteous Russian had gone off after having paid for my punch as well as for his own! Did he imagine that I meant to barter my instruction for the price of the beverage to which it related? May this page meet his eye, and discover to him, at last, the true cause of my unceremonious behaviour.

VII.

By daylight I was dimly awake, and dreamily aware of the singing of a bird outside my window. Of all the bird-songs that ever I heard this was the briskest, most high-strung, most dandified: giving my drowsyhead the fancy that some elfin exquisite was busy arranging his cravat, parting his hair, and pointing the ends of his moustache before a dew drop mirror; uttering the while a brilliant series of fairy witticisms upon the follies of society. I fell asleep again, and dreamed incoherently, though not unpleasantly, despite my cramped position: but awoke soon after to see the pure sunshine lighting up the fir-trees on the opposite hillside, and to hear the inner voice of the brook babbling to itself beneath the window. Even then I should not have got up, had not a steady tide of weeping set in from the babies in the adjoining room.

No matter how early I rise in Saxony, I never fail to find people up before me. It was now but little after five o'clock; and two elderly hypochondriacs were dipping up the iron water from the spring in the front court, while a pallid young lady, blanched, I suppose, from indulgence in city dissipations, was pacing slowly up and down the walk, sipping fresh milk out of a tall tumbler. For my own part, being in search of an appetite, I started up the steep zigzag hill-path, and steered a breathless course heavenward, through dewy heather and blueberry bushes, and over difficult rocks and grassy knolls. The world enlarged around me as I climbed, though the feathery arc of white cloud which spanned the blue overhead grew no nearer for all my pains. At length I attained a small semicircular stone erection, which from below, had seemed to crown the hill, but which now turned out to be somewhat below the highest point. It commanded, nevertheless, a comprehensive view of the Schandau valley, still hazy with the remnants of last night's mist. The pine-trees on the ridge of the hill opposite seemed almost within reach of my outstretched arm. Below, some four or five hundred feet, appeared the flattened roof of the Badehaus; and there were the hypochondriacs, pigmies now, still lingering over the iron-spring; and a young lady, a couple of inches high, pacing slowly to and fro, and occasionally sipping milk from an infinitesimal tumbler. There, too, comes a microscopic Karl, and begins to set a breakfast-table, with tiny white cloth, and glistening plates no bigger than heads of pins. This pebble, which I hold in my hand, were I to cast it down, would utterly overwhelm and crush out the entire establishment—Badehaus, hypochondriacs, Karl, iron-spring, young lady, breakfast-table, and all! Heavens! what power for wholesale destruction lurks in this arm of mine. Yet, tremble not, poor mites, I will not annihilate ye; moreover, were one of you but to turn his eyes hitherwards, it is I who would appear insignificant, and you the giants.

Fresh and invigorating was the atmosphere at this height, polluted by no human exhalations, but seeming to be the essence of last night's stars, dissolved for my use by this morning's sunshine. After swallowing my fill of it, I left the little stone semicircle, and took my way along the ridge of the hill towards the river. Looking downwards, there were the red-tiled roofs of the villas almost beneath my feet; further out, the brook, flowing on hastily between its green banks, and at one time rushing out in white foam beneath a dark archway. Beyond still, the road, with its line of houses of older and quainter growth, seeming to rest their aged shoulders against the perpendicular hill-wall behind them. Long narrow flights of stone steps mounted straight upwards from the kitchen doors of the villas, leading to heights of backyard on a level with the tops of their chimneys. There was one villa, high up on the opposite hillside, where it made a white break in the dense growth of firs, which was romantic with battlemented turrets and mullioned windows, and dignified with an elaborate staircase of dressed stone, winding through several landings to the porticoed doorway. Farther on, surmounting the extreme spur of the ridge and abreast of the village, was the little Schloss-Bastei Restauration, with its flag flying, its camera-obscura like a black pill-box, and its vine-covered beer-garden, where I had quaffed many a refreshing stoup after a dusty tramp from Dresden, chatting the while with bright-eyed, good-humoured little Marie.

Before long, I found myself at the end of my own ridge, apparently overhanging the red-roofed irregular town, and sat down on one of the hospitable benches established there. A wooden railing afforded a not unnecessary precaution against tumbling over into the front yard of the little villa on the roadside below. The villa, plain enough in itself, was surrounded by a small garden full of roses; and its porch was heavily overgrown with woodbine. Out of this porch presently issued a woman and a little girl, and walked about the garden picking the beautiful flowers. The woman was simply clad in white, and had a green bow on the bosom of her dress—as if she were a humanisation of the villa. Her hair, however, was not red, but black.

Beyond the town flowed the river Elbe, and winding westward, gleaming white, swept round the broad base of Lilienstein, five miles away. The great rock, from this point of view, resembled an old woman sitting closely huddled up beside the river in a green cloak, her grey head bowed forwards on her knees. On the railroad, just across the stream, an engine was steaming itself out of breath in the effort to set in motion an innumerable train of freight waggons. Above the railroad was a showy, glistening, bannered edifice, perched brand new on its raw green terraces; above this again, a yellow stone quarry; and higher still, the pine-fringed summit against the sky. Ferry-skiffs, gay with awnings, and full of passengers by the early train from Dresden, were being poled across; the landing-place, however, was shut out from my view by the intervention of the line of hotels which is drawn up so officiously along the river margin. The most prominent feature in my immediate neighbourhood was the church steeple, which bulged out irregularly, like an insufficiently swaddled infant. None of the streets in the town were visible; but the green tops of the trees planted along them rose up above the ruddy roofs, seaming them into uneven quadrilaterals. Meanwhile, from the chimneys the smoke of a hundred breakfasts began to rise, reminding me that my own was still uneaten. I returned along the ridge of the hill to my semicircular bastion, whence descending, as it were, through the very tops of the gloomy fir-trees, I sat down to table, warm and glowing, with an appetite for the largest of beefsteaks. The hypochondriacs and the milk-drinking lady had wandered away; several people, singly or in parties, were breaking their fast beneath the trees; excursionists were strolling past, and Sunday was getting fairly under way. By the time I had lit my morning cigarette the yard was quite alive, and those who had parted latest the night before were now hypocritically complimenting one another upon the freshness of their appearance. After a cool half-hour, I resumed my hat and staff, and leisurely began the ascent of the Schiller-Hoehe, on the other side of the road.

VIII.

It was a ten minutes' easy climb. The well-built, easily-graded path went zig-zagging upwards beneath the tall dark pines, bordered with dewy green ferns, purple-tipped heather, huckleberry bushes, and tufts of narrow-leaved grass. At the turns of the ascent were benches, either constructed from a slab of stone laid across two uprights, or hewn in the solid rock whenever it jutted out conveniently. Enterprising climbers had worn short-cuts straight upwards from corner to corner of the path, tempting to look at, but, as short-cuts, fallacious, unless men were made on the principle of a balloon! and, on reflection, I have come to the conclusion that they must have been created by people on the downward trip. Saxons will climb, and climb to good heights; but it is indispensable that the incline should not be arduous. In the present case the gradual slope was further modified by putting in three or four stone steps at the end of each short stretch; and if all should prove insufficient, there were always the benches to fall back upon.

The profound stillness which prevailed here at this hour had an exquisite charm. Through openings between the trees I caught lovely green glimpses of the valley below. I met no one until, when nearly at the top, I came upon two peasant girls, each with her basket, sitting down to rest. I gave them "good morning," and one of them responded with sober courtesy. A few steps further on I was startled, emerging from such a depth of seclusion, at coming abruptly in sight of an open, commonplace road, with a cart rumbling along it; and beyond, broad fields sown with potatoes and cabbages, and scattered over with half-a-dozen women-cultivators. Still keeping to the path, I soon came to the "Schiller-Hoehe" monument itself.

In itself, it certainly did not amount to much—a square shaft of grey stone, on a pedestal, the whole less than ten feet high. On the side towards the valley was a medallion of Schiller's head, and a date—1859: and all four sides, both of shaft and pedestal, were crowded with the names of visitors, and the dates of their visits. Round about, at a respectful distance, were placed wooden benches, apparently for the purpose of facilitating the study of so remarkable a work of art. Accordingly, I sat down, and fixed my eyes upon it. Three small ragged boys, dismayed at my solemnity, gave up their irreverent gambols, and retreated into the woods. Finding myself once more solitary, I filled a pipe with sweet Lone-Jack, and smoked, and dutifully meditated upon the poet, who, I suppose, composed some one of his poems or tragedies on this spot.

After a while I heard an approaching step, weighty and sedate; and soon appeared a stout, elderly gentleman in wide black clothes, who, upon seeing me, paused to deliver a gravely ceremonious bow; being under the impression, probably, that I was a sort of deputy tutelar genius of the grove, employed during the poet's absence. I returned his salute with all the dignity I could command. He advanced towards the monument, and inspected, though with a rather embarrassed and mechanical air, the medallion and the date. It was easy to perceive that he was a morbidly considerate man, and shrank from subjecting the affair to a rigid criticism, while even the deputy tutelar genius was looking on. Moreover, finding nothing to admire, and being altogether too honourable a person to counterfeit admiration, he was not long in making up his mind that his only proper course was to retire. This he accordingly did, as sedately as he had come; by no means forgetting to deliver me a second ceremonious bow (which I returned) before passing out of sight.

Hereupon ensued another interval of silence and solitude: I finished my pipe; and so soothing was the murmuring of the pines, and the wild domestic twittering of the birds, that I think I should have yielded to the temptation of compensating my bad night with a nap, had not my drowsiness been scared away by the sudden advent of a bevy of laughing, prattling, sky-larking young women, upon whom the solemnity of my demeanour produced not the slightest effect. So, finding that they were determined to take possession of the place, I resigned my deputy-tutelarship perforce, and retired in my turn. Following a downward-bending track, I stumbled upon a small cave, partly hollowed out of the natural rock, but owing most of its attractions, such as they were, to masonry. Schiller's Grot it was called, in black letters upon a white ground. Of course, Schiller may have sat in it: there is a pretty outlook over the valley from a point near at hand; and the Grot is ostentatiously fitted up with a semicircular stone seat, which, however, can hardly date back to Schiller's time. Be that as it may, the place, when I visited it, was peculiarly unsavoury, and nothing less than a Noachian deluge would have kept me in it a moment. I rambled on, and soon came to another coign of vantage, a little lower down than the first, but overlooking a wider prospect. Wooden benches were provided here also, and a signboard, mounted on a pole, informed the visitor that this was Friedens-Platz.

The Saxon custom of sentimentalizing over all their pretty places, and branding them with lackadaisical titles, is not altogether agreeable to a foreigner. It destroys the finest aroma of natural beauty to have it coarsely insisted upon and crammed down your throat by some vulgar fellow who happens to have been beforehand with you in discovering it. Every one, it seems to me, ought to be allowed to believe, if it suits his fancy to do so, that whatever charm he finds in nature is virginal for him; that it has not been previously breathed upon, handled, catalogued, and labelled by an impure rabble—spectacled and professional enthusiasm-mongers—who never can rid themselves of their itch for besmearing everything with which they come in contact with the slime of their own offensive personality. The Saxons, though they carry the matter to the greatest extreme, are not the only nation blameworthy in it. Let a man name his house, if he likes; it is his own, and should suggest him, and the name helps it to do so. But what is the use of giving to eternal mountains and everlasting rivers the puny patronymics of our so-called great men, whose pigmy reputations are astonishingly long-lived if they endure five hundred years? If such things must be directly named at all, let the name be simply descriptive, like those the Indians give. There is much talk nowadays, about the wholesome effect of a sense of humour and a perception of the ludicrous; and Englishmen, Americans, and others pride themselves upon the possession of these qualities. But nature, I imagine, must often find us humorous in another sense than we intend; and bears our tiny impertinences with a smile too broad for us to see. A rage for what is called conciseness is the vice of the time, and circumlocution has been made a bugbear. The truth is that our conciseness, which is a literal and not a real conciseness, leads to the worst kind of circumlocution, which is not real circumlocution at all. To be truly consise is, once to express clearly one idea; circumlocution is primitive and majestic, and must lie at the bottom of all right perception of truth. Such polemical essays, however, are not particularly suited to a Friedens-Platz.

IX.

Whatever other people's feeling may be, there is no doubt that Saxons like a pretty place all the better for having a lackadaisical name. It gives them their cue, and they dispose themselves accordingly. I had not more than got through the above diatribe, when a Saxon family appeared—a man and wife, child of four years, and nurse. They looked at the prospect with complacency, it is true; but the signboard was their primary admiration. "Friedens-Platz!" they repeated one to another, in a congratulatory tone, and then took another look with new eyes. Friedens-Platz— yes, yes! Observe once more, the peculiar peacefulness of the valley; and methinks the sky is calmer, and the breeze gentler here than elsewhere. Blessed signboard! to think that we might have come and gone and never known wherein the charm of this spot consisted, or whether it had any charm at all. It is all in the signboard—peace be unto it, and to the poetic insight that placed it there!

These people did not stay there very long, and I sat them out. My next visitors were a woman and two men—pleasant, respectable people, and, I think, Swedes. The woman was not only very good-natured, but incredibly loquacious and voluble; and so agreeable were the tones and inflections of her voice, that, although not understanding a syllable she uttered, I found an indescribable charm in listening to her. The effect was magnetic and soothing. Here was a good opportunity for studying the influence of mere speech, apart from all knowledge of its meaning, upon the ear and sentiments of the hearer. Undoubtedly it has great significance—is at least as important to language as the material of a building is to its architectural design. It was only my guess that this language was Swedish: it may just as well have been Hawaian or Persian. Whatever it was, it tripped along at a great pace, in a kind of short four-footed canter; no drawling or dwelling upon syllables; little sibilation, but plenty of sh'ing, tt'ing, and pp'ing. While the woman thus held forth, one of her companions sat quietly listening, giving occasional vent to an assenting or annotatory grunt; the other kept walking restlessly to and fro, interpolating a sentence here and there. I sat for half-an-hour, my back turned upon the party, apparently absorbed in the view—really so, in fact; for the flow of babble did not interfere with my appreciation of what I saw, but chimed in with it. Very likely, on the other hand, it was I who interfered with the Swedes.

Small sounds below in the valley were distinctly audible at this height. The first-fiddle of the Badehaus band was tuning his instrument in the front court. Then came the slow jar of a cart, and now the driver cleared his throat. The road was visible for a considerable distance, winding up the valley like a smooth buff riband, the brook flowing light and dark beside it, in pleasing contrast with the bright, moist green of the grass and the swarthy tint of the pine-clad hill. The whole valley was a westward curving furrow, ploughed by some immeasurable giant. The summit of the opposite hill was bald above its side-growth of trees, just like the head of an elderly man in a counting-house. White villas dotted the slope, even to the top: riverwards lay Schandau, wedged between its valley walls, and massed around its steeple. Against the horizon, on all sides, uprose abrupt pinnacles of rock and jagged detached boulders, the like of which abound throughout this region. Lilienstein was hidden by the woods behind me; but the crest of Wesenstein, across the river, reached into sight. A faint odour of pine-leaves hung in the air, though the breeze was scarcely strong enough to blow it about.

X.

I left Friedens-Platz to the babbling Swedes, and walked along the ridge of the hill, as on the back of some enormous animal. The stillness of the woods was such as to make the heart beat: each lusty blade of grass, and leaf, and tree, and vegetable, stood so motionless, yet so deeply alive. At length the path brought me to the verge of the narrow precipitous cañon, through which the road runs after passing the bend above the Badehaus. I managed to clamber out upon an almost inaccessible boulder, which had been partly detached from the face of the cliff, and dizzily overhung the road. Here a deep ledge, cushioned with heather, served me admirably for a chair, and a projection lower down gave a rest for my feet. I was indistinguishable from the road, and invisible from behind, yet myself commanded everything. It was a fall of about three hundred feet to the road below.

Facing me was a magnificent bastion of rock, rising to a higher level than mine, and split and cleft in every conceivable direction. Wherever root could cling, the stern surface was softened and enriched with small trees, bushes, or heather; which last, being very plentiful and in full purple bloom, gave a delicious tone to the slopes. The rock itself was various in tint; reddish where little exposed to rain and sunshine; in other places grey; and mottled elsewhere by lichens, like a Persian rug. One kind of lichen, not uncommon, showed in broad splashes of sulphur yellow. All these colours, harmonizing among one another, were tuned to wholly different keys by sunshine or shadow. In many parts, the sunlight caught the bastion obliquely, illuminating the projecting points in sharp contrast with the rest. The silent immobility of rocks is profoundly impressive, and this surface-play of light and colour but emphasizes their real unchangeableness.

The broader clefts or gorges, extending from top to bottom of the bluffs, were verdant and rich with crowded foliage, and seemed to invite ascent: for wherever a tree can grow, there man fancies that he, too, has a right to be. Great boulders had in many places fallen from above, and lay buried in green beside the brook. For centuries had they lain there, and slowly, silently, and beautifully had nature healed their scars, and clothed their nakedness with moss, heather, and leaves of all kinds. Trees pressed in lovely jealousy to the brookside, eager to see their tender images mirrored there. How sweetly and closely they mingled together, branch within branch and leaf to leaf, each with its own beauty beautifying its neighbour! How rich were their contrasting shades of green! How melodiously did they whisper to one another, when the breeze gave them tongue! How well each leaf and bough turned sun and shade to advantage, and how inspiring was the upward impulse that filled each one! If trees, as some maintain, are emblems of men, it must be the men of the golden age!

Those which grew beside the brook had, in some cases, attained a large size, but only the smaller ones had been venturous enough to scale the cliffs and peer fearfully over the hollow verges. Trees have a fine and novel effect when seen from above with the sun shining on them. The edges of the successive layers of branches catch the yellow light, and the structure and character of the tree, as it tapers upwards to a point, is thus more clearly defined than when viewed from below or on a level. But their fascination is in all respects inexhaustible. Where they overhung the brook, its warm brown tint was deepened to black; but through the midst of the gloom its wrinkled surface snatched at the light in magic sparkles: nature never omits what is needful to complete her harmony. I could hear the gurgle of the stream, however, more distinctly than I could discern the stream itself. All sounds were so echoed up between the rocky walls, that they reached my ears as plainly as if originating but a few yards off.

A hill-top is a real, and not an apparent—a moral

as well as a physical—height. I doubt whether a murder, seen from a great elevation, would move the beholder to any deeper feeling than pity. Men's deeds appear of importance proportioned to their doer's size. I should like to be informed, however, which requires the finer structure of mind—the power to appreciate nature in great, or in little? to be able to see the beauty of a grand prospect, or of a mossy stone shadowed with fern? Certainly, an uneducated man, who would gape with admiration at the former, would see nothing worthy attention in the latter. It is true, on the other hand, that refinement loves not the little to the exclusion of the great, but great and little both: neither does vulgar admiration necessarily vulgarize its object. Nevertheless, who can discern minute beauties, may recognize, in great, qualities invisible to the untrained eye; and the uneducated man, perhaps, loves not solely or chiefly the grandeur of the prospect, but rather the sensation of moral and material elevation—the feeling grander than the grandeur—the crown and culmination of it.

XI.

A precipice possesses a strange charm; it is in a manner divine, being inaccessible to man, with his belittling civilization. But if steep places lead our upward-gazing thoughts heavenwards, they also remind us of the devil when we shudder on their brink. What is the spiritual significance of the phenomena of gravitation? Something profound and universal, I fancy. I have never experienced the common desire to jump from great heights; but had I, as a malefactor, to choose my form of death, I would cling to some such great boulder as that on which I was now sitting and bid the executioner use his lever. Then headlong downwards would we thunder to the valley's far bottom; and, falling underneath, I should be provided with both a grave and a gravestone ere I were well dead. But that the general adoption of this expedient for settling with condemned criminals would soon deprive us of all our overhanging cliffs—to say nothing of scaring away superstitious tourists and picnickers from our valleys — I would respectfully recommend it to the consideration of the Board.

What I most liked about my boulder (apart from such reflections) was its isolation: the thought that nobody could find me out, or get to me if they did. I was separated from my kind; and though greatly in the minority, I felt that the advantage was on my side. I had banished them, not they me. Moreover, I indulged myself with the persuasion that I was the first who had ever set foot on that spot, and that a long time would elapse before any one came after me; and then I amused myself with speculating on what manner of man he, my successor, would be; whether he were yet born; whether he would be a Frenchman out of the next war; or whether æons would go by, and Europe be known by another title before he came. Pending these questions, I took out my pipe and smoked, where no man ever smoked before. My isolation, it must be confessed, had not separated me from the faculty of enjoying good tobacco, as other men enjoyed it; or, for that matter, from being shone on by their sun and breathing their air. After all, therefore, it amounted to very little—every human soul stands on a pinacle of its own, eternally individualized from all his fellows; but our plainest badge of brotherhood is this very individuality, which the love and life that the good God gives us show to be but a means to His end, and otherwise insignificant.

An excursion carriage rattled by, seeming to make slower progress than it did. I watched it from its first appearance round the southern bend till it disappeared just beneath my feet; and on its reappearance, till it went out of sight beyond a roadside cottage about a quarter of a mile northward. The driver blabbed his guide-book formulas as they passed, pointing here and there with his whip; and the people stared dutifully at the rocks, and straight at my boulder, but without noticing the strange fungus upon it. At one moment, I might have dropped the ashes of my pipe right into the open mouth of the senior member of the party. Some time after this, three pedestrians came in sight ; two at the southern bend of the road, and one at the northern. The curve of the valley was such that, at the rate they were going, they would not come in view of each other until within a few yards of their meeting-point; this point being a little to the right of my position, and about opposite a decayed bridge ; which, by the way, must have been built for no other purpose than to be fished from ; for its further end almost impinged upon the vertical face of the opposite cliff—up which not even a Bertram Risinghame could have conveyed himself.

As the three pedestrians drew near, I perceived the two southerners to be tramps; but the northerner was an ambitious young man in a black frock-coat, ruffled shirt-front, and straw hat on the back of his head. He strode along with a magniloquent step, declaiming, with passionate emphasis and at the top of his compass, some passage of blank verse. His gestures were very striking: he held his head well up, flung his arms about, slapped his breast, and made his voice resound through the cañon. Meanwhile the two tramps shuffled along, as unconscious as was he of mutual proximity.

"This young fellow," said I to myself, "evidently

has a mind to be an orator and a statesman. He feels the seeds of greatness within him. Now he imagines himself in the Senate, confronting the opposition. That point was well given! Bismarck is getting old: who knows whether I do not here behold his successor?" The young orator was now within a couple of rods of the bridge, and suddenly he and the tramps came face to face. I watched with painful interest. His voice quavered and sank; he cleared his throat, put his hands in his pocket, and whistled. Bismarck, or any truly great man, would have kept on louder than ever—nay, would have compelled the tramps to stop and hear him out! But this young man feared to appear ridiculous; and the savage sincerity which Mr. Carlyle ascribes to all great men is not reconcilable with any such timidity. A great man must be capable of spending his life in a position which a small man would find intolerably ridiculous even for a minute's lease.

XII.

I climbed gingerly back to the mainland, and leaving my boulder for ever, made my way by degrees to the road, and followed it for about a mile. At one point, the brook made a little *détour*, enclosing a lawn of the softest and most vivid green I ever beheld. Straight upwards from it sprang a smooth gray bluff, near two hundred feet in height, throwing a deep, cool shadow, sharply defined, over half the plot. Two peasant women were mowing the grass with sickles, and the wind that had begun to rise was taking great liberties with the skirts which, at best, scarcely covered the knees of their stout bare legs. Along the summit of the cliff overhead a procession of long-shanked trees were straggling against the sky. Further on, I came to the entrance of a wood-path, whose shady invitation I could not resist; and in a few minutes more I found myself in the heart of a pine forest.

I sat down upon a mossy stump, such as poets write of; indeed, mossy stumps and stones have become so hackneyed in literature that I am shy of further enlarging upon them. The pines were from sixty to one hundred feet high, growing palm-like, with all their foliage at the top. Their music, therefore, sounded far away, like the murmur of an ocean in the clouds. Their thick, dark foliage strove to veil from the sun the slender nakedness of their long, graceful limbs; but he peeped through them nevertheless, and made beautiful sport of their shyest secrets. Around their roots was a sweet omnipresent dampness, encouraging moss to flourish, and display its most delicate tints. There was no grass or flowers to speak of, but plenty of low bushes, and green creeping vines, and elegant ferns. The forest was full of clear twilight, in which the occasional shafts of sunlight burnt like celestial torches.

Still bearing eastward, the forest gave way to high rocky fields, crossing which I presently sighted a stupendous four-sided mountain of stone, standing solitary and apart, its bare walls ascending far above the tops of the tallest trees, and scarcely suffering even lichens to gain foothold on them. Deep fissures, crossing one another almost rectangularly, gave the great mass the appearance of having been piled together of blocks, in comparison with which the huge shafts of Stonehenge would be mere dominoes. On the summit was a sparse growth of scrawny pines, looking as though they had lost flesh from exposure and anxiety at the peril of their position. In short, this might have been the donjon-tower of some Atlantean castle, the remainder of which had either been overthrown and annihilated, or was buried beneath the sand out of which the lonely tower arose.

But whether or not the antediluvian theory be tenable, at all events this rock has been used as a stronghold in modern times—that is, within the last three centuries. A band of robbers lived here, and the rock is full of traces of their occupation. A place more impregnable could scarcely be imagined. After toiling up an arduous sandy path, as steep as the roof of a house, until pretty well out of breath, I came to the base of the "Stein" itself. The way now lay up perpendicular fissures, through narrow crevices, underneath superincumbent masses, and along dangerous precipices, where precarious footholds had been cut out in the solid stone. Still further up, hands rather than feet came into play, and three or four extra pairs of arms and legs might have been employed to great advantage. How the robbers ever got their booty up this ascent, or had strength left for anything except to lie down and faint after they had done so, is hard to understand. At length, however, I reached the great cave formed by the leaning together of the two principal boulders of the pile. It was about twelve feet wide at the base, and four times as high to the crotch of the roof. The end opposite the entrance was blocked up with fragments of rock and rubbish. A large oblong pit, dug in the solid stone floor, was used, I presume, either to keep provisions and booty in, or as a dungeon for captives. It had been formerly covered over with a wooden flooring, the square holes in the rock which held the ends of the beams being still visible.

From this, which may be called the ground-floor of the robbers' dwelling, to the upper stories, there was no natural means of access. The old fellows, therefore, by wedging short sticks of wood one above another into an irregular fissure, extending nearly from the top to the bottom of the Stein, constructed a primitive sort of staircase, traces of which yet remain. Some enterprising modern, however, has introduced a couple of ladders, whereby the ascent is greatly facilitated. Above, I found, at various well-chosen points, the marks of old barricades, showing that these brigands had some sound notions on fortification, and had resolved, moreover, to sell their lives dearly, and to fight to the last man. It is inconceivable, though, that any force unprovided with the heaviest artillery could have made the slightest impression on such a stronghold as this. In those days of bucklers and blunderbusses, a new-born babe might have held it single-handed against an army.

It was very windy on the summit, and an excess of wind ruffles up the nerves, blows away common sense, baffles thought, and tempts to rashness and vain resentment. The place, too, was a maze of sudden crevasses, just wide enough to fall into, and utterly impossible to get out of. What a ghastly fate to be lodged in one of them, remembering that the Stein is visited hardly once a month in the height of the season! I was already so hungry that the mere thought of such a catastrophe put me out of all conceit with the robber-fortress. Accordingly, I made the best of my way earthwards; and, having previously taken my bearings, I steered for a neighbouring farm-house, where a smiling old lady, white-capped, yellow-petticoated, and bare-legged, fetched me a tumbler of cool creamy milk, nearly twelve inches high.

XIII.

On my homeward journey, I happened upon a long, winding, shadow-haunted pass, such as abounds in this region, and which reminded me (as, indeed, did the whole Saxon Switzerland) of our own Yellowstone Valley, modelled on the scale of one inch to the foot, or thereabouts. The white-sanded bottom was so narrow that space was scarcely left for the slender path to follow the meanderings of the rivulet, which tinkled, concealed, beneath luxuriant overgrowths of forget-me-not and fern. Up to the sky on either side climbed the rugged walls, shaggy with fir and hemlock, and thatched below with grass-tufts and shrubs. The fallen fragments, which ever and anon blocked the way with their surly shoulders, were iridescent with green moss, and dampness seemed to exude from the rocky clefts. The footpath was criss-crossed with pine-roots till it resembled an irregular parquet-floor. Sometimes the boulders had so fallen together as to enclose spacious hollows, the crevices of which had been stopped up with sand and pebbles and vegetable decay. I might have lived very comfortably in many of these caves: they were overrun with raspberry and blackberry vines, and within were cool and dry, with clean sanded floors: but I saw no troglodytes.

At one point a broad nose of rock jutted over the pathway full fifteen feet, like a ceiling; and so low-studded was it, that I could easily touch its flat surface with my upraised hand. There was something fascinating about this freak, and, at the same time, provocative of a smile—old nature making a humorous pretence of imitating the works of man! But the grotesque pranks she plays with that soft-hearted white sandstone of hers are indescribable and endless. In many places the surface of the rock is honeycombed and otherwise marked as if by the action of water. I am not acquainted with the geological history of this strange tract, but I should fancy it might have been the compact sandy bed of some great lake, which having broken its boundaries, and gone seaward by way of the Elbe, the sand-bed caked and cracked and hardened, and became traversed with ravines and gullies, worn by downward percolating streams. The lake must have subsided gradually, to produce the horizontal markings which are everywhere apparent. I have often seen precisely similar formations to this of the Saxon Switzerland at the bottom of dried-off mud-ponds. Beyond the mouth of the Elbe are great shoals and bars, composed of the same kind of sand as that which I trod underfoot in this shadowy ravine.

It should not be called a pass, for it was a place to linger and pause in—to enter at sunrise, and scarcely depart from by moonlight. It seemed wholly secluded; I met neither foot nor foot-print throughout its whole length. Even the sky might not be too familiar; looking upwards, but a narrow strip of blue was visible, and the overbending trees fretted even that with emerald lattice-work. However, I could not support life on raspberries and water: the afternoon was more than half gone, and I had no idea how far off the Badehaus might be. Hastening onward, the narrow walls of the ravine suddenly opened out right and left in a vast circular sweep, and I stood within a grand natural amphitheatre, rising high and descending low above and beneath. My station was about a third of the way up, in what might be called the dress-circle. The area below was crowded thick with summer foliage—oaks, elms, beeches, and underbrush in profusion. These were the players—gay fellows in nodding caps and green fluttering cloaks. The audience was composed of a stiff and sedate assemblage of dark-browed hemlocks, standing rigid and erect each in his rock-bound seat. Not one of them all was sitting down; but whether they were merely standing on ceremony, or whether (as, judging from their gloomy and unyielding aspect, seemed more likely) they had started up to demand the condign punishment of some unlucky wretch who had outraged their sense of decorum, I had no means of determining. At all events, my arrival seemed to have put an abrupt stop to the proceedings, whatever they may have been; there was no voice or movement anywhere, save as created involuntarily by the mysterious wind. On my shouting across, however, to a sombre giant on the opposite side of the amphitheatre, to know the title of the drama which was under representation, he answered me, indeed, but with an unreal tone of hollow mockery, and in such a manner as to leave me no wiser than I was before. Manifestly I was looked upon as an interloper who had slipped in without paying for a ticket, and self-respect demanded that I should retire at once.

The theatre, vast as it was, had only two doors—that by which I had entered, and another just opposite. To reach this I must make half the circuit of the enclosure, the direct route across the arena being impracticable, owing to the savagely precipitous nature of the descent. The path which had hitherto guided me now bearing to the right, I followed it in that direction, passing almost within reach of the outstretched arms of hundreds of the inhospitable hemlocks. Presently the sun, which, hidden behind a cloud, had sunk almost to the upper verge of the rocky rampart, shone out with mellow lustre, flinging my shadow far away into the centre of the arena, where the green-coated actors treated it with great indignity, bandying it from one to another, tossing it up and down, and more than once letting it tumble heedlessly into some treacherous pitfall. Meanwhile the wind, which had caused me no small annoyance already that afternoon, was maliciously making the rounds of the house, and stirring up every individual in it to a sibilant utterance whose import there was no mistaking. It was my first—and will, I fancy, be my last—experience of being hissed out of a theatre; and I could not help resenting the injustice of the proceeding. Yet, after all, why should I consent to be ruffled by the senseless clamour of a lot of trees? If I have misrepresented them at all, it has been on the side of eulogy; and should I ever have occasion to mention trees in future, it will be with the proviso that every one of them—the oldest, biggest, and respectablest more particularly—are no better than incorrigible blockheads at bottom.

XIV.

To the banks of the Elbe I came at last, with a dusty distance of three or four miles still lying between me and Shandau. But the scenery hereabouts is novel and striking: the stone quarries extending up and down the river for many leagues; and the heaps of sand and débris, rising to an average height of perhaps a hundred feet, and sloping sharply downwards to the water's edge, are a remarkable if not a strictly picturesque feature. The path—if the informal track which leads a risky life along the base of these lofty dumping-grounds can be called such—yields wearisomely to the feet, and a wary look-out must be kept to dodge the heavy stones which are continually bowling downwards from the summit. At intervals there are slides, compactly constructed of masonry and worn very smooth, by which the square blocks quarried from the cliffs are shot to the water's edge, to be taken on board by canal-boats and floated to Dresden, all the modern part of which is built of this material. The supply is practically inexhaustible, but that does not prevent the cliffs from suffering in appearance; and before many years a voyage up the Elbe will be no longer attractive. It is a nice question in economy, whether it be worth while to rob Saxon Switzerland to pay Dresden. Perhaps only the stone contractors would answer it unhesitatingly in the affirmative. It reminds me of the little boy who was courted by his friends as being the possessor of a fine cake. With the praiseworthy purpose of at once concentrating and augmenting their regard, he made the cake a part of himself by eating it. But, strange to say, his friends ceased to visit him from that day forwards, and the cake gave him a stomach-ache.

I took my dinner that evening at the Forsthaus, one of that row of hotels which rampart Schandau. Hot and noisy as they are to live in, their bill of fare is to Herr Boettcher's as a novel by Thackeray to a schoolboy's composition. I dined on a terrace beneath the trees, with the river just beyond. At dark every table had its great astral lamp, and the gentlemanly proprietor amused himself and his guests by making blue, red, and green fires on the stone steps.

Next morning, as I stood with my valise on the platform of the railway station at Krippen, a fellow—he keeps a small tobacco store on See Strasse in Dresden—stepped up to me, and, after requesting the favour of a light from my cigar, supposed, in a cheerful tone, that I was returning to town by the approaching train.

"No," said I, "I left Dresden finally yesterday morning. I am now for Prag; and never expect, sir, to see you, or buy your cigars, again!"

The train came in, the cigar vendor assisted a pretty young woman, with small shapely feet, into a second-class carriage; the whistle blew and the train moved off.

I have remembered and reproduced this disappointing little episode, because of the emblematic likeness it bears to my experience of Dresden. The city, like the young woman, enchants at first sight, but is presently detected in familiar association with sentimental vulgarity, and betrays an appetite for gross and crude fare: whereupon our parting regrets are narrowed down to the somewhat equivocal one that, despite certain picturesque passages of physical contour, so little in the capital of Saxony is honestly regrettable.

STRAHAN & CO.'s
RECENT PUBLICATIONS.

By GEORGE MAC DONALD.

THE WISE WOMAN;
A PARABLE.

By GEORGE MAC DONALD,
Author of "Alec Forbes," "David Elginbrod," etc.

Post 8vo. Cloth, 10s. 6d.

"It is told in language so strikingly simple that it may be read with benefit by the merest child; yet it is pregnant with truths which may be pondered with profit by those of mature years. It may be described, in a sentence, as an exposition of the text, 'We are made perfect by suffering.'"—*Glasgow Herald*.

"We breathe in the new book the clear, bracing, almost intoxicatingly pure moral atmosphere which we remember so well in the old one ('Phantastes'). In 'The Wise Woman,' as in the older allegory, there is the inexorable but tender unveiling of the weak spots which more or less spoil all our lives, and make sorry failures of so many of our best attempts. Here, too, we recognise the high imagination—tender, delicate, ethereal—which recalls the saying of an acute critic, who remarked that Mr. Mac Donald always reminded him more of Mendelssohn than of any writer. . . . On the whole, it may be said that this parable of 'The Wise Woman' shows Mr. Mac Donald to us as he is when he is most individual, most truly himself; and for this reason it is likely to be held very precious by the crowd of admirers and disciples which, during the term of his literary life, this charming writer has gathered around him."—*Liverpool Albion*.

"In all such compositions the charm lies not in the conception, which is easy enough, but in the execution, which is extremely difficult; and in this latter Mr. Mac Donald excels. He has a wealth of fancy, which luxuriates in an overflow of apt and beautiful images, and a clear, strong light of meditative wisdom, which prevents them from running altogether wild. The result is a very pleasing and instructive book. It is but a fragment, and ends abruptly. We have observed before that Mr. Mac Donald, like

PATERNOSTER ROW.

unpractised extempore speakers, **finds great** difficulty in bringing his stories to an end; but perhaps **this rather** enhances the general effect of undefined mystery, which **constitutes** one of **the attractions of the tale."**—*The Guardian.*

"Children **ought to** like this book very **much.** The moral will easily suggest **itself to them**; but it is not obtruded and italicised, and **we need hardly say of a** 'parable' written by Mr. Mac Donald that the story **in which it is** thinly veiled is full of graceful **and** pretty thoughts. **What can be more** charming than the picture **in** the opening chapter of **a shower of** summer rain, 'when the very sheep felt it blessing them, **though it** could **never** reach their skin through the depth of their long wool, and the veriest hedgehog—I **mean** the one with the longest spikes—came **and** spiked himself **out to impale as** many of the drops as he could?' **What quaint** wisdom **in the remark** that Agnes's self-conceit gradually devoured all **the good that was** in her,—'for there is no fault that does **not** bring its **brothers and** sisters **and** cousins to live with it;' and again in the saying that '**when we are** cross all our other faults grow busy, and poke up their ugly heads like maggots.'"—*The Standard.*

By MRS. PFEIFFER.

POEMS.

By EMILY PFEIFFER,
Author of "Gerard's Monument."

Fcap. 8vo.   Cloth extra, 6s.

"There is a touch of genius in Mrs. Pfeiffer which comes out most distinctly in her more thoughtful poems. . . . On the whole, her best poems are her sonnets—some of these **are,** to our mind, among the finest sonnets in the language. . . . There is a great weight of **truly-**blended thought and feeling in many of the poems; and in not **a few of** the sonnets, where the thought and feeling are so closely intertwined that **it** is impossible to separate one from the other. There are flights of true imagination, of which almost the greatest of English sonnet-writers might, and possibly would, have been proud."—*Spectator.*

"Mrs. Pfeiffer **has been known for some** years amongst the *illuminati* **as a poetess of great refinement and** power of expression; **and her present volume will serve to increase** her reputation."— *Hereford Times.*

BY THE AUTHOR OF "GINX'S BABY."

THE DEVIL'S CHAIN.

By EDWARD JENKINS, M.P.,

Author of "Ginx's Baby," etc.

TENTH THOUSAND.

Small Crown, 8vo.   *Cloth extra*, 5s.

"All our readers know 'Ginx's Baby,' and some of them are familiar with its successors from the same hand. This book surpasses all these efforts of the social and Christian reformer put together . . . . It ought to prove to the pledged total abstainer and temperance reformer alike the most powerful human weapon ever wielded by them . . . . No one who reads a page of it will lay it down in a hurry, and no one who has read it will ever again treat the great curse of our age with indifference."—*Edinburgh Daily Review.*

"This book outvies in interest the most sensational of novels, and is sure to be widely read both in Britain and in America."—*Dundee Advertiser.*

"This powerful and well-sustained story contains ample evidence of being the work of a man of genius."—*Scotsman.*

"'The Devil's Chain' is boldly written, and full of dramatic incident . . . . Mr. Jenkins's book will be more fruitful for good than any discussion in the House of Commons . . . . 'The Devil's Chain' will do valuable service for the temperance cause, and it will certainly create a sensation in literary and political circles."—*Sheffield Independent.*

"In 'The Devil's Chain' Mr. Jenkins has given another illustration of the originality of his genius, as well as of his courage as a reformer. He has undertaken to unmask and to assail the demon of strong drink, and the result is the most powerful contribution which has yet been made to the literature of the temperance party."—*Nonconformist.*

"Mr. Jenkins deserves our thanks for the fearless manner in which he has handled some of the most appalling social evils of our time. Of all these evils none are more horrible than intemperance; and it will indeed be well if 'The Devil's Chain' helps to chain down the demon of drink."—*Northern Echo.*

PATERNOSTER ROW.

By the Right Hon. W. E. GLADSTONE, M.P.

THE CHURCH OF ENGLAND AND RITUALISM.

Reprinted from "The Contemporary Review," and Revised.

Demy 8vo.   *Cloth*, 2s. 6d.   *Paper Cover*, 2s.

A CANDLE LIGHTED BY THE LORD:

A LIFE STORY FOR THE OLD AND THE YOUNG, AND THE RICH AND THE POOR.

By a New Author.

Fcap. 8vo.   *Cloth*, 1s. 6d.

"'A Candle Lighted by the Lord' is a touching history of little Jenny. How she found peace, lighted a dark home, blessed father and mother, is admirably told—without exaggeration or precocity. It wins its way to the heart."—*The Freeman.*

"'A Candle Lighted by the Lord' is a simple story of a child's conversion, told in plain language that will strike the intelligence of religiously disposed persons. The picture of the heroine—a ragged street girl—and her motherly love and care for her little sister, is even pathetic here and there. The description of the miserable home is, it is to be feared, only too graphic, as innumerable recent cases in the police records show."—*Lloyd's Weekly Newspaper.*

"This is the story of the good and useful life of a girl who was rescued when a child from dirt, poverty, and drunkenness, and slowly led on by the example and precepts of Christian people to an earnest and Christian life herself. Nowhere in the volume is teetotalism mentioned, but the moral of the story is unmistakable, and is its highest recommendation."—*Warrington Guardian.*

By Dr. C. J. VAUGHAN.

THE LORD'S PRAYER:

A COURSE OF SERMONS PREACHED IN THE TEMPLE CHURCH.

By C. J. VAUGHAN, D.D., Master of the Temple.

Small Crown 8vo.   Cloth, 3s. 6d.

"They are the well-weighed utterances of an intelligent, cultivated, devout, and catholic divine; and they reach, as they are in the first instance addressed to, men from whom the average preacher might find it sometimes hard to get audience."—*Bath Chronicle.*

"'The Lord's Prayer' is an exposition, from the author's point of view, of what ought to be thought, believed, and felt by persons who use this, the oldest and most catholic form of prayer in use among Christians. It would be easy to extract—indeed there has often been extracted—from the Lord's Prayer a whole system of divinity; but although his opinions on theology are sufficiently definite, Dr. Vaughan's purpose in these discourses is practical rather than theological; and readers, to whatever school they may belong, will be none the worse—they may be all the better—to have pressed home upon them, in the earnest and searching words of the Master of the Temple, the import of what is often, even by very pious persons, repeated unthinkingly."—*Scotsman.*

By FREDERICK S. WILLIAMS.

THE MIDLAND RAILWAY:

ITS RISE AND PROGRESS.

A NARRATIVE OF MODERN ENTERPRISE.

By FREDERICK S. WILLIAMS,
Author of "Our Iron Roads."

Demy 8vo, **with 7** Maps and 120 *Illustrations.* Cloth, 20s.

PATERNOSTER ROW.

BY K. F. VON KLÖDEN.

THE SELF-MADE MAN:

AN AUTOBIOGRAPHY.

TRANSLATED BY A. M. CHRISTIE.

Vol. I., demy 8vo.   With Portrait.   Price 14s., *cloth.*

The *Saturday Review,* in a recent notice of the German edition of this work, thus speaks of it:—"We are much mistaken if this autobiography does not take rank as a classic. It is a masterpiece of ingenuous self-portraiture and graphic narrative. In its warmth and simplicity it reminds us of Mr. Smiles' 'Life of Stephenson,' with the zest of autobiography superadded."

Vol. II., completing the work, in the press.

BY MRS. BROCK.

THE FINEST OF THE WHEAT;

OR, THE BREAD OF FORGIVENESS.

BY MRS. BROCK.

Small Crown 8vo.   *Cloth extra,* 3s. 6d.

"This book forms really pleasant reading. It has been got up with great taste, and is divided in such a manner as will readily yield itself to disconnected reading. It is suffused with tender thought, savoured with Evangelicalism, and is broad enough to be welcomed generally."—*Nonconformist.*

PATERNOSTER ROW.

www.ingramcontent.com/pod-product-compliance
Lightning Source LLC
Chambersburg PA
CBHW022121290426
44112CB00008B/758